Design Analysis of Chihuahuan Polychrome Jars from North American Museum Collections

Mitch J. Hendrickson

BAR International Series 1125
2003

Published in 2016 by
BAR Publishing, Oxford

BAR International Series 1125

Design Analysis of Chihuahuan Polychrome Jars from North American Museum Collections

ISBN 978 1 84171 501 8

BAR Publishing is the trading name of British Archaeological Reports (Oxford) Ltd.
British Archaeological Reports was first incorporated in 1974 to publish the BAR
Series, International and British. In 1992 Hadrian Books Ltd became part of the BAR
group. This volume was originally published by Archaeopress in conjunction with
British Archaeological Reports (Oxford) Ltd / Hadrian Books Ltd, the Series principal
publisher, in 2003. This present volume is published by BAR Publishing, 2016.

Printed in England

BAR
PUBLISHING

BAR titles are available from:

BAR Publishing
122 Banbury Rd, Oxford, OX2 7BP, UK
EMAIL   info@barpublishing.com
PHONE   +44 (0)1865 310431
FAX   +44 (0)1865 316916
www.barpublishing.com

ABSTRACT

Chihuahuan polychrome jars acquired by museums in the early and middle part of the 20th century represent a wealth of untouched data for modern research. The aim of this thesis is to demonstrate the utility of unprovenienced ceramics to inform several levels of archaeological investigation. Using a design analysis of layout and motif depicted on three polychrome types (Ramos, Babícora, and Villa Ahumada) housed in the Royal Ontario and Wilderness Park Museums, this study will address: 1) the issue of trait overlap in the Chihuahuan typology; and 2) the existence of decorative patterns within the ceramic tradition that may reflect temporal and spatial variation, as well as the impact of cultural forces. With the recent increase in projects undertaken in Chihuahua, the incorporation of museum collections is a timely and necessary endeavour in order to properly evaluate the role that this region played in North American prehistory.

ACKNOWLEDGEMENTS

For nearly every jar examined in this study there is a person who needs to be thanked, either in whole or in part, for helping with the completion of this tome. To begin I would like to thank my scholarly mentors. First, Dr. Jane H. Kelley for asking me to be part of the last incarnation of the Proyecto Arqueolⅎgico Chihuahua. While my research was spawned in the museum, the field seasons spent in Mexico provided the physical and intellectual context needed to situate my 'floating dataset'. Without this experience, my research would have sunk beneath the waves of art historical description. Second, I would like to thank my advisor, Dr. Nicholas David, for being patient and steering me onto the path of wisdom and away from the cliff of hanging participles. My sentences now say what they mean or vice versa, and I will gladly take this knowledge into my next life as a travel writer. Third, Dr. Gerry Oetelaar provided numerous challenges to my data, conclusions, and thought processes. Everyone needs a devil's advocate, and I appreciated every session. Last, thanks also to Dr. Dan Mato who sat in on my committee at the last minute.

For my dataset, I must thank Mima Kapches at the Royal Ontario Museum and Marc Thompson at the Wilderness Park Museum for allowing me to analyze and photograph their respective ceramic collections. The El Paso Archaeological Society also provided me with work space and the opportunity to visit Mr. Harold Naylor and Mr. Kenneth Burlingham, both of whom took time from their schedules to meet with me during my stay in El Paso. The City of El Paso and the Royal Ontario Museum graciously allowed the use of my own photos, the majority of which are included within the body of this work. I am indebted to Monica Webster for 'enjoying some quality time' with the collections in El Paso. Her assistance in measuring the WPM pots after a busy field season sped up the process so we could speed our way home.

Thanks go out to my keepers in Toronto, Leslie F. and Dave S, and to Ben Brown in El Paso. They kept things on the cheap for me, which allowed for better film processing,

The conferences that I attended were supported by funding from the University of Calgary, The Province of Alberta Grant, and the Museum of Man in San Diego. The Jornada Mogollon conference run by Pat Beckett and the Museum of Man Casas Grandes World symposium set up by Grace Johnson were memorable and crucial experiences. Starting with the Casas Grandes symposium at Paquimé, these conferences succeeded in solidifying my ideas and presentation skills necessary to get my point across.

During the writing process, the numerous drafts were read and re-read by Dr. Nicholas David, Dr. Jane Kelley, Liz Holt, Bonnie-Jean Hendrickson and Art MacWilliams. I appreciate their comments, candor and support.

My sanity throughout this process was maintained by the crew at the Wine Shop (Tim, David, Rob) and the Puritans, Vladimir and Robert, and those members past and present. Whoever said driving, drinking, and singing was a bad thing never hung out with these people.

From the archaeology department, thanks go out to Matthew Boyd, Liz Robertson, Dan Meyer, Charles Mather, Nancy Saxberg, David Blower, Monica Webster, Pete Dawson, Evelyn Siegfried, and Andrea Waters. Not from department, I want to thank Art MacWilliams, Maria Sprehn, Christine Van Pool, Karin Burd Larkin, Sue Fairburn, Dave Phillips and many others too long to list. In order to succeed in academia, you truly need an armada of friends. I have such a fleet.

At home, I would like to thank my family, Bonnie-Jean, Reg, Tim and Tom Smith for being there for me, feeding me, wining me, and caring about my mental state for three years plus. In the end, I have to say that we had the technology and we made it work.

Finally, I would like to thank my two. Without the numerous discussions over coffee, wine, or blue bowl, this thesis would never have fermented into its present state. Particularly, I want to thank Elizabeth. You provide the motifs that make my structure complete. Thanks for everything, Lizard.

DEDICATION

To Mr. John Liandzi

Who wasn't let down by my slow start

TABLE OF CONTENTS

ABSTRACT i
ACKNOWLEDGEMENTS ii
DEDICATION iii
TABLE OF CONTENTS iv
LIST OF TABLES v
LIST OF FIGURES v

CHAPTER ONE: INTRODUCTION
    Why Chihuahua? 1
    What We Know of Private Pots 2
    The Utility of Whole Vessel Analysis 2
    Thesis Outline 3

CHAPTER TWO: CHIHUAHUAN PREHISTORY AND THE HISTORY OF CERAMIC RESEARCH
    The Environment 4
    The Archaeological Record 5
    Ceramic Period Chronology 9
    Cultural "Boundaries" 12
    Cultural and Ceramic Definitions 13
    History of Ceramic Research 14
    Role of Ceramic Traits in Chihuahuan Research 19
    Problems Within the Chihuahuan Tradition 25

CHAPTER THREE: DESIGN ANALYSIS: THEORY, METHOD AND MODEL CONSTRUCTION
    The Importance of Raising Questions 28
    Introduction to the Study of Design in Ceramics 28
    Application of Design Analysis to the Museum Sample 31
    Products of the Design Analysis 34
    Constructing Explanatory Modules for Decorative Variation 34

CHAPTER FOUR: DATA COLLECTION AND METHODOLOGY
    History of the Collections 37
    Data Recording 37

CHAPTER FIVE: DATA PRESENTATION
    Terminology and Research Focus 44
    Design Analysis 44
    Secondary Comparative Tests 60

CHAPTER SIX: ANALYSIS OF DESIGN AND PRESENTATION OF EXPLANATORY MODELS
    Type Descriptions 73
    Design Horizons in the Chihuahuan Tradition 84
    The Question of Forgeries 93

CHAPTER SEVEN: CONCLUSION
    Perspectives and Questions 96

BIBLIOGRAPHY 97

LIST OF TABLES

Table 2.1   The Chihuahuan Chronology
Table 2.2   Basic type descriptions and variant categories for Ramos, Babícora, and Villa
                Ahumada polychromes according to Sayles and Di Peso, Rinaldo and Fenner
Table 5.1   Relative frequency of layouts by polychrome type and museum sample (ROM and
                WPM)
Table 5.2   Relative frequency of motifs by polychrome type and museum sample
Table 5.3   Number of different motifs per jar by polychrome type and museum sample
Table 5.4a-d   Frequency of motifs by layout for each polychrome type and the museum sample
Table 5.5a-d   Actual count of the number of different motifs recorded by layout class in each
                polychrome type and museum sample
Table 5.6   Comparative frequency of motifs between Continuous and Segmented layouts for
                each polychrome type and the museum sample
Table 5.7   Comparative frequency of layouts for each polychrome type and the museum
                sample according to the presence of BoR
Table 5.8   Comparative frequency of motifs for each polychrome type and museums sample
                according to the presence of BoR
Table 5.9   Comparative frequency of BoR for each polychrome type and museum sample
                according to motif and layout styles
Table 5.10   Distribution of effigy classes by polychrome type and museum sample
Table 5.11   Frequency of layout classes and style for effigy jars by polychrome type, museum
                sample and effigy class
Table 5.12   Comparative frequency of motifs in effigy jars for each polychrome type, museum
                sample, and effigy class
Table 5.13   Comparative frequency of motifs among effigies by layout style and class
Table 5.14a-b   Comparative frequency of motifs in Hooded and Bird Effigies by polychrome type
                and layout style
Table 5.15   Distribution of layout class and style by BoR in effigy jars for each polychrome
                type, museum sample, and effigy classes
Table 5.16   Comparative frequency of motifs and motif styles by BoR in effigy jars for each
                polychrome type, the museum sample, and effigy classes
Table 5.17   Relative frequency of polychrome type, layout and motif styles, BoR and effigies
                between the ROM and WPM
Table 5.18   Distribution of layouts in the Paquimé Collection by polychrome type, effigy class
                and presence of BoR trait
Table 5.19   Distribution of effigy classes by polychrome type from Paquimé
Table 6.1   Relative frequency of multiple bands for each polychrome type
Table 6.2   Relative frequency of vertical shapes for each polychrome type

LIST OF FIGURES

Figure 2.1   Map of Chihuahua
Figure 2.2   Plan map of Paquimé with diagnostic features of the Chihuahuan culture
Figure 2.3   Sample of Chihuahuan polychrome vessel shapes in the ROM collection
Figure 2.4   Sample of effigy vessels from the WPM collection
Figure 2.5   Basic type descriptions for the Chihuahuan polychrome ceramics
Figure 2.6   Ramos, Babícora, and Villa Ahumada polychrome jars from the WPM collection
Figure 2.7   Sayles' proposed evolution of Chihuahuan polychrome tradition
Figure 2.8   Geographical extent of the Chihuahuan culture
Figure 2.9   Chronological development of ceramic types for the Chihuahuan polychrome
                tradition
Figure 2.10   Shell and bone artifacts from Paquimé showing decoration commonly found on
                Chihuahuan polychrome ceramics
Figure 2.11   Examples of the 'classic' shape of Chihuahuan jars from the WPM collection
Figure 2.12   Variation in jar forms present in the WPM collection
Figure 2.13   Effigies carved in other media recovered from Paquimé

Figure 2.14   Babícora 'Reverse' Hooded effigy jar from the collection of Sr. Guilfrido Robles

Figure 2.15   Example of a band layout with and without motifs

Figure 2.16a-c   Sequence of decoration and layout classes identified by Kidder and Di Peso

Figure 3.1   Methodological and theoretical trajectory for the analysis of Chihuahuan whole vessels from the ROM and WPM collections

Figure 3.2a-d   Layouts and Layout Styles recorded in the design analysis

Figure 3.3a-h   Examples of Motif and Motif styles recorded in the design analysis

Figure 4.1   Physical dimensions recorded for each vessel from the ROM and WPM

Figure 4.2   Shape characteristics recorded for each vessel from the ROM and WPM collections

Figure 4.3   Examples of altered and reconstructed jars from the WPM collection

Figure 4.4a-c   Decorative decoding process used in the design analysis

Figure 4.5   Layout classes and styles recorded for the ROM and WPM collections

Figure 4.6   Potential overlap in layout categories identified from the Casas Grandes classification scheme

Figure 4.7a-l   Simple style motifs recorded in the design analysis

Figure 4.8a-g   Complex style motifs recorded in the design analysis

Figure 4.9   Examples of black-bordered red motifs from the WPM collection

Figure 5.1   Levels of design analysis for the museum sample

Figure 5.2   Summary of layouts recorded on each polychrome type and the museum sample

Figure 5.3   Summary of Motifs present in each polychrome type and the museum sample

Figure 5.4   Summary of motif frequency by layout for Ramos Polychrome

Figure 5.5   Summary of motif frequency by layout for Babícora Polychrome

Figure 5.6   Summary of motif frequency by layout for Villa Ahumada Polychrome

Figure 5.7   Summary of motif frequency by layout for the museum sample

Figure 5.8   Relative frequency of motifs by layout class

Figure 5.9a-b   Comparison of relative motif frequencies for each layout style with and without the Zig-Zag class

Figure 5.10   Summary of motifs by polychrome types and museum sample with 2-line layouts

Figure 5.11   Summary of motif frequency by polychrome types and museum sample with 3-line layouts

Figure 5.12   Summary of motif frequency by polychrome types and museum sample with 4-line layouts

Figure 5.13   Summary of motifs by polychrome types and museum sample with Zig-Zag layouts

Figure 5.14   Summary of motif frequency by polychrome types and museum sample with Semi-Panelled layouts

Figure 5.15   Summary of motif frequency by polychrome types and museum sample with Panelled layouts

Figure 5.16   Summary of motif frequency by layout style for the polychrome types and museum sample

Figure 5.17   Summary of motif frequency for the polychrome types and museum sample according to the presence/absence of black borders around red motifs

Figure 5.18   Summary of motif frequencies in effigy jars for polychrome types, layout styles, and presence of BoR

Figure 6.1   Decorative characteristics of Ramos Polychrome

Figure 6.2a   Ramos polychrome jars from the ROM decorated with Segmented layout / Complex motifs

Figure 6.2b   Ramos polychrome jars from the WPM decorated with Segmented layout / Complex motifs

Figure 6.3a   Ramos polychrome Effigy jars from the ROM decorated with Segmented layout / Complex motifs

Figure 6.3b   Ramos polychrome Effigy jars from the WPM decorated with Segmented layout / Complex motifs

Figure 6.4   Decorative characteristics of Babícora Polychrome

Figure 6.5a   Babícora polychrome jars from the ROM decorated with Continuous layout / Simple motifs

Figure 6.5b   Babícora polychrome jars from the WPM decorated with Continuous layout / Simple motifs

Figure 6.6a   Babícora polychrome jars from the ROM decorated with Segmented layout / Complex motifs

Figure 6.6b	Babícora polychrome jars from the WPM decorated with Segmented layout / Complex motifs
Figure 6.7	Babícora Effigy jars from the ROM decorated with Continuous layout / Simple motifs
Figure 6.8	Decorative characteristics of Villa Ahumada Polychrome
Figure 6.9a	Villa Ahumada jars from the ROM decorated with Continuous layout / Simple motifs
Figure 6.9b	Villa Ahumada jars from the WPM decorated with Continuous layout / Simple motifs
Figure 6.10	Villa Ahumada jars from the WPM and ROM decorated with Segmented layout / Complex motifs
Figure 6.11	Villa Ahumada Effigy jars from the ROM decorated with Continuous layout / Simple motifs
Figure 6.12	Polychrome jars decorated representing Design Horizons A and B from the WPM and ROM
Figure 6.13a-b	Models of temporal development and direction of influence of the Chihuahuan polychrome types using the Design Horizon concept
Figure 6.14	Comparison of effigy classes between Design Horizons A and B from the museum sample
Figure 6.15	Macaw effigies and painted macaw designs
Figure 6.16	Proposed development of layout through Design Horizon A and B with associated motifs
Figure 6.17a-b	Evolution of vertical division (Panlled layout) and secondary bands in the Chihuahuan polychrome tradition
Figure 6.18	Regional distribution of polychrome types and Design Horizons in each area
Figure 6.19	Variation in "P" Triangle motifs from the ROM, WPM, and Paquimé vessels
Figure 6.20	Anomalous examples of Chihuahuan polychrome jars from the ROM and WPM
Figure 6.21	Chihuahuan polychrome vessels from the collection of Mr. Harold Naylor

## CHAPTER I

INTRODUCTION

Chihuahuan archaeology is presently experiencing a surge of new research (see Schaafsma and Riley, eds. 1999) unrivalled since the completion of the Amerind Foundation excavations at Paquimé (Casas Grandes) in 1961. Over the past decade this research has provided vital information of regional development from both the core area around Paquimé (Whalen and Minnis 1999) and the periphery of the Chihuahuan culture area (Kelley et al. 1999; Cruz and Maxwell 1999). But even with these advances archaeologists studying the ceramic assemblage still lack a detailed understanding of the temporal sequence and the geographic spread of the polychrome types. With heightened interest in Chihuahuan prehistory over the past decade, the opportunity presents itself to explore not only new questions of variability within the ceramic tradition but also to include a previously ignored, but eminently useful, data set: the museum-curated ceramic collection.

Due to the copious amount of Medio period (ca 1200-1450 A.D.) polychrome pottery housed at museums in Canada, the United States, and Mexico, a database exists for inventive ceramic research that few culture areas can claim. Two of these collections, housed at the Royal Ontario Museum (ROM) in Toronto, Ontario, and the Wilderness Park Museum (WPM) in El Paso, Texas were examined with the intent of meeting three specific goals (and two perspectives):

- to test the established parameters of the Chihuahuan ceramic typology at the level of decoration within the jar form (etic/temporal);
- to expand our perceptions beyond type association to address models of decorative variation at the level of the tradition (emic/social/spatial), and;
- to demonstrate that, through these analytical perspectives, the museum collection can be partially re-contextualized into its archaeological milieu and should be considered a significant resource for future research.

A design analysis comparing layout and motif characteristics found within three of the Chihuahuan polychrome types (Babícora, Ramos, Villa Ahumada) is presented as an effective method for accomplishing these goals.

Why Chihuahua?

Due to the relative isolation of Chihuahua from the rest of Mexico, the study of Chihuahuan archaeology has proved more popular historically to researchers from the United States and Canada than it has to those from within Mexico. Chihuahua represents a rather barren landscape, both literally in the imposing Chihuahuan desert and archaeologically in its lack of high' culture markers, such as the cities, temples, and roads that litter central and southern Mexico. Beneath the mounds and dunes scattered in farmer's fields and montane valleys is evidence of one of the most important yet poorly understood cultural regions of North America. The significance of this culture, first brought to the world stage by Charles Di Peso and the Joint Amerind Foundation excavations between 1958-1961, is that it is a hybridization of Puebloan and Mesoamerican material and social characteristics. As a result of this diversity, arguments for the origins of these people have included migration of Toltecs (Di Peso 1974), or Chaco Canyon Anasazi (Lekson 2000). In addition to the intriguing questions of broader origins, the Chihuahuan culture is represented by an excellent material culture database, including the elaborately painted ceramic jars.

Chihuahuan polychrome ceramics are selected for this study for both historical and practical reasons. First, whole pots have already played a small but significant role in past research through the endeavours of Kidder (1916), Carey (1931), Sayles (1936) and Di Peso (Di Peso et al. 1974a). In these accounts, whole vessels were used by these archaeologists to provide a basic description of decorative characteristics that eventually led to the formation of the Chihuahuan typology. The cultural implications of this decorative patterning, however, have been largely unexplored. Second, the Chihuahuan polychromes are part of a distinct and easily recognizable ceramic assemblage. This fact was noted in the earliest discussions of these artifacts:

> Casas Grandes pottery is a rare achievement of early ceramic art. It is distinguished by beauty both of form and decoration, and by perfection of technical skill, (Harcum 1923:4),

> [the pottery] ranks as one of the most notable in the culture history of aboriginal America (Chapman 1923:25),

> Casas Grandes pottery is different; it has no known relatives (Hough 1923:34) and,

> It is very fine, harmonious in color, and in accuracy of line work is not surpassed by any other class of Southwestern ceramics (Kidder 1924:318).

Third, the elaborate decoration of this distinct ceramic culture provides an extensive range of possible contrastive analyses from individual elements to overall designs. Finally, perhaps the most critical feature in selecting Chihuahuan polychrome ceramics for this study is that they *can* be selected. The number of vessels housed in museums throughout North America provides an excellent database that needs to be addressed within the context of archaeological research programmes.

The greatest drawback to using these museum-based collections is the lack of known provenience and is likely responsible for their poor representation within past Chihuahuan archaeological endeavours. This situation is not unique to Chihuahua, as Cantwell et al.'s (1981) comprehensive attempt to demonstrate the utility of the museum collection to anthropology and archaeology contains only one example (Winter 1981) where provenience-less artifacts are used as the primary evidence for archaeological interpretation. Ultimately, the stopping point for many archaeologists seeking to utilize curated collections is that, without context, the potential for cultural interpretation is restricted or marooned within the realm of art historical description. To disregard this data set completely, however, is to turn away potentially invaluable evidence that might expand our current understanding of prehistoric developments. Instead of ignoring these data, it is the archaeologist's responsibility to seek new methods to properly incorporate artifacts without the binding force of provenience.

What We Know of Private Pots
Prehistoric whole pots located in the cluttered drawers of museums and on the dusty shelves of private collectors contain a wealth of untapped and highly informative information ready to be accessed. Devising a way to apply these data sets to archaeological investigation is particularly important for the study of Chihuahuan prehistory because of the numerous collections in North American museums. Among the largest collections are those housed at the San Diego Museum of Man, the Arizona State Museum at Tucson and the National Museum of Natural History in Washington, D.C. Historically, we could include the substantial private acquisitions of individuals such as Ledwidge, Houghton, and Lea in El Paso, Texas, and Genin in Mexico City (Brand 1933:60). Given the wide access to these collections and the length of time that we have known of their existence, it is surprising that so little effort has been put into using this data for archaeological purposes.

The majority of museum acquisitions were purchased in the first three decades of the 20th century, a period associated with both the cessation of the numerous Mexican revolutions and lack of employment due to mine closures (Brand 1933:59). Prior to the enforcement of laws that would curb 'illegal' trafficking in antiquities, whole pots fetched prices ranging from,

> two and five pesos for a whole Chihuahua polychrome olla, and five to fifteen pesos for the effigy pots and more exotic forms. Dealing through local collecting agents are the big buyers, usually foreigners residing in Chihuahua, Mexico City and the border towns, (Ibid.:59-60).

Interestingly, several of the WPM vessels incorporated in this thesis still have the price written in pencil ranging from $7 to $15. Modern prices for individual pieces are

drastically inflated with private owners being offered up to US$35,000 from wealthier collectors or museums (Harold Naylor 1999, personal communication).

A result of this trade of Chihuahuan ceramics into public and/or private collections is that only rarely do we encounter pots with detailed information of their original provenience. Donald Brand, whose work in Chihuahua established the basic foundation of the region's prehistory, acknowledged this shortcoming in the museum collections suggesting that, "...a negligible amount [of pottery] has been procured through licensed excavations," (Brand 1933:59-60). However, basing his conclusion on a series of extensive surveys, he did suggest that the majority of these vessels likely came from the Casas Grandes valley which is home to the region's type site, Paquimé (Casas Grandes),

> ...it can be stated safely that fully three-fourths of the Chihuahua material outside of Mexico came from the vicinity of Casas Grandes, La Ascencimn, Janos, Corralitos, and Ramos – perhaps in that order (1933:60-61) (Figure 1.1).

While Brand's inference provides a potential spatial location for these collections, the geographical spread of this pottery and its associated culture complex are actually much greater in scope. For the time being, the lack of provenience information for these vessels is outweighed by the fact that we are presented with the opportunity to use a rarely encountered artifact form, the whole vessel.

The Utility of Whole Vessel Analysis
Ceramics, whether whole or broken, are one of the most significant artifact forms because they are inherently complex units for archaeological analysis, providing traits ranging from chemical composition of the raw material, processes of manufacturing, external decoration and use (Shepard 1956:2). Given the greater propensity to find sherds in archaeological contexts, it is not surprising that the majority of ceramic research has focussed on this ceramic form. Complete jars have also played an important role in both archaeological and ethnoarchaeological research (e.g., Raymond et al. 1975, Hardin 1984; De Boer 1990; Longacre 1991), and can be used effectively to deal with a much broader range of research objectives. Like the sherd, the pot can be evaluated according to type, motifs, paste, and manufacture, but it has the added benefit of affording the archaeologist a more 'complete' picture of the prehistoric artisan's perception of the object and its role in society. Chilton, in fact, argues that the complete jar plays a critical role in archaeology, "as units of analysis [the whole vessel] is very important in the interpretation of human behaviour because vessels were likely the most common units of meaning in prehistoric societies" (1998:146). The archaeologist lucky enough to use whole vessels also need not estimate such traits as vessel size,

shape, or rim form, which are required in sherd-based analyses. More importantly, it is possible to assess the 'complete' qualities of vessel decoration not (normally) feasible with the broken form. Because the whole vessel is the complete representation of the ceramic process it allows us the opportunity to directly investigate the decorative content and ordering principles of design with a higher degree of confidence.

The obvious drawback to relying on whole vessels is that they are rarely encountered within archaeological contexts. As a result of the infrequent discovery of complete pots, it has been argued that any analysis of the complete form should include traits that can be measured on both sherds and vessels alike (Froese 1985:229). This is an important point to consider in re-contextualizing data from the museum collections since the results will ultimately have an effect on informing changes in the typology and the further classification of sherds. In addition to taking advantage of the unique characteristics of the complete pot (i.e., layout), the design analysis presented here will also emphasize traits (i.e., motifs) recognizable on sherds.

THESIS OUTLINE

Before we can begin to consider the implications of using these museum collections for archaeological studies, the whole jars will first be re-contextualized within their cultural milieu in Chapter II. Background for these context-less artifacts will be established through a review of chronology, geography, and cultural characteristics of the associated Medio period occupation (1200-1450 A.D.). In addition to laying out the basic cultural patterns, the methodological implications of the history of Chihuahuan ceramic research will also be discussed, including the role that decoration has played in the reconstruction of prehistoric activity. The chapter will conclude with a summary of the cultural and typological problems that face current research and how these issues can be addressed through the design analysis.

Chapter III will outline the theoretical and methodological components of design analysis to be used to evaluate the museum collections. A contrastive approach involving different design levels, design styles and secondary tests is adopted to provide the framework for identifying decorative structures that transcend the type concept and are recognizable throughout the tradition. Models of temporal, spatial, and social variation are introduced to explain any regular patterning that appears within the museum sample data.

The history of the museum collections and description of the variables used in the data collection and analytical process are explained in Chapter IV. Presentation of these variables is outlined in detail within Chapter V, looking specifically at the motif and layout frequencies present on the three polychrome types. Variables are both examined individually and compared against one another at the level of type and across the tradition. Secondary tests of the association of motif and layout with decorative (presence of black outlines around red motifs) and formal (effigy jars) characteristics are also examined in detail. The final part of this chapter details the layout and type information for the whole vessels recovered from Paquimé. These jars are incorporated into this study because they represent a sample with known provenience.

The discussion of the data in relation to typology and testing of temporal and spatial models is the focus of Chapter VI. Broad decorative similarities shared between types are clustered into Design Horizons, which form the basis for making stylistic associations of time and regional distribution. In addition, the implications of decorative evolution are presented within the context of the larger archaeological picture and changes in the Medio sequence. The final aspect to be discussed in this chapter is the issue of pot authenticity and likelihood that forgeries exist in the museum collections.

CHAPTER II

CHIHUAHUAN PREHISTORY AND THE HISTORY OF CERAMIC RESEARCH

THE ENVIRONMENT

Chihuahua, encompassing an area of 247,000km², is the largest state in Mexico (Figure 2.1) and shares borders domestically with the states of Coahuila, Durango, Sinaloa, and Sonora, and internationally with New Mexico and Texas (Schmidt 1973:9). The landscape is composed of three primary physiographic regions, roughly from west to east: the Sierra Madre Occidental proper; Basin and Range on the eastern flank of the Sierra; and creosote-dominated Chihuahuan desert (Phillips 1989:375-376). Climate in Chihuahua is arid to semi-arid and is characterized by significant micro-diversity (Schmidt 1973:16). Within this generally dry environment is an abundance of natural resources that have been used to support both the prehistoric and historic inhabitants. The desert (<1520m in elevation), grassland and oak savannah (1670 to 2120m), and pine forest (2150m+) zones each contain distinct floral, faunal and mineral resources capable of supporting both prehistoric and historic populations.

THE ARCHAEOLOGICAL RECORD

The prehistoric sequence in Chihuahua extends over 10,000 years and is divided into three cultural periods: Paleo-Indian, Archaic and Ceramic (Table 2.1). Research on each period increases proportionally from the earliest period with the greatest emphasis being placed on the Ceramic period.

Paleo-Indian research is restricted to discoveries of individual Clovis (Di Peso 1965; Kelley 1991b) or Folsom (Ayeleyra 1961) projectile points. As a result, our knowledge of the earliest occupation in Chihuahua is very limited (Phillips 1989:378). The Archaic period is slightly better understood and is associated with concentrations of flaked stone artifacts, seasonal habitation of rock shelters, hilltops or lakesides, and shows a reliance on deer, antelope, and rabbits, as well as seed and plant production (MacNeish and Beckett 1987; MacNeish ed. 1993; Beckett and MacNeish 1994). Unfortunately, the Archaic Chihuahuan Tradition identified by MacNeish and Beckett (1987) is based on sites excavated in the Chihuahuan desert of New Mexico and Texas. Archaic sites have been identified in Chihuahua in various locales such as deserts, mountains, and lakesides (Phillips 1989:378-79), however, only the *trincheras* (hill terrace) site at Cerro Juanaqueña (~3000 B.P.) has been extensively excavated (Hard and Roney 1998). This large site contains 468 man-made terraces, many used for residential occupation, and numerous charred remains of maize, squash and other economic plants, and an extensive ground stone assemblage

suggesting that the site was extensively used for seed processing (Ibid.:1662-3). The area north of Laguna Bustillos has also produced hundreds of Archaic points, while fewer have been located in the Santa María and Babícora drainages (Kelley 1991b). Further excavation of Archaic sites in Chihuahua is required to test the parameters established for this period across the international border.

Study within the Ceramic period follows a similar trajectory to the entire sequence with the quantity of research increasing towards the later occupations. Brownware ceramics are estimated to appear in Chihuahua at approximately 100 A.D. (Phillips 1989:377), however, other than J. Charles Kelley's (1956; 1971) identification of the Loma San Gabriel villages of farmer-foragers in southern Chihuahua, very little is known of the people responsible for this technological innovation or introduction. Clear evidence of permanent settlements in north and central Chihuahua becomes more visible during the Viejo period (beginning ~600 A.D.) with the regular occurrence of roundish semi-subterranean pithouses and red-on-brown wares (Di Peso 1974:107-127; see Kelley et al. 1999b; 2000a for more recent accounts). These round structures are found isolated or in clusters and can vary in size with an average of 3.5m and a maximum of 8m in diameter (Di Peso 1974:149; Kelley et al. 2000a:32). Pottery from these sites is characterized by plainware, textured, and painted types that are produced in a fairly restricted range of vessel forms and sizes (Di Peso et al. 1974a:4). The subsistence is divided between products such as corn, beans, and squash, as well as wild plants, and supplemented by hunting local species including deer, antelope, birds, and perhaps some fish (Kelley et al. 2000a:46).

Overall, research on the Viejo period is more extensive than the preceding periods; however, the number of excavated sites represents a miniscule portion of those recorded through survey over the past decade. The exceptions to this trend are the significant efforts of the Proyecto Arqueológico Chihuahua (PAC) under Kelley and Stewart (1991a; 1991b; Kelley et al. 1999b; 2000a). The PAC has not only improved our understanding of this important era but has also unearthed possible evidence of a site transitional between the Viejo and Medio periods. The Calderon pithouse village site (800-900 A.D.) located in the upper Santa María drainage has produced painted ceramics that appear to bridge the gap between the earlier red-on-brown wares and Medio period types such as Babícora polychrome (Jane Kelley 2000, personal communication; Kelley et al. 2000b). Di Peso, relying on the stylistic comparison of data from Paquimé and the Convento sie, a large Viejo period settlement north of Viejo Casas Grandes, hypothesized a similar transition in decoration between Viejo and Medio period ceramics (Di Peso et al. 1974a:4). These studies represent important attempts at comprehending a cultural

Figure 2.1 Map of Chihuahua

Periods	Di Peso Chronology	Revised Chronology
11,000-10,500 to 9000 B.P.	Paleo-Indian	
3500 B.P. To A.D. 300	Archaic	
A.D. 300 to 1450	Ceramic	
Plainware	A.D. 200-700	A.D. 300-700
Viejo		
Convento phase	A.D. 700-900	A.D. 700-1150
Pilon phase	A.D. 900-950	
Perros Bravos phase	A.D. 950-1060	
Medio		
Buena Fe phase	A.D. 1060-1205	A.D. 1200-1450
Paquime phase	A.D. 1205-1261	
Diablo phase	A.D. 1261-1340	
Tardio	A.D. 1340-1686	A.D. 1450-1598

Table 2.1 The Chihuahuan Chronology

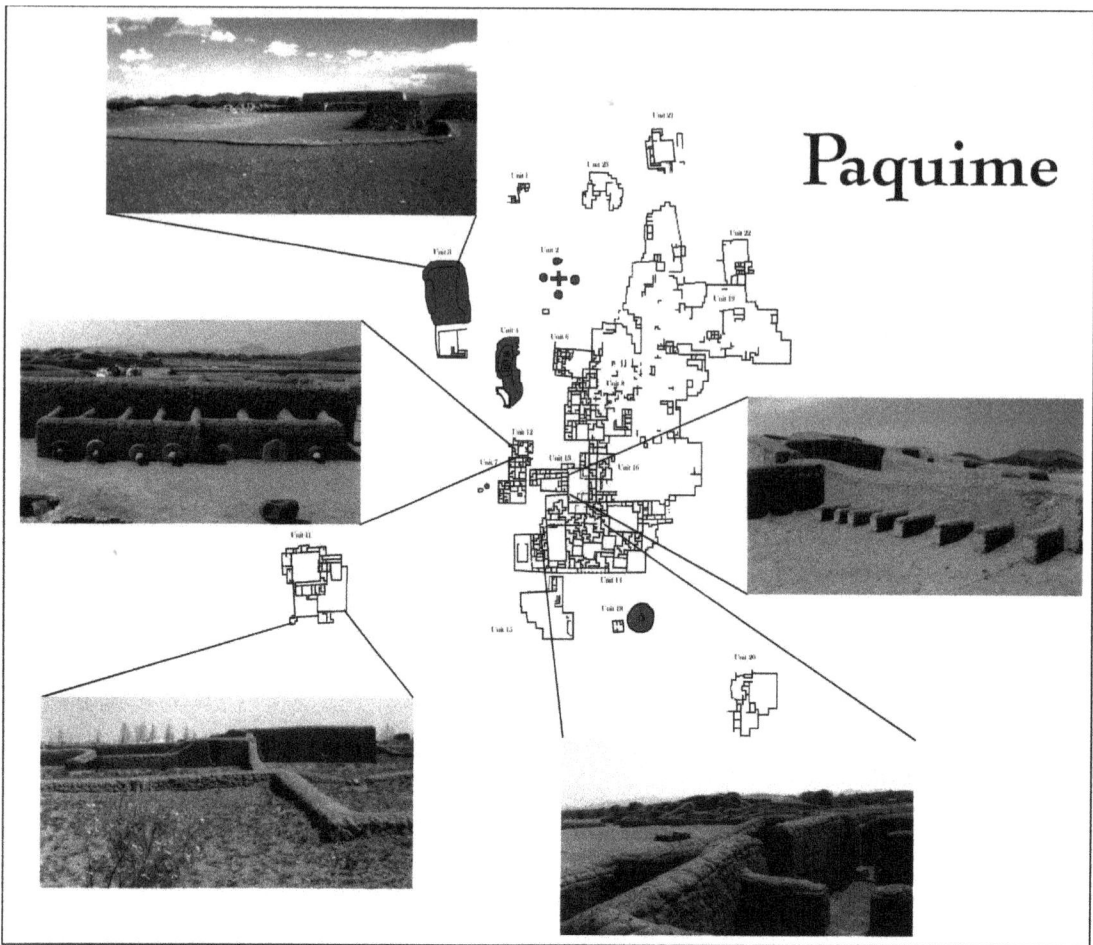

Figure 2.2 Plan map of Paquime with diagnostic architectural features of the Chihuahuan culture, clockwise from top – ballcourt, turkey breeding pens, remains of multi-story walls in Unit 14, t-shaped doorways, macaw breeding pens (map provided by Art MacWilliams)

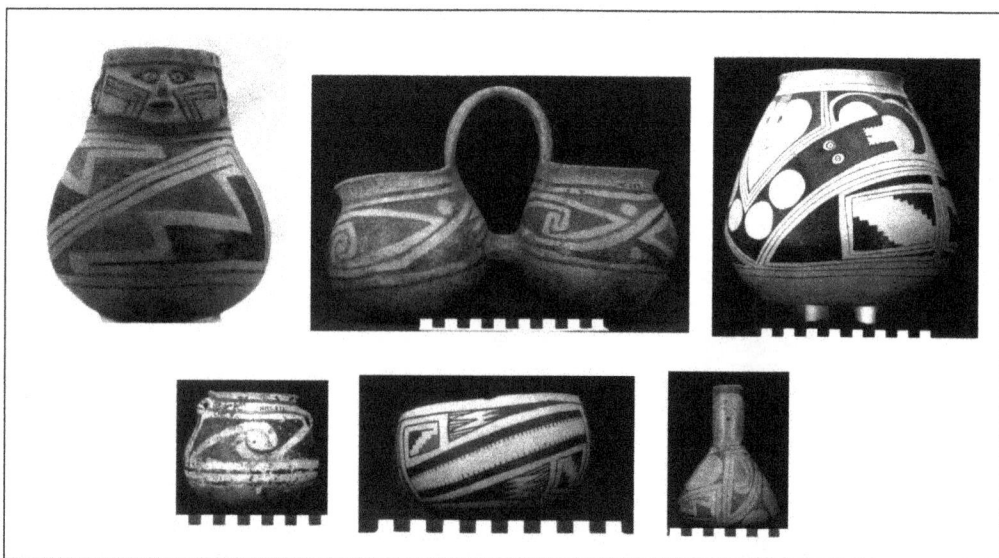

Figure 2.3 Sample of Chihuahuan polychrome vessel shapes from the ROM collection (top row – l to r - #33 Babicora polychrome Hooded effigy, HMC 257 Carretas polychrome double jar, #46 Ramos polychrome jar, bottom row - #189 Villa Ahumada polychrome jar, HMC 198 Ramos polychrome bowl, HMC 178 Ramos polychrome bottle

continuum throughout the Ceramic period rather than restricting the focus to a select portion of the Chihuahuan sequence.

The vast majority of archaeological research in Chihuahua is focussed on the diverse and highly visible material remains associated with the Medio period. Medio occupation sites are primarily differentiated from their Viejo predecessors through the appearance of contiguous, rectangular surface structures of puddled adobe, and the florescence of polychrome pottery. Architecturally, this period is distinguished through the combination of T-shaped doorways, raised hearths, alcove platforms, as well as the appearance of large open plazas, canals, macaw and turkey breeding areas, ceremonial mounds, and I-shaped ball courts (Di Peso 1974:379-433; Phillips 1989:382). Figure 2.2 illustrates several of these architectural features from the site of Paquimé, situated along the Río Casas Grandes south of the modern town of Casas Grandes. This immense site covered approximately 36 hectares and was excavated by Charles Di Peso and the Joint Amerind Foundation between 1958-1961 (Di Peso 1974:370). Di Peso's eight-volume treatise, *Casas Grandes: A Fallen Trading Center of the Gran Chichimeca* (Di Peso 1974), represents the greatest single work on the archaeology of Chihuahua and is largely responsible for the site's predominant role in discussions of regional development.

Another important difference between Medio and Viejo period sites is the significant increase in long-distance trade items. Foreign goods, recovered in substantial quantity from Paquimé have been sourced to the US Southwest (turquoise, serpentine, ceramics), west Mexico (marine shell, ceramics), and southern Mexico (scarlet macaw feathers) (Di Peso 1974:620-633). The prodigious quantity of such material, including 109,249 pieces of marine shell and 114 pounds of serpentine, has contributed to the belief that Paquimé was an important trade center controlled by *puchteca* (Di Peso et al. 1974b:170,188; Di Peso 1974:290-295) or local elite (Whalen and Minnis 1995; 1996). This theory has led to much speculation on the direct involvement of Paquimé in this trade and the actual extent of its power within Northwest Mexico. J. Charles Kelley (1986) argued that the goods found in Chihuahua are evidence for a direct interaction with the Greater Aztatlan trade network centered on the west coast of Mexico, and provided the link between US Southwestern and Mesoamamerican groups. Such direct contact, however, has yet to be discovered archaeologically. From an internal perspective, Minnis (1989) questioned the spatial extent of Paquimé's hegemony over such goods. In combination with Whalen (Minnis and Whalen 1995; Whalen and Minnis 1999), they have demonstrated restricted areas of Paquimian control based on the distribution of trade items and public architectural features and have identified primary (30km radius) and secondary zones (60-90km radius) of interaction. Archaeologists are still grappling

with the actual level of long-distance interaction and distribution of power in Chihuahua, however, the overarching implications of this data are that these people in the Casas Grandes core were deeply involved in a broad regional system.

The Medio period assemblage contains a distinct suite of locally produced artifacts including full-grooved stone axes, copper crotals and bells, and, most importantly, the finely crafted polychrome ceramic wares (Figure 2.3). Decoration of ceramics changes significantly during this period in both style and technique. In addition to the widespread combination of black and red paint, other new developments include the application of slipped backgrounds, use of negative painting, a greatly expanded repertoire of overall designs, and the adoption of zoo- and anthropomorphic symbols, such as the plumed serpent (Di Peso et al. 1974a:2). The sudden florescence of polychrome painting is matched by an increased variety of shapes produced by potters (i.e. bowls, jars, *cajetes* [neckless jars], bottles, effigies) and greater vessel capacity (upwards of 79 litres) (Ibid.:3-4). The most distinct vessel class is the effigy, which can take the form of a variety of animal, bird, lizard, or human figures (Figure 2.4). These decorative and formal characteristics represent two key components of the classification system devised to better understand this period in Chihuahuan prehistory.

Medio Period Typology
Twenty-two plainware, textured, and painted types have been identified from the Medio period assemblages based on traits of paste colour, surface finish, and decoration (Di Peso et al.1974a:77-316). Each of the eight polychrome types, Babícora, Carretas, Corralitos, Dublan, Escondida, Huerigos, Ramos, and Villa Ahumada, were divided according to the presence of slip, differences in paste colour, surface finish, paint, and decorative style. From the earliest research on these ceramics, the number of traits, specifically individual motifs or characteristics of paste, shared between types has been a problematic issue in the study of Chihuahuan pottery (see Sayles 1936a). While this overlap is likely attributed to the cumulative nature of a typology developed by several different scholars (Kidder 1916; Carey 1931; Brand 1933; Lister 1946) over a period of 50 years, Di Peso's (Di Peso et al. 1974a) rigorous evaluation of the Paquimé ceramic assemblage identified similar decorative regularities. Figure 2.5 illustrates the parameters of type definition followed by archaeologists working with the polychrome assemblage from Chihuahua. Based on the analysis of sherds and whole vessels, Di Peso proposed that overlapping type characteristics required further division of the types into smaller variant categories (Ibid.). The justification for these variants, however, is quite subjective and relies on single trait differences that are more commonly associated with a completely different type. For instance, both Babícora and Villa Ahumada are assigned Paquimé

Figure 2.4 Sample of effigy jars from the WPM collection (top row l to r - #176 Ramos polychrome Hooded Effigy, #177 Ramos polychrome Human Face effigy, #193 Babicora polychrome Hooded effigy, bottom row - #165 Ramos polychrome Animaleffigy, #164 Ramos polychrome Snake effigy, #168 Ramos polychrome Bird effigy).

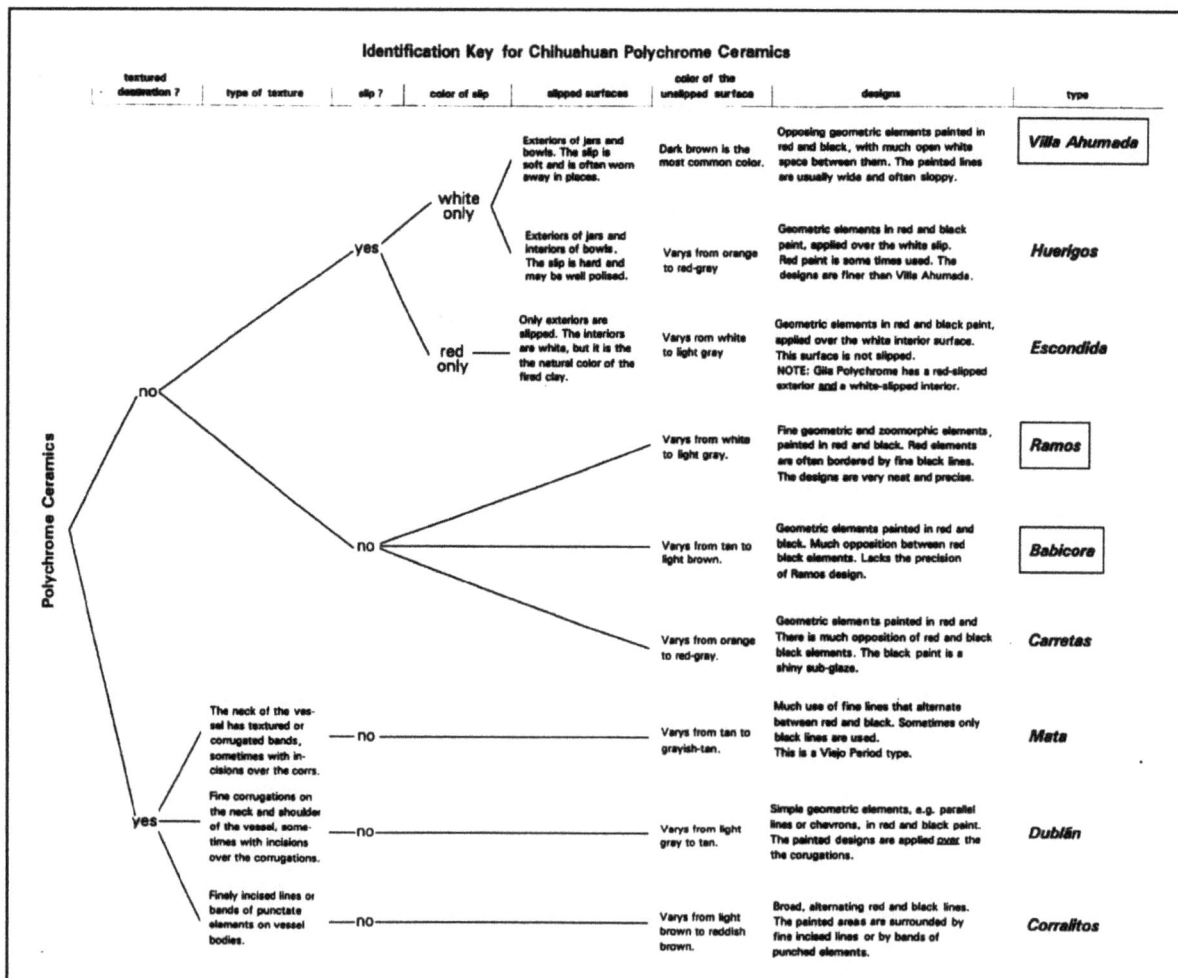

Identification Key for Chihuahuan Polychrome Ceramics

textured decoration ?	type of texture	slip ?	color of slip	slipped surfaces	color of the unslipped surface	designs	type
			white only	Exteriors of jars and bowls. The slip is soft and is often worn away in places.	Dark brown is the most common color.	Opposing geometric elements painted in red and black, with much open white space between them. The painted lines are usually wide and often sloppy.	Villa Ahumada
				Exteriors of jars and interiors of bowls. The slip is hard and may be well polised.	Varys from orange to red-gray.	Geometric elements in red and black paint, applied over the white slip. Red paint is some times used. The designs are finer than Villa Ahumada.	Huerigos
			red only	Only exteriors are slipped. The interiors are white, but it is the natural color of the fired clay.	Varys rom white to light gray.	Geometric elements in red and black paint, applied over the white interior surface. This surface is not slipped. NOTE: Gila Polychrome has a red-slipped exterior and a white-slipped interior.	Escondida
no		no			Varys from white to light gray.	Fine geometric and zoomorphic elements, painted in red and black. Red elements are often bordered by fine black lines. The designs are very neat and precise.	Ramos
					Varys from tan to light brown.	Geometric elements painted in red and black. Much opposition between red black elements. Lacks the precision of Ramos design.	Babicora
					Varys from orange to red-gray.	Geometric elements painted in red and black elements. There is much opposition of red and black elements. The black paint is a shiny sub-glaze.	Carretas
yes	The neck of the vessel has textured or corrugated bands, sometimes with incisions over the corrs.	no			Varys from tan to grayish-tan.	Much use of fine lines that alternate between red and black. Sometimes only black lines are used. This is a Viejo Period type.	Mata
	Fine corrugations on the neck and shoulder of the vessel, sometimes with incisions over the corrugations.	no			Varys from light gray to tan.	Simple geometric elements, e.g. parallel lines or chevrons, in red and black paint. The painted designs are applied over the the corugations.	Dublán
	Finely incised lines or bands of punctate elements on vessel bodies.	no			Varys from light brown to reddish brown.	Broad, alternating red and black lines. The painted areas are surrounded by fine incised lines or by bands of punched elements.	Corralitos

Polychrome Ceramics

Figure 2.5 Basic type descriptions for the Chihuahuan polychrome ceramics (from Whalen, June 1999)

8

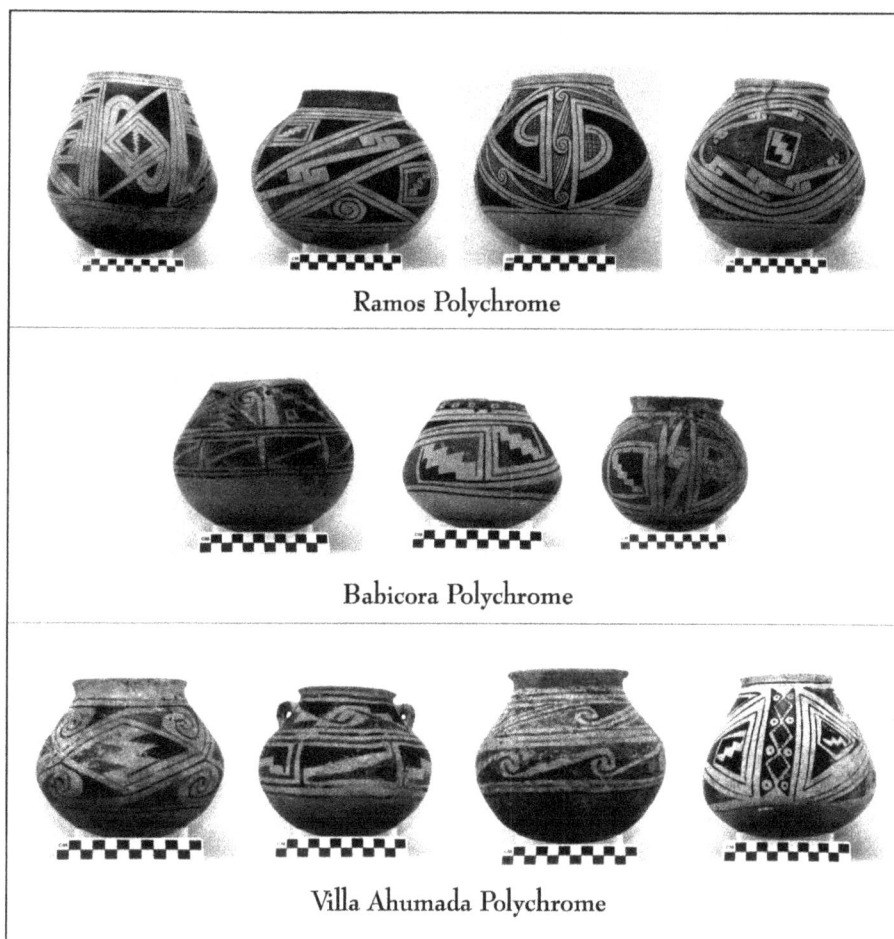

Figure 2.6 Ramos, Babicora and Villa Ahumada polychrome jars from the WPM collection (top row - l to r - #187, #72, #87, #90; middle row - #111, #52, #75; bottom row - #143, #146, #150, #194)

and Ramos variants that are essentially decorated like Ramos polychrome but contain a darker paste or white slip (Ibid.:183; 299). Due to the difficulty in applying the variant classes, archaeologists working with ceramics normally restrict their focus to the level of type. The conflicting traits listed in individual type descriptions (i.e., variants of Babícora is identified by Di Peso), and the problem of affixing variant status on incomplete vessels (i.e. Ramos Capulín variant is defined by the presence of red framing lines around the main design) has caused most archaeologists to disregard Di Peso's categories.

An analysis of decorative variation would ideally include the suite of polychrome types, however, only Ramos, Babícora, and Villa Ahumada (Figure 2.6) are found in quantity within museums. The descriptions for each of these types as described by Sayles and Di Peso are summarized in Table 2.2. Regardless of the fact that this study incorporates both whole vessels and Di Peso's classification system, variant categories will not be employed as it is felt that these sub-classes will complicate discussion of decorative variation.

Summary of Prehistory

Each stage of the Chihuahuan sequence contains intriguing research questions, yet the diversity, abundance, and visibility of Medio period sites is responsible for the overwhelming efforts expended to better understand its role in North American prehistory. From this brief summary of the temporal and cultural background of the Chihuahuan polychrome ceramics we are presented with the basic framework for re-integrating the museum collections. The focus of this discussion will now address in greater detail the development of the regional chronology, the geographical extent of the Medio period assemblage, and I also address issues of terminology.

CERAMIC PERIOD CHRONOLOGY

In contrast to the well-dated cultures of the US Southwest, chronology in Chihuahua remains very much in the fledgling stage. Prior to the application of radiocarbon dating, the most commonly used technique in Chihuahua was through ceramic cross-dating. Foreign types found in localized contexts, especially the well-

9

Trait	Ramos	Babicora	Villa Ahumada
Sayles			
Surface	Ivory, white to brown	Dark cream to light brown or tan	Brown to tan
Slip	None	None	White
Paint	Rich scarlet to maroon, black to dk grey	Dull red, black or greyish-brown	Deep red to orange, black
Effigies	Human - hooded, reclining, true human face Animal, Bird, Fish - Hooded, side-appended; -snake, horned lizard, owl, macaw	Human - hooded, true effigy Animal and Bird - side-appended	Human - hooded, often with painted arms; Animal, Bird, Fish - side-appended, legs often added to animal;
Decoration	- highly elaborate, balanced colours; - repeated elements occupy wide strip/panel around vessel; - opposed keys, steps, scrolls, club-shaped designs, tapering triangles; - elements are hatched, cross-hatched, filled with dots - solid colours often outlined by fine line of a different colour	- Solid red and black designs boldly executed, often opposed; - interlocking scrolls and bent lines, dots, circles; - many lines finely drawn, similar to Ramos; - solid colours sometimes outlined by fine line of a different colour	- Solid red and black designs boldly executed, often opposed; - interlocking scrolls and bent lines, dots, circles; - many lines finely drawn, similar to Ramos; - solid colours sometimes outlined by fine line of a different colour
Comments	Classic type of the Chihuahua series with all aspects of form and decoration taken to the highest level of artistic development and variety	Overall this type appears to be a transition type including styles of both earlier types and Ramos characteristics	Execution of designs in finely drawn lines, use of elements found in Ramos suggests possible introductory type
Di Peso			
Variant	Standard - light-coloured paste, reliance on black linework, red elements oultined by black, fine brushwork Capulin - precise brushwork, lack of black borders on solid red elements, greater use of red lines B/W - no red paint, same design scheme	Standard - painted with thick lines, balanced red and black designs, and multi-pointed flags; similar to Carretas, Huerigos, and Dublan poly Paquime - similar to Ramos in style and technique, fine lines, negative circles, and occasionally red elements oultined in black	Standard - as described by Sayles (see above) Ramos - same style as Standard Ramos but with white slip Capulins - good brushwork, similar to Ramos Caplin, with no black borders around red elements Memmott - red paint only used in narrow line above and below layout

Table 2.2 Basic type descriptions for Ramos, Babicora and Villa Ahumada polychromes according to Sayles (1936) and Di Peso, Rinaldo and Fenner (1974)

dated Southwest wares, were used as markers to provide the Chihuahuan types with a rough temporal context (see Brand 1935). After Di Peso's excavation at Paquimé, the finer aspects of internal regional chronology shifted to architectural stratigraphy (building superposition), architectural typology (component features and total building structure) and, to a lesser degree, on tree-ring dates, obsidian hydration, and ceramic cross-dating (Di Peso et al.1974a:78-79; Scott 1966:73). Oddly, given the large size and depth of deposits at Paquimé the use of ceramic stratigraphy was thwarted by the lack of sortable excavated contexts,

Little, if anything, was gained by a comparison of painted decoration within the Medio Period alone. This was primarily due to the lack of a sample of floor sherds representative of each of the three phases. However, in viewing sherds of each type and variant sorted by specific provenience, no observable differences were noted in the details of design. The main contrasts, rather, came as a result of differential distribution of variants by unit provenience (Di Peso et al. 1974a:99).

Regardless of the inability to incorporate the ceramic data into an internal chronology, Di Peso still proposed finer temporal distinctions within the Medio Period based on a

proposed seriation of building construction (see Table 2.1). This chronology represents the temporal foundation for Di Peso's interpretation that Paquimé was founded by Mesoamerican warrior-priests, the *pochteca*, who moved north in search of trade goods in the 11th century A.D. (Ibid.:290-295).

Di Peso's original chronology has since been the subject of intense scrutiny starting with LeBlanc (1980), Stewart (1984), and Lekson (1984), however perhaps the most salient argument against his conclusions was presented in Dean and Ravesloot's (1993) paper, 'The Chronology of Cultural Interaction in the Gran Chichimeca'. Their re-examination of the tree-ring samples from Paquimé determined that the earliest date for the site was 150 years too early, placing the span of the Medio period between 1200 and 1450 A.D. (Ibid.:96). This change was corroborated by the presence of Gila polychrome pottery, a 14th century Puebloan type from central Arizona, and other foreign ceramic wares located in the excavated contexts at Paquimé (Ibid.:86; Stewart 1984). The most significant impact of this research was the decreased likelihood that Paquimé, and inevitably the entire culture area, was the result of the arrival of Mesoamerican migrants to the region. By moving the date 200 years younger, Paquimé is too late to be the result of Toltec expansion (Braniff 1986:79) and too early to have

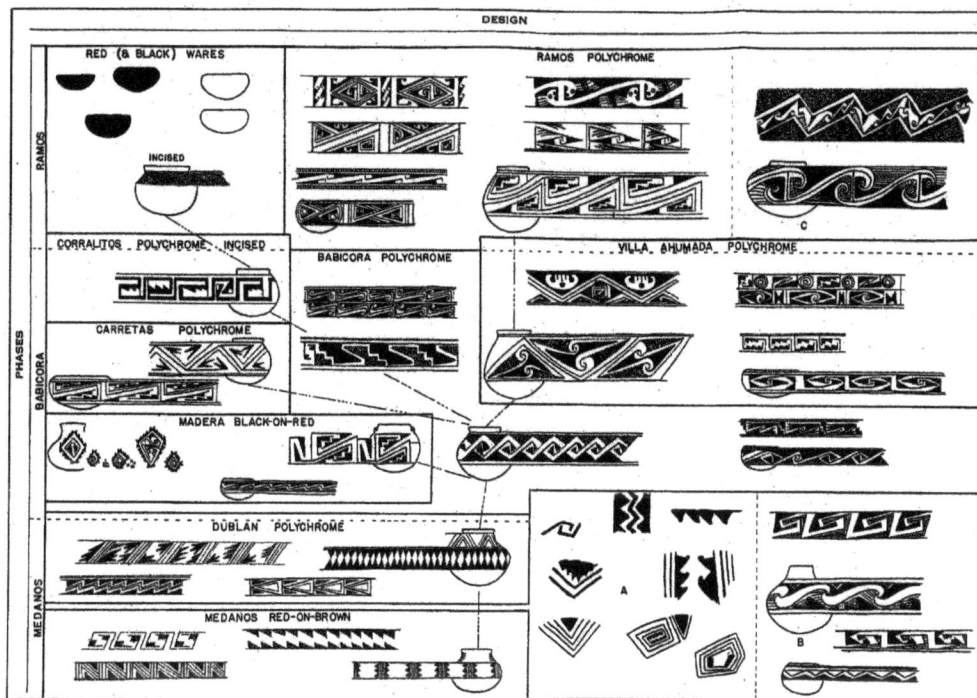

Figure 2.7 Sayles's proposed evolution of design in the Chihuahuan polychrome tradition (from Sayles 1936)

interacted significantly with the Aztec (Dean and Ravesloot 1993:103). One consideration raised by Nelson (1992) is that the groups on the northern periphery of the Mesoamerican cultural sphere flourished during the period between the wane of Toltec and rise of Aztec cultures. Interestingly, the 'new' dating for the Medio period corresponds to that suggested by Brand (1933:92-93) who proposed, based solely on ceramic cross-dating, that the climax of the site and culture occurred during the 14th to 15th centuries.

Another significant change to Di Peso's Medio period chronology has been to set aside the Buena Fe, Paquimé, and Diablo phases defined by the architectural building sequence (Schaafsma and Riley 1999:7). The reason for this backlash is that these temporal divisions have proven impossible to verify through either absolute or seriation dating techniques. Radiocarbon dating cannot be used to ratify these micro-distinctions because the 2-sigma statistical standards used to bracket the resultant date often eclipse the 250-year window of the Medio period. Comparable problems exist in the application of dendrochronology (Joe Stewart, personal communication, July 1999). While Dean and Ravesloot were able to correlate the few pine tree-rings from Paquimé to the well-established Southwest sequence, formation of a comparable reference for Chihuahua is hindered due to the lack of provenienced samples and the predominance of unusable wood types from prehistoric sites (Scott 1966:75-76). This problem can be attributed to the massive logging of old growth in the region and that the majority of wood found in Chihuahuan sites is juniper,

which cannot be connected to the tree-ring series established in the US Southwest.

A definitive artifact-based seriation has similarly eluded researchers attempting to corroborate the phases produced through architectural stratigraphy and building typology. The greatest obstacle with the Paquimé data is that, as a result of the collapse of multi-story roomblocks, pieces of the same vessel were often found within different rooms and associated with more than one architectural episode (Di Peso et al. 1974a:79). Each type was found in the lowest levels of the excavation and Di Peso interpreted this to indicate contemporaneous appearance and continuous production throughout the Medio period (Ibid.:80-84). More recent attempts to seriate the ceramic data from Paquimé into these phases have met with little success. One exception is Whalen and Minnis's (1996) re-examination of type frequencies across the site, which produced clusters of 'early' and 'late' Medio ceramics. Unfortunately, these clusters have not been directly studied to discern the presence of temporally sensitive markers such as motifs, paste, or surface finish. While this study indicates that temporal variation is present in the ceramic data, there is no other justification to continue dividing the Medio period into three phases.

By contrast with the work undertaken at Paquimé, Carey (1931), Sayles (1936a), and Carlson (1982) each formulated a polychrome seriation based on relative frequencies of pottery or decorative style from survey and museum collections. Figure 2.7 illustrates the progression

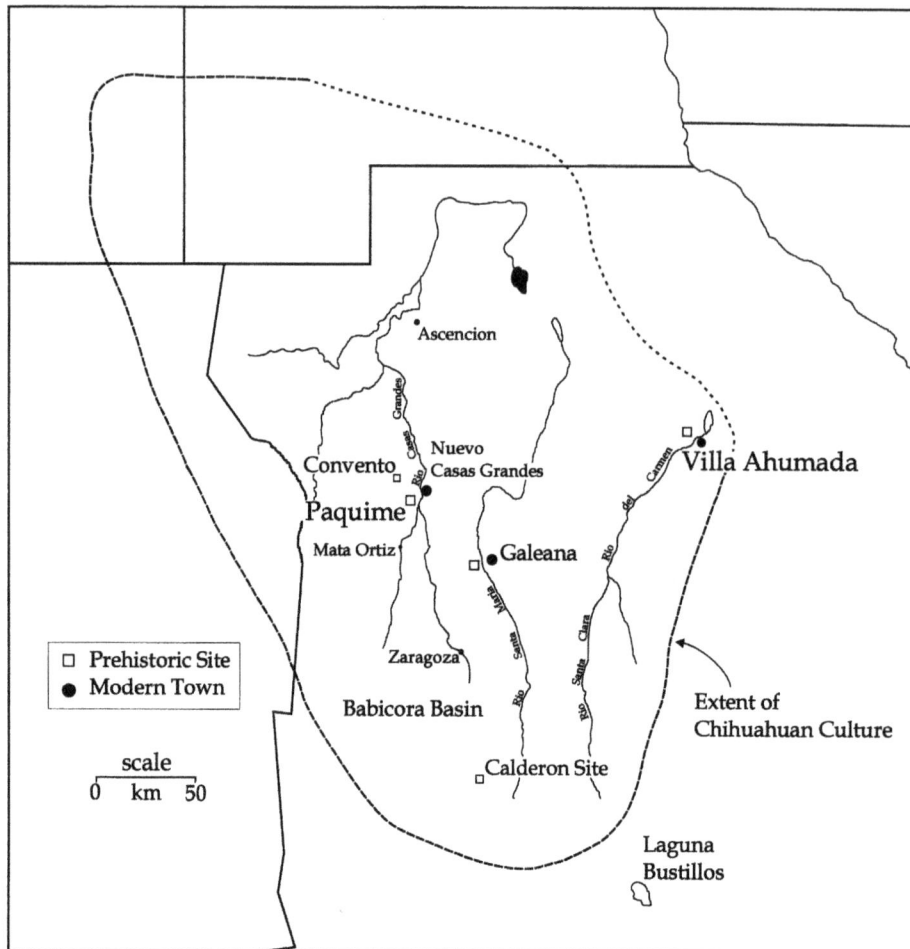

Figure 2.8 Geographical extent of the Chihuahuan culture. Dashed line indicates shared cultural traits with Jornada Mogollon (El Paso Phase). (based on Brand 1935; Schaafsma and Riley 1999:7)

of types devised by Sayles according to changes in painted design. These sequences offer useful comparative models but cannot substitute for an undisturbed, deeply stratified site with a clear ordering of ceramic types. Until we locate such a site, we must continue examining trait relationships between and within types with the hope of uncovering a micro-seriation comparable to that accomplished in the Mimbres area (Shafer and Taylor 1986; Shafer and Brewington 1995) or at Moundville (Steponaitis 1983).

A direct result of the shift in dating for the Medio period was the dismissal of Di Peso's Tardio period, which he associated with the foundation of the historic puebloan groups in the US Southwest and Northern Mexico (1974:766-779). The majority of discussion of this final period deals with Iberian impact on the native populations. The archaeological evidence from his Robles phase (A.D. 1340 to A.D. 1519) is poorly represented and, on the whole, it is little differentiated from that produced during the previous period (i.e., similar pottery types, architectural style, etc.). Current opinion favours the elimination of this chronological division for lack of

supporting data (Art MacWilliams, personal communication, May 1998).

CULTURAL "BOUNDARIES"

Medio period sites are found throughout central and west central Chihuahua with numerous sites in the Sierra Madre Occidental, the high elevation basin-and-range country on the eastern flank of the Sierra, and in the Chihuahuan desert. The distribution of these sites was originally compiled from the surveys completed by Bandelier (1890), Carey (1931), Brand (1933), and Lister (1946) in the late 19th- to mid-20th centuries. The spread of this culture was defined by the presence of the painted ceramics in conjunction with architectural features, and ground/chipped stone artifacts from surface inventories. Of the ceramic remains, it was the spread of the painted wares, specifically Casas Grandes Polychrome (later dubbed Ramos polychrome), Huèrigos Polychrome, and Villa Ahumada Polychrome, that proved to be important markers of the spatial distribution of the Chihuahuan culture (Brand 1933:79-80). More recent survey projects by Whalen and Minnis (1999), Kelley and Stewart (1999b), and Cruz Antillon and Maxwell (1999) have

12

refined the limits of Medio period culture to its presently accepted distribution (Figure 2.8). The only distinct break in the Chihuahuan assemblage has been identified on the southern frontier where, according to surveys by the Proyecto Arqueológico Chihuahua (Kelley et al. 1999a:65), the material culture extends no further south than the town of Buena Vista on the upper Santa Maria drainage. In contrast, the Chihuahuan assemblage becomes heavily mixed as a result of interaction with groups to the north, and west. Areas where the cultural boundary is blurred are found in Sonora at Cerro de Trincheras (McGuire and Villalpando 1993), within the Black Mountain/Animas/ Cliff phases of southeastern Arizona and southern New Mexico (Carpenter 1996; Douglas 1995, 1996), and in the El Paso phase of eastern Chihuahua/western Texas (Schaafsma 1979; LeBlanc 1980; Bradley and Hoffer 1985; J.C. Kelley 1986; Cruz Antillón and Maxwell 1999).

Several localized variations in material components, especially in the painted ceramics, have been identified within the homogenized zone that defines the culture. For example, the same ceramic types, including effigy vessels, found on the southern edge of the Medio distribution and in the core area around Paquimé are differentiated by the nature and finishing of the pot surfaces, yet are decorated in a similar style (Carey 1931:338). Amsden (1928:339) proposed that the Babícora Basin sites represent an earlier occupation than that found around Paquimé on the basis of differences of southern pottery, which contained a darker paste and were "less finely" painted than northern examples. While dating has not corroborated this hypothesis, Amsden's insight is important to this discussion as it recognizes that the variability found between polychrome ceramics may be indicative of regional production centers.

CULTURAL AND CERAMIC DEFINITIONS

Cultural Terminology

Before turning this discussion towards the history of ceramic research in Chihuahua it is necessary to select a consistent cultural terminology. Chihuahuan (Brand 1935:290; Sayles 1936a:iv) and Casas Grandes culture (Brand 1935:290; Lister 1960:123; Di Peso 1974; Phillips 1989:383) have been bandied about equally and interchangeably within the archaeological literature. The primary difference between these terms is mostly a matter of perspective: Chihuahuan culture recognizes the wide distribution of the material remains throughout the region, while Casas Grandes culture emphasizes the importance of the site of Casas Grandes (Paquimé). Little problem existed in employing either term prior to the Paquimé excavations between 1958-61. Soon afterward, however, the site became the lynchpin for ascribing cultural development throughout the area (Di Peso 1974; Phillips 1989; Schaafsma and Riley 1999:6). While the overall impact of Paquimé is not disputed, the emphasis that has been given to a 'Casas Grandes' culture presents

a stilted perception of regional prehistory, to the detriment of recognizing independent growth within this vast area. For the purpose of this thesis the term Chihuahuan culture, as suggested by the PAC (Kelley et al. 1999a:63), is used because of its broader ranging implications for regional development.

In addition to the inclusive terms, more expansive labels have been suggested to relate the Chihuahuan culture within the Greater Southwest. For example, extra-regional terms such as Chichimecan, Gran Chichimecan, and O'otam were proposed by Di Peso (1974:48-57),

> to force us to break down our mental obstacles and think about a world without a United States-Mexican border, as is only appropriate for the vast time of prehistory and for most of the historic period as well (Cordell 1993:222).

While such concepts are necessary to properly frame the inherent similarities between the groups consolidated within this large area there is no need to extend the archaeological implications of the Chihuahuan culture into a pan-regional framework at this time. Paquimé and the prehistoric inhabitants of Chihuahua were definitely part of a broad interaction sphere, however, we know substantially less about the internal relationships within the region. Once the local developments are understood it will be possible to reconsider Di Peso's broader terms to incorporate this region into the larger framework of North American prehistory.

Ceramic Terminology

In selecting a proper name for the ceramic assemblage we must recognize its role in prehistoric society. For example, what do the different ceramic types represent, either individually or as a set? Does the polychrome pottery represent the works of a widespread, uniform culture that existed for 250 years? Or, do the different types denote a series of distinct, yet closely related, culture or ethnic groups? The wide geographical distribution and shared decorative features between the types support the argument that they are part of a distinct school as suggested by Di Peso (Di Peso et al. 1974a:1-2). Due to the modern implications of a 'school', the term 'tradition' will be used here in reference to the polychrome types as it has less association with direct information transfer or regulated production.

The early literature referred to the local ceramics interchangeably as Chihuahuan and Casas Grandes (Bandelier 1886:28-29; Kidder 1924:318; Harcum 1923:4; Carey 1931:328; Brand 1933:59). Since this thesis is directed toward both diachronic and synchronic processes from an assemblage that is potentially from a very wide span of space and time, the term Chihuahuan tradition will be employed.

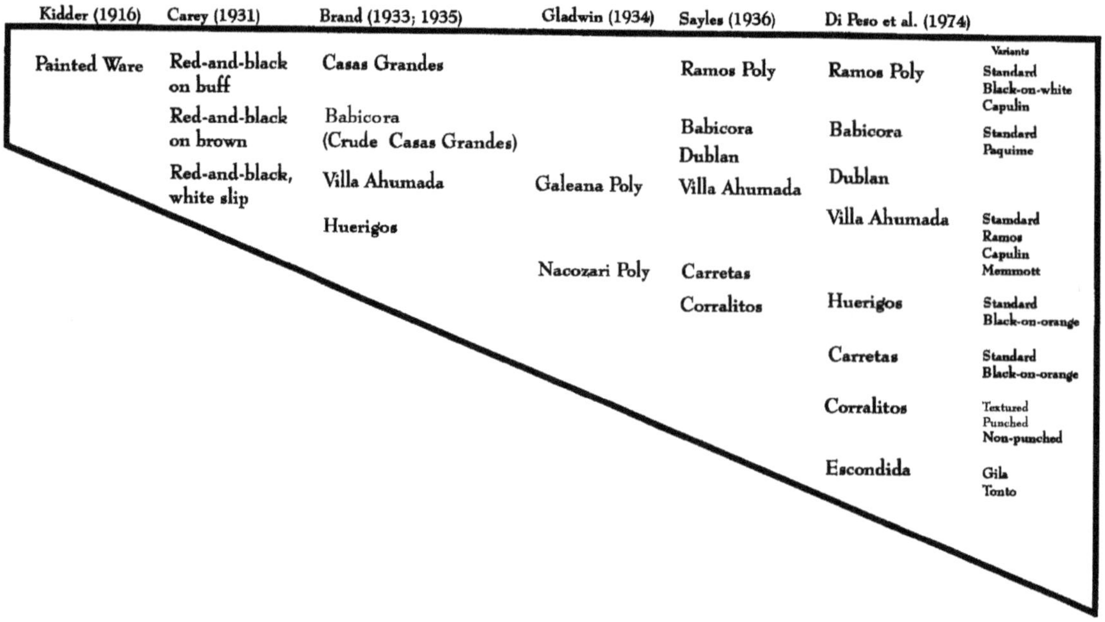

Kidder (1916)	Carey (1931)	Brand (1933; 1935)	Gladwin (1934)	Sayles (1936)	Di Peso et al. (1974)	Variants
Painted Ware	Red-and-black on buff	Casas Grandes		Ramos Poly	Ramos Poly	Standard Black-on-white Capulin
	Red-and-black on brown	Babicora (Crude Casas Grandes)		Babicora Dublan	Babicora	Standard Paquime
	Red-and-black, white slip	Villa Ahumada	Galeana Poly	Villa Ahumada	Dublan	
		Huerigos			Villa Ahumada	Stamdard Ramos Capulin Memmott
			Nacozari Poly	Carretas	Huerigos	Standard Black-on-orange
				Corralitos	Carretas	Standard Black-on-orange
					Corralitos	Textured Punched Non-punched
					Escondida	Gila Tonto

Figure 2.9 Chronological development of ceramic type names for the Chihuahuan polychrome tradition

Museum Collections from the Medio Period

The chronological and archaeological information presented above provides the necessary background for re-integrating museum collections into their original milieu. This broad survey illustrates the cultural complexity of the Medio period and touched on issues, such as a lack of temporal control and political control, that need to be addressed in future research. The next section will examine the nature of the applications of ceramic data to archaeological inference as well as outline the fundamental role that the study of design has played in this research.

HISTORY OF CERAMIC RESEARCH

The goal of reviewing the history of ceramic research is twofold; firstly, it will delimit the form and progression of research undertaken over the past 100 years in the region; secondly, it will identify critical issues or gaps in our knowledge or in the methods that have been used. A further benefit of this review is that intuitive hypotheses made by early scholars, either forgotten or set aside, can be re-examined and tested against new data sets. Finally, this summary will play an important role in assessing the range of archaeological questions that the museum collections can be used to address.

The Role of Polychrome Pottery

"Of this civilization Casas Grandes Pottery is one of the most notable extant records" (Harcum 1923:11).

This statement heralding the arrival of the Chihuahuan pottery at the National Museum of Natural History, Washington, D.C., attests to the impact and importance of this ceramic tradition. Ironically, despite the ubiquity of this material and the seventy-odd years since this observation, archaeologists have made little headway in understanding the complexity of the Chihuahuan polychromes. This fact is surprising given the in-depth discussions (see Graves 1998) of interaction (Plog 1980), ideology (Crown 1994), and use in food consumption (Mills 1999) published for contemporary cultures across the international border. Having said this, large quantities of ceramic data *have* been collected and analyzed in detail, specifically, Di Peso's (Di Peso 1974) excavations at Paquimé. The problem in this case lies not with the quantity of material but the paucity of post-excavation synthesis to address questions beyond classification. Outside of Paquimé, recent research has greatly expanded our knowledge of regional ceramic variability based on sherd collections obtained from survey and excavation (i.e. Hill 1992; Minnis and Whalen 1995; Kelley and Stewart 1991a; 1991b). Again, these studies are focussed on understanding regional diversity and are slowly coming to the point where cultural issues will become the primary concern.

In general, ceramic research in Chihuahua can be clustered into two basic groups; the first, and most common focussed on culture historical issues aimed at defining the typology and chronology; the second emphasizes cultural factors such as interaction and, to a much lesser degree, ceramic production. While these are not mutually exclusive groups, the kind of information taken from the ceramics and the levels of cultural interpretation make them distinct.

Internal Developments, Typology and Interpretation

The root of ceramic investigation is the organization of its constituent parts into categories (i.e., typology) and the establishment of a developmental sequence (i.e., chronology). Culture history in Chihuahua remains a critical issue today, especially with the absence of a readily identifiable micro-seriation of the Medio period. This section will address the development of the typology and the debate surrounding the temporal developments of the Chihuahuan tradition.

The Beginning of Classification

The development of the Chihuahuan typology spans nearly 100 years of archaeological research beginning with Alfred Kidder's (1916) description of the whole vessels from the Peabody Museum. Figure 2.9 illustrates the changes in painted ceramic nomenclature that have taken place during the evolution of this typology. Using surface finish as the determining factor, Kidder documented four categories in his classification: rough dark ware, polished blackware, redware and painted ware (Ibid.:253). These basic divisions were later expanded by Carey (1931) according to generalized categories of vessel shape and decoration using field and museum collections. Carey also recognized that these distinct pottery forms belonged to a recognizable ceramic tradition,

> ...as the pottery from the known sites of the Casas Grandes valley is homogeneous in form, technique, and design, museum collections of unknown provenience were examined. These collections have a certain value in that, according to Mexicans who had secured such material from the mounds and sold it, they were all obtained within a radius of thirty miles from the ruins of Casas Grandes, (1931:339).

The importance of Kidder and Carey's research for this study is that their reliance on whole vessels provides an early example of the incorporation of this kind of data set into archaeological analysis.

Efforts to understand the origins of this distinct ceramic tradition often relied on comparison of material with neighboring areas in the US Southwest and from the closest centers in Mexico. Generally, the Chihuahuan ceramics share much more in common with northern groups and the sudden proliferation of these wares is not attributed to a sudden influx of Mesoamerican influence or migration. Amsden (1928), Carey (1931) and Brand (1933) attempted to delineate regional distributions for the ceramics based on type frequency between valleys, providing the first spatial associations for the tradition. At this time the polychrome ceramics were divided into Casas Grandes, Peripheral Casas Grandes, Villa Ahumada, and HuOrigos types according to decorative technique, paste, areal distribution and, to a lesser extent, on stratigraphic relationship (Brand 1933:79-80;

1935:90). Peripheral Casas Grandes is distinguished from Casas Grandes ware by the inferior decorative technique, poorer clay, lack of life-designs, and it has a southerly distribution centered in the Babícora basin (Brand 1933:79). These surveys narrowed the geographical locus of each type, however, very little was known about the temporal relationship between these ceramics. One exception proposed by Brand (Ibid.) was that the artistic skill and complexity of decoration in Casas Grandes polychrome (or Ramos) represents the pinnacle (i.e. later) ceramic type.

Working from this initial breakdown of types, Gladwin and Gladwin (1934) and Sayles (1936a) broadened the classification to include Dublan and Carretas polychromes, Madera Black-on-red, Medanos Red-on-brown, Corralitos Incised, and changed the official appellations of Casas Grandes to Ramos polychrome and Peripheral Casas Grandes to Babícora. Each type was described in more explicit terms according to formal traits such as decoration, technique, and vessel form, and was associated with a type-site and geographical distribution. While there is considerable spatial overlap of the polychrome types throughout northwestern and west central Chihuahua, Sayles suggested that possible centers of production for individual types based on type frequencies at sites throughout Chihuahua. In addition to outlining the ceramic traits in greater detail, Sayles also furnished the first chronological ordering of the types based on similarities and contrasts of design style. Further studies by Lister (1939) contributed to the knowledge of type distribution throughout Chihuahua as well as providing a seriation comparable to that defined by Sayles.

This research established the basic parameters of the material remains in Chihuahua that, twenty years later, would become the diagnostic artifacts of the Medio period. The excavation of Paquimé would change the face of Chihuahuan archaeology and literally open the region's archaeology to a much wider scholarly and popular audience.

Charles Di Peso and the Chihuahuan Typology Explosion

The Joint Amerind excavations at Paquimé (1958-1961) remain the most detailed attempt to address questions of typology and chronology from any Chihuahuan site. Based on nearly 800,000 sherds and several hundred whole vessels, Di Peso, Rinaldo, and Fenner's analysis (1969; 1974a) established the regional standard for all subsequent research on Chihuahuan ceramics. Even today the information from the eight-volume site report represents a formidable database that has only recently been digested by archaeologists working in the region (McGuire 1993:35). Description of each artifact type is very intensive; however, the interpretation of these data is rather limited and dwells on descriptive frequencies of particular traits rather than in-depth comparison. This restricted analysis is likely attributable to the overwhelming size of the database and difficulties in interpreting the complex site formation processes.

The three key changes resulting from this research that have already been introduced in the discussion of Medio period typology and chronology are: 1) the increase in descriptive information for each polychrome type (i.e., identification of decorative similarities and differences); 2) splitting and expanding the typology to include numerous variants within each type; and 3) and the division of the Medio period into phases.

As discussed earlier, the Casas Grandes ceramic volume provided a comprehensive list of nearly every conceivable trait found on sherds or whole vessels. Unfortunately, the Di Peso's Ceramic volume is largely restricted to descriptions and broad comparisons of decorative and formal similarities between types (Di Peso et al. 1974a:84-100). The problem with these relationships, such as the decorative similarities shared between Babícora, Dublan, and the Standard Variant of Villa Ahumada, is that the actual data supporting this association is never explicitly stated.

The second change proposed by Di Peso was to split the types into variants. Many scholars, including myself, have questioned the utility of smaller classes, primarily on the grounds that variants cannot be used to categorize sherds. In a recent test of the Medio period typology Hendrickson (2001) indicated that the identification of a variant (black-bordered red motifs) often ignored the diagnostic markers attributed to a different type (such as dark paste, or design layout) in the classification system. Gloria Fenner (personal communication June 1999), one of the original analysts of the ceramics recovered from Paquimé, also cautioned against the over-simplification and direct application of the intricacies of the typology to distant collections. Ultimately, since the meaning of the variants is not understood at their source it seems inappropriate to use them for classifying assemblages from other sites. Indeed, if the role of typology is to answer specific questions of time and space (Brew 1946; Adams and Adams 1991:240), the utility of making such micro-distinctions with no identifiable goal must be disputed or addressed in greater detail.

Perhaps Di Peso's most significant, and controversial, contribution to our knowledge of Chihuahuan prehistory was the proposition of temporal periods and phases. Strangely, the enormous excavations did not produce a decipherable ceramic seriation to support the architecturally-defined phases. Because each of the ceramic types was found at the lowest levels, Di Peso was led to conclude that the Medio polychrome types were produced contemporaneously from the earliest part of this period (Di Peso et al. 1974a:80-84). This result may also be a result of the complex site formation processes, which involved the collapse of three to four story roomblocks.

Challenges to both the chronometric dates of the Medio period and the architecturally-derived phases have succeeded (see Dean and Ravesloot 1993; Whalen and Minnis 1996), however, a proper seriation is still required to test the validity of Di Peso's hypothesis of contemporary appearance. Secondary evidence such as the evolution based on decorative changes proposed by Kidder (1916), Carey (1931), and Sayles (1936a), and the presence of Escondida polychrome, which is derived from Salado culture Gila and Tonto polychromes (1300-1450 A.D.) (Crown 1994: 19-20) can also be added to suggest some form of internal temporal variation in the ceramic assemblage.

Post- Paquimé Progress
Nearly a decade later, Roy Carlson (1982) discussed the Chihuahuan wares in a synthesis of ceramic development and historical relationships between US Southwest and Northwest Mexican traditions. From this broad perspective, Carlson identified relationships between the Chihuahuan and Mimbres painted wares based on decorative characteristics such as life designs, and examined the contribution of Chihuahuan polychromes to later traditions (Ibid.:213-215). More importantly for the present discussion, Carlson challenges Di Peso's view of the temporal sequence for the Medio period and the contemporaneity of the polychrome types. Based on ceramic cross-dating of US Southwest wares found at Chihuahuan culture sites and the lack of radiocarbon dates, he argued that the Medio period likely spanned from A.D. 1275 to 1400 (Ibid.:216). Carlson (Ibid.:212) admits that there is considerable disagreement in the temporal placement of the individual polychromes and proposes, contra-Di Peso, date estimates for the production of each type. According to his ceramic sequence, Babícora, Dublan, and Escondida polychrome were produced from A.D. 1275 to 1400, while Villa Ahumada, Carretas, Huérigos, and Ramos polychromes spanned the period of A.D 1350 to 1450 (Ibid.:213). The problem with this proposed seriation, which revives the idea that the types did not appear *en masse*, is that no explicit reasoning is provided to justify this sequence. Even with the lack of supporting data, the importance of this paper is that it re-affirms the need to continue addressing variation within the Chihuahuan ceramic assemblage.

A secondary suggestion that emerged from Carlson's regional comparison was that the geometrically-based decoration found on pottery may have been derived from existing motifs on non-ceramic objects, such as basketry (Ibid.:203). This translation of the form of one medium (i.e,. basketry) into a new medium (i.e., ceramics), known as skeumorphism (Vansina 1984:56), is a common occurrence and can be expressed not only in decoration but also in technological applications (see Lechtman 1977; Callaghan and Allum 1989). Unfortunately, a substantial sample of comparably decorated media has not been discovered in Chihuahua to test this hypothesis,

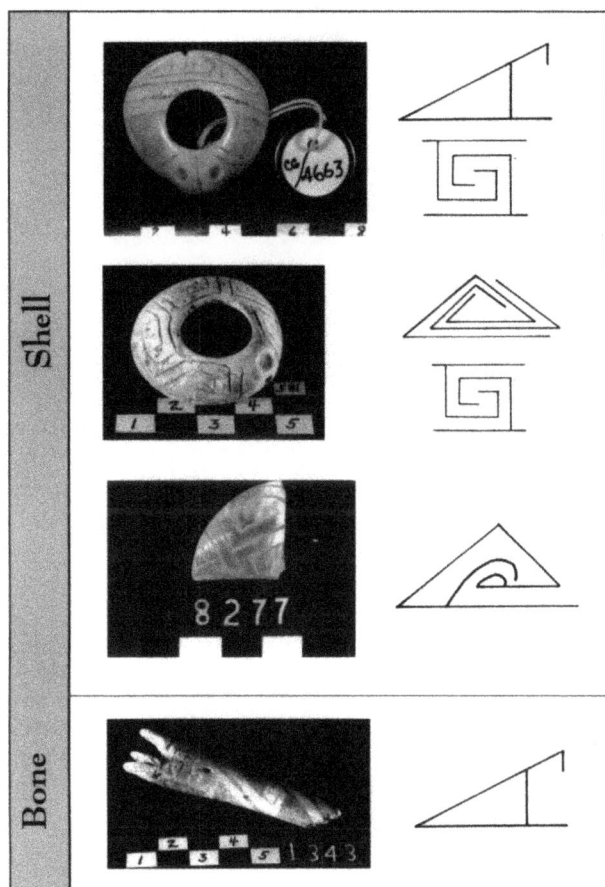

Figure 2.10 Shell and bone artifacts from Paquimé showing decoration commonly found on Chihuahuan polychrome ceramics
(photos courtesy of INAH Chihuahua)

and the majority of examples recovered archaeologically (see Figure 2.10) are not textile-based. Similarities have also been identified between pottery decoration and rock art (see P. Schaafsma 1999) found scattered throughout Chihuahua and west Texas, specifically in relation to life figures such as the plumed serpent and human forms.

Intensive field research in Chihuahua has only become a reality in the past decade with the survey and excavation undertaken by Minnis and Whalen (see summary in Whalen and Minnis 1999), Kelley and Stewart (1991b), Cruz and Maxwell (1999) and Leonard (1999, personal communication). As a result we now have a larger base of radiocarbon dates (Hill 1992; Kelley et al. 1999a; Kelley et al. 2000a) and have compiled extensive collections to begin to assess regional type distribution and decorative variation between types.

Slowly the picture of regional development in Chihuahua is being uncovered and it is possible to change our focus to address new lines of archaeological inquiry. Current graduate topics incorporating polychrome pottery include ceramic production and gender roles (Malagon 2001), social complexity and religious organization (Rakita 2001), and status and ideology (Van Poole 2001). This trend represents an important movement beyond etic typological concerns to a more cultural view of how the ceramics were integrated into Chihuahuan culture.

Origins and External Relationships
Research using ceramics to delineate inter-regional relationships has focussed on understanding the origins of Chihuahuan culture and also outlining the extent of Paquimé's influence as the economic and political capital of the region (i.e. Woosley and Olinger 1993). The basis for the comparative approach is the idea that the Chihuahuan ceramics represent a related body of material culture. Carey (1931:328) pointed out that, "if sufficient homogeneity of cultural traits exists within the region to permit the whole to be designated a culture area, then analytical comparison of contiguous areas may be made". The primary methods for measuring interaction are based on the spread of artifacts outside of their 'home' culture area, through the presence of foreign wares within Chihuahuan culture sites, or the degree to which diagnostic decorative types or techniques are shared between groups (Plog 1980:54). The study of cultural interaction is not restricted to ceramic data and must include other cultural components such as architecture (i.e., ballcourts, breeding pens), specific cultural practices (i.e., burial type), and settlement patterns (see Di Peso 1974; Ravesloot 1988; Minnis 1989).

Foreign Contact and Origins
Carey (1931:327) first suggested that archaeologists needed to address the internal developments and then examine the relationships between the Chihuahuan peoples and neighboring groups. Given the sudden florescence and fusion of diverse cultural traits in the Chihuahuan culture it is not surprising that much research has focussed on the second part of Carey's research goals. Historically, the most heated debate surrounding the origins of Paquimé and the Chihuahuan culture has centered on the nature and extent of Mesoamerican contact and its subsequent influence on the US Southwest (J. Charles Kelley 1966, 1986; Phillips 1991; Di Peso 1974; Pailes 1978; 1980). The most ardent supporter for a Mesoamerican origin was Di Peso who hypothesized (1974) that Paquimé was the product of a migration of the Toltec merchant class, or *puchteca*, who founded the city as a trading post between the US Southwest and Mesoamerica. He viewed the presence and scale of architectural features (i.e. macaw breeding pens, ball courts, mounds) and substantial stores of trade items as requiring a powerful, non-local elite to explain such progress (see summary in McGuire 1993).

Arguments for direct Mesomamerican contact are complicated, however, when considered within the history of developments within the US Southwest and the distribution of 'Southern' traits in Chihuahua. Foreign traits such as I-shaped ballcourts, marine shell, T-shaped doorways, and scarlet macaws are found to pre-date the

Medio period at sites in the Hohokam area of southern Arizona (Gregory 1991:165-166). There is also little evidence of widespread distribution of trade goods from the south into Chihuahua. Brand's (1935:288) broad survey of NW Chihuahua recorded infrequent Mesoamerican artifacts such as spindle whorls, metal objects, and terra cotta figurines. In a recent examination of Paquimé, the proposed hub of *puchteca* activity, Lekson (1999) has argued that the distinctive architectural features at Paquimé represent the culmination of three centuries of Puebloan development. Unfortunately, there has been little research aimed at determining a northern origin for the Medio period developments. The few studies that addressed this topic have used the similarity of Chihuahuan buildings to Puebloan architecture (i.e., multi-story rectangular roomblocks, t-shaped doorways) and have posited a southward migration of Mimbres (LeBlanc 1980; Carlson 1982:212-215) or Anasazi groups (Lekson 2000). The problem with these studies that attribute the origins of Medio occupations to distant migration is that they fail to take into consideration the existence of Viejo sites, which have a similar distribution to Medio period occupation throughout Chihuahua.

Polychrome pottery has played an important role in understanding the roots of Medio period culture, mostly because painted decoration can illustrate long-held trends as well as quickly incorporate new ideas of content and technique. Evidence of southern influence is suggested by the addition to the local tradition of the plumed serpent image, erotic imagery, abundance of effigy vessels, negative painting technique, and red and black as the main paint colors (Kidder 1916:267; Brand 1933:95; Di Peso et al.1974a:90). Following Di Peso's goal to define a southern origin for the Medio Period florescence, he proposed that the combination of decorative traits from the Paquimé assemblage reflects specific Mesoamerican ritual complexes (1974:554-571). For example, the cult of Quetzalcoatl is seen in the use of the plumed serpent, a hooded effigy with an open mouth was seen as representing Xipe Tótec, god of springtime, and two-faced jars that are interpreted as symbolizing the Warrior Twins (Ibid.:552-571). The problem with these inferences is that similar iconographic depictions appear in the Mimbres Black-on-white ceramics that pre-date the Medio period (see Thompson 1999). Such associations with well-established and elaborate Mesoamerican cults may be correct; however, this data can only be used to validate the transmission of ideas and not the migration of *puchteca* or other southern groups.

Overall, the assignment of the Chihuahuan tradition to Mesoamerican origins has been rejected since the initial studies undertaken by Kidder (1916) and Brand (1933). It was argued that the small cluster of southern decorative and formal traits represent only a minor part of a tradition that is predominated by geometric motifs and design fields (i.e. use of framing lines, repetition of elements) commonly found among Puebloan ceramics (Brand 1933:94). The great variety of vessel forms produced in the Chihuahuan tradition also conforms to the range of shapes associated with Southwestern cultures (Ibid.). Even the effigy vessel, which stands apart in the Chihuahuan assemblage, cannot be directly associated with Mesoamerican contact since effigies have been found in west Mexico, east Texas, and the Mississippi valley, as well as infrequently in other parts of the US Southwest (Di Peso et al. 1974a:87; Steponaitis 1983). Chihuahuan ceramics are therefore likely derived from northern predecessors and incorporated traits from contemporary traditions. For instance, the decorative and formal characteristics present in Escondida polychrome are directly related to Gila and Tonto polychrome types of the Salado tradition centered in east-central Arizona (Di Peso et al. 1974a:226).

While circumstantial evidence of decoration or form provides intriguing possibilities for arguing contact or influences, it cannot be used to verify the appearance of Mesoamerican *puchteca* traders or migratory bands of potters interacting with the people of Chihuahua. How Mesoamerican and more localized influences such as the Salado phenomenon were integrated into the ceramic assemblage remains uncertain. At present, we can state with confidence that the Chihuahuan tradition is local in origin and the ceramic evidence of decoration and vessel form indicates a history of interaction either directly or indirectly with new technological or symbolic ideas.

Trade Wares and Integration

While the source of the Medio period florescence is unclear, Di Peso's argument, based on the immense quantity and variety of non-local goods, that Paquimé was an important trading center cannot be denied. Foreign ceramic wares represent an important marker of interaction between the Chihuahuan culture and its close and/or distant neighbours. Interestingly, Di Peso suggests that ceramic trade was equally important during the Viejo period (especially with Mimbres Black-on-white) as in later Medio period contexts (Di Peso et al. 1974a:141). The range of interaction, however, grew exponentially during the later period as pottery found at Paquimé suggests interaction with seven regions, including Arizona (Tucson polychrome), Durango (Mercado red-on-cream) and Nayarit-Jalisco (Early Nayarit polychrome) (Ibid.:141-143). As with discussion of the impact of foreign influence on the Chihuahuan tradition, there is much speculation as to the importance of these trade wares. Di Peso (Ibid.) originally believed that these ceramics added to the stature of Paquimé as an important trade center. In a recent review of this data, Douglas (1992:20-21) suggests that because of the variable frequency and distribution of foreign ceramics in the roomblocks, these wares are more properly seen as prehistoric curios rather than prestige items. The justification for this assumption is based on the fact that there is little change in non-local pottery as the site increased in scale.

A further method for interpreting regional interaction has focussed on the role of Chihuahuan pottery as trade ware. The Chihuahuan ceramics, but particularly the painted types, have been discovered archaeologically as far away as Mexico City, Colorado, western Sonora, Texas, and New Mexico (Di Peso 1974:622-23). The predominance of Ramos polychrome in these assemblages, in association with ceremonial architecture and other 'prestige' goods, has been used to argue the extent of influence that Paquimé exerted over a particular site and measure its sphere of influence within Chihuahua (Carey 1931:338; Woosley and Olinger 1993). Interaction has also been identified with three regional phases on the edges of the Chihuahuan culture area: the Animas phase in southeastern Arizona (Carpenter 1996; Douglas 1995, 1996); the El Paso phase of the Jornada Mogollon in west Texas/southern New Mexico (J. Charles Kelley 1986; Schaafsma 1979; LeBlanc 1980; Bradley and Hoffer 1985); and, to a lesser degree, the Salado phenomenon centered in eastern Arizona (Crown 1994; Nelson and LeBlanc 1986) and Trincheras culture of eastern Sonora (McGuire and Villalpando 1993). Understanding the relationship between the Chihuahuan culture and the peoples from each of these regions has proven more complex than simply identifying outlier enclaves acting as subjects to the Paquimian Empire. For example, Ramos polychrome has been discovered in quantity at sites in southern Arizona and New Mexico, however, these pots were produced locally and not imported from Paquimé; the assemblages at these sites therefore reflect local production of a non-local style (Woosley and Olinger 1993:123-5). That the potters at these sites were producing Ramos polychrome and other non-local types remains important, but this fact changes our perception of a subservient relationship with Paquimé. In fact, a similar situation appears at Paquimé where Salado polychrome types (Gila and Tonto) were being imitated at the site (Escondida polychrome) (Crown 1994:28). There is no concrete evidence to suggest that the production of Escondida resulted from the movement of peoples or ideas into Chihuahua. In fact, following Crown's suggestion that the Salado culture may reflect an ideological phenomenon, it is more likely that the situation in Chihuahua represents an influx of new socio-religious concepts (Ibid.:215-217).

Summary of the History of Ceramic Research
This review has broadly defined the role of polychrome ceramics in the Chihuahuan literature. While the range of such research is limited in comparison with work undertaken in the US Southwest, we are presented with an array of questions that need to be addressed of our datasets, such as: how are the types related? Is there a developmental sequence of ceramic types? Were the ceramics used as trade items? Attention will now be focussed on the study of vessel form and decoration in

the literature to identify more specific questions that can be addressed by a design analysis of museum collections.

ROLE OF CERAMIC TRAITS IN CHIHUAHUAN RESEARCH
Presented below is a brief summary of the use of vessel form and design in the Chihuahuan literature. Variables that have played an important role and will be examined in detail include the jar form and its sub-class, the effigy vessel, and the decorative levels of motif and layout. Since the goal of this thesis is to undertake a design analysis of three Chihuahuan polychromes, the greater part of this discussion will be spent outlining the study of painted decoration.

Shape
Chihuahuan polychrome vessels are most commonly associated with the jar (*olla*), effigy, and bowl forms (Kidder 1916:256-260) as well as more elaborate and intriguing shapes such as drums, *cajetes* (neckless jars), cruciforms, and bottles. Unfortunately, the infrequent discovery of these latter forms requires that we consider them as curiosities within the material complex rather than a useful data set for understanding changes across the Chihuahuan cultural landscape (Carey 1931: 344; Wheat 1948-49; Di Peso et al. 1974a:85-92). This being said, the jar and effigy forms are abundantly found in museum collections or from excavated contexts and have been employed extensively for making hypotheses about prehistoric developments in the region (Di Peso et al. 1974a:79).

Jars
The jar has long been recognized as the most characteristic form among the Chihuahuan ceramics (Kidder 1916:256; Brand 1935:291). The typical form of a jar as illustrated in Figure 2.11, has been described as being roughly 7-1/2 to 8 inches in height with a

> high, gently sloping upper body; rounded shoulder; full, round bottom; and point of greatest diameter set very low. The rim is slightly out-curved, ending in a plain round lip (Kidder 1916:256).

While this 'classic' shape of Chihuahuan jars is undeniably the most common ceramic form, there is substantial variation in the basic jar shape, which Rice defines as "a necked (and therefore restricted) vessel with its height greater than its maximum diameter," (Rice 1987:216). Figure 2.12 presents a sample of the variation in size, body shape, and rim form of polychrome vessels housed in museums.

The importance of jars in Chihuahuan research is primarily attributed to their predominance in collections and, secondly, because this form appears in the lowest levels of excavated Medio period sites (Carey 1931:345). Jars have therefore been the key form in most analyses of

Figure 2.11 Examples of the 'classic' shape of Chihuahuan jars from the WPM collection (l to r - #167 Ramos polychrome, #27 Ramos polychrome, #40 Ramos polychrome, #64 Ramos polychrome)

Figure 2.12 Variation in jar forms present in the WPM collection (top row - l to r - #52 Babicora polychrome, #152 Villa Ahumada polychrome, #58 Babicora polychrome, #171 Ramos polychrome, bottom row - #33 Ramos polychrome, #67 Ramos polychrome, #126 Villa Ahumada polychrome, #174 Ramos polychrome)

whole vessels and, as a result, played a significant part in the development of the classification system. Studies focussing explicitly on the variation in jar shape are very limited in the literature. Di Peso's (Di Peso et al. 1974a) study represents the most significant contribution to this aspect of ceramic research. He recorded eight qualitative and six quantitative traits in the Casas Grandes ceramic volume (Ibid.:18-19); however, this data has not been properly evaluated or compared with other ceramic traits to test for any distinctive patterning of manufacture. Little is also known about the function of Chihuahuan polychrome vessels, as it is highly unlikely that these vessels were used for cooking (some pots showed evidence of post-fire deposits of carbon on their exterior). Other proposed functions for these elaborately painted artifacts include gambling or trade, and several are

included with burial offerings or, in one particularly large example, as a container for one crushed individual (Di Peso et al. 1974a:77; Ravesloot 1988). In general, the characteristics of jar form (i.e. height, rim diameter, rim thickness) have been largely overshadowed by the content of design, the exception to this trend being the closely-related effigy class.

Effigies

The presence of effigy vessels in Chihuahuan sites has long been recognized as an important feature of this ceramic tradition (Kidder 1916; Carey 1931:339-343; Brand 1933:77). While this form is not unique within the US Southwest, it is its conspicuous abundance throughout Chihuahua and the form's potential ties to southern and eastern cultures that has attracted so much attention

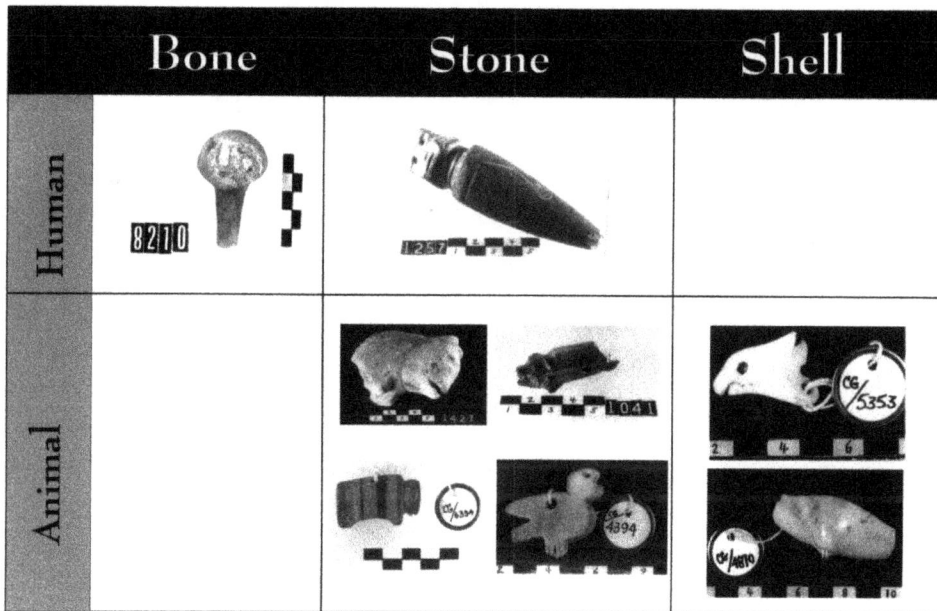

	Bone	Stone	Shell
Human			
Animal			

Figure 2.13 Human and animal effigies carved in bone, stone, and shell from Paquimé (photos courtesy of INAH Chihuahua)

(Brand 1935:293; Di Peso et al. 1974a:90-91; see Kelley et al. 2000a:12). Equally important are the formal relationship that the effigies share with the basic jar form described above (Kidder 1916:256), and that they appear to be decorated using the same decorative principles. Interestingly, representations of effigies are not restricted to the ceramic medium, and human or animal figures are commonly found in shell, bone, and stone media throughout northwest Chihuahua (Figure 2.13) (Di Peso et al. 1974b:62; Kelley et al. 2000a:45).

All effigy vessels are constructed by adding appendages to the side or neck of a basic jar template. Kidder (1916:256) originally defined three effigy classes based on the position of these appendages, 'side-appended' (features modelled to the side of the vessel), 'hooded' (features attached to the rim or neck), and 'true' (hooded effigy in seated position with arms and legs appended to the side of the vessel). Each effigy class contains both human and animal representations and, with the exception of the scarlet macaw, the distinguishable animals represented in effigy form are native to the Chihuahuan landscape (i.e. bears, badgers, ducks, fish, snakes, turtles, quails, owls). Di Peso split Kidder's primary categories into the more specific classes of hooded, human face, reclining human, animal, snake, bird, fish, and horned lizard effigies (Di Peso et al. 1974a:90-91). The difference between these classifications is essentially an emphasis on either construction or subject matter. While Di Peso's terminology will be used during the analysis of the museum collections, discussion of each class is more easily summarized according to the formally based categories defined by Kidder.

The majority of Di Peso's effigy classes, including animal, bird, horned lizard, snake, and human face, fit within the side-appended category (see Figure 2.4, #165, #164, #177). Side-appended vessels are perhaps the most diverse effigy class and are found with twin animal heads, sets of legs, entire bodies, head and tail combinations, or facial features attached to the exterior surface of a jar. A related form included in this class are repoussé snakes (Figure 2.4, #168), which are constructed by partially extruding the wall of the pot outwards to or appliquéing a snake or pair of entwined snakes around the vessel. Painted decoration on side-appended effigies is rather variable with some appendages worked into the flow of the design, while on other pots the painted design appears to be a secondary concern to the shape of the pot.

Hooded or raised neck effigies are constructed through the attachment of a human or animal 'hood' or head to the neck of a jar (Figure 2.4, #193). By contrast with side-appended effigies, the hooded class is much more homogeneous in form with the primary difference being the subject matter of the hood rather than variation in construction (Kidder 1916:258). The lack of appendages on the sides of these effigies also accounts for the more static structure of decoration painted on the vessel surface. Brand argued that the importance of this effigy class is that it has no counterpart in Mexico and therefore may represent a local development (1935:288). Studies from the lower Mississippi show a limited distribution of this form; however, the construction and content of these vessels were substantially different from those produced in Chihuahua (Di Peso et al. 1974a:90-91).

The 'true' effigies identified by Kidder are equated with the reclining effigy and modified hooded effigy in Di

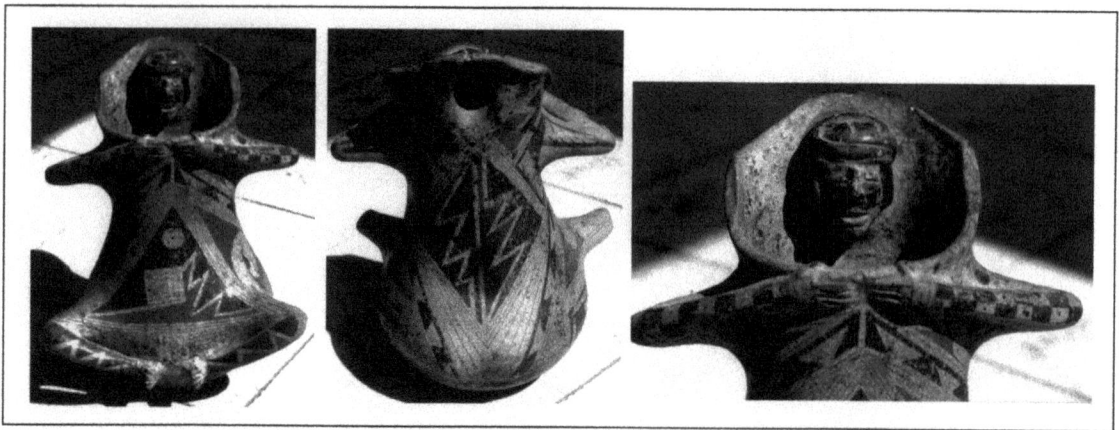

Figure 2.14 Babicora 'Reverse' Hooded effigy jar from the collection of Sr. Guilfrido Robles

Peso's classification (Figure 2.4, #176). Hooded effigies within this class have appended legs and arms, and are restricted to human depictions of females or males, in an array of seated postures, often holding children, bowls, genitals, or smoking. Painted decoration on the back and sides of these pots is often very elaborate and very dense, which Kidder (1916:259) interpreted as simply representing the "horror vacui" of leaving open space on the vessel. Other interpretations of these decorations are that they represent clothing (King in Di Peso et al. 1974b:81-92) or tattoos (Sprehn 2000, in press). Neither true nor hooded effigies of humans appear to be portraits of individuals because of the fairly conventionalized manner of facial construction and painted designs applied to the faces. One example that may represent a death mask or woman in child birth (David Friedel, personal communication November, 2000) is a reverse-hooded effigy (hood is attached to 'back' of the vessel and the face is pushed through) recovered at the San Juan Mounds in the Babícora basin (Figure 2.14). This vessel is important because of the individualized facial representation in the hood and it is the only known vessel to incorporate this construction technique.

The role of effigies remains uncertain yet we can be confident they were likely imbued with important socio-religious meaning. Several effigies were found in association with burials at Paquimé (Di Peso et al. 1974b:363-366; Ravesloot 1988) but there is no conclusive patterning to this practice. Future investigation of this subject is likely impossible given the extensive work of looters searching for pottery among graves throughout Chihuahua. The only 'developed' hypothesis to explain the social role of these vessels is Di Peso's dubious inference that hooded effigies represent Mesoamerican gods such as Quetzalcoatl and Xipe Tótec.

Interpreting the role of this diverse vessel form is complicated by the fact that the museum collections contain different quantities of the three basic forms and there is no consistency in the relative frequency of each. For instance, the Peabody collection analyzed by Kidder

(1916:257) contained mostly side-appended effigies with two heads, a head and tail or dual low relief serpents. Carey's (1931:342) examination of the Lumholtz collection at the San Diego Museum of Man, the State Museum of New Mexico, and excavated materials had a greater ratio of hooded effigies and slightly less side-appended pots. Human hooded effigies were also the most common effigy form of the forty-seven painted effigies recovered from the Paquimé excavations (Di Peso et al. 1974a:90). On account of this variability it has been difficult to determine the relative importance (i.e., temporal, spatial, social) of each effigy class produced by Medio period potters. It may be that the museum collections, and especially the early ones, might be from one site or locality; however, we cannot assume that this is the case.

Decoration

The decorative variation and complexity in the Chihuahuan polychrome pottery is responsible for the emphasis placed upon this artifact class in the archaeological literature. Research using unpainted and textured wares yields important information on day-to-day activities such as cooking and storage (see Stark et al. 1998), however, as outlined in Chapter I, there are several immediate advantages in selecting polychrome wares. Included among these benefits are the diversity of design levels that can be selected for analysis, the important role that decoration has played in Chihuahuan archaeology, and the possibility that the study of decoration may provide important clues to better understanding the symbolic or ideological constructs of Medio period society. The following discussion will define and examine the role of the layout and motif, which represent the most commonly studied decorative characteristics in the Chihuahuan literature.

Layout

A layout is here defined as the framework of lines that provide the basic design structure on the surface of a vessel. The predominant layout in the Chihuahuan tradition is the continuous band (Figure 2.15), composed

22

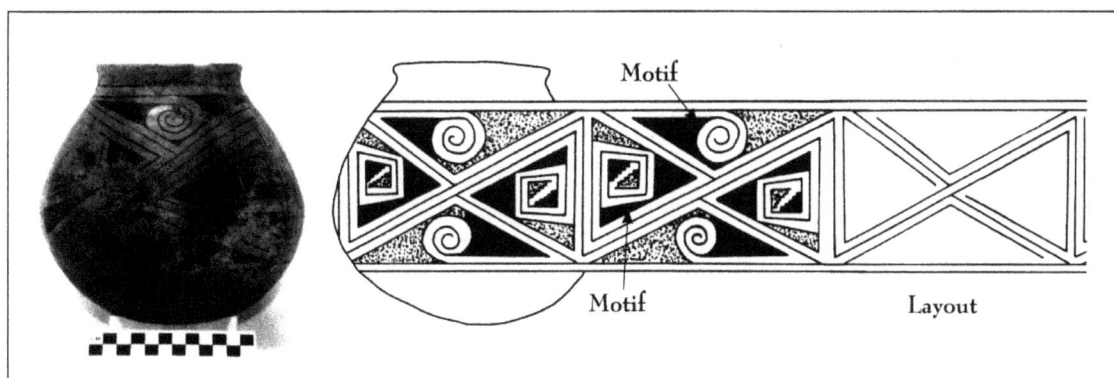

Figure 2.15 Example of a band layout with and without motifs
(photo - WPM #82; layout adapted from Di Peso et al. 1974:271, fig. 290-6, 51)

of an upper and lower border that encircles the exterior of the pot (Di Peso et al. 1974a:94). Multiple bands, with upwards of three related layouts are often found stacked on the exterior of jars. A second format used on jars is the overall layout, which covers the entire exterior surface of the vessel (bottom included); however, vessels decorated in this manner are considerably less common and are not tested in this study.

Kidder (1916) was the first to analyze the band layout pattern and identified the construction patterns used to create the design framework. According to his examination, the initial partition of a band is into two sides, or panels, and is strictly adhered to in all 'phases of Casas Grandes art' and on each of the different vessel forms (Ibid.:261). Following this initial step, the bands are further divided into a number of triangular spaces and filled with motifs (Ibid.:261-262; Brand 1933:78). Kidder (1916:262) also noted that dual representation is a basic trend in both the general tendency for a layout to occur twice around the pot, and that most designs are represented through opposition.

The Chihuahuan band layouts were originally divided into diagonal, diamond, or zigzag formats (Kidder 1916:261-262.), and then later revised by Di Peso who identified eleven primary band layouts (i.e., Blank, Simple [here called Basic], 2-line, 3-Line, 4-Line, Semi-Panelled, Panelled, Net Pattern, Zig-Zag, Repeated Figure, and Miscellaneous each containing an extensive list of variants (Di Peso et al. 1974a:7-14). Figure 2.16 illustrates the sequence of decoration and layout categories identified by both Sayles and Di Peso. Typically, the discussion of layout in the Casas Grandes Ceramic volume (Ibid.:94-99) is limited to the identification of broad patterns within the assemblage and does not question why these relationships occurred. For instance, Panelled bands were the most numerous (21.6%), specifically among variants of Ramos and Villa Ahumada, while 2-Line bands were slightly less common (18.7%) (Ibid.:94). In fact, even though Di Peso, and Sayles years earlier, recognized that specific pot types tended to be decorated using particular layouts neither

undertook an in-depth comparison of the individual frequency of layout by type. Regardless of these methodological problems, the basic parameters for layout construction in the Chihuahuan tradition are fairly clear for researchers interested in understanding variation at this level of decoration.

Motifs
Motifs are composed of a series of decorative elements used by the artisan to fill the divided spaces within a band layout. The quality and kind of decoration are both distinguishing features of the Chihuahuan tradition and is an amalgam of Puebloan and non-Puebloan (read southern) characteristics, filled with striking black and red oppositions (Kidder 1924:319). The basal unit of decoration found throughout the painted wares is the triangle, which appears individually and as the template for more elaborate motifs.

Looking through the numerous studies that have focussed on ceramic decoration, there is little continuity in the identification and recording of motifs. Carey examined nine motifs (elements) on Chihuahuan polychrome vessels: key designs, interlocked spirals, step designs, triangles, opposed stepped figures, negative painted circles, club-shaped elements, life forms and plumed serpents (1931:346-347). Di Peso recorded a much broader range of motifs such as circles, bulls-eyes, lines, macaws, feathers, triangles (with hooks and spirals), barbed, and unusual motifs such as the 'hikuli' and Chupícuaro diamond (Di Peso et al. 1974a:94-98). Recent studies of motif variability, such as Van Pool's examination of the University of New Mexico collection, have expanded the number of identifiable designs to over 80 motifs (Van Pool 2000, personal communication). The contrast between these studies is likely attributable both to differences in the interpretation of what constitutes a motif and to the size of the sample being studied. The result of the existence of multiple classification systems is that we still lack a basic understanding of motif frequency and patterns for the polychrome types. While studies such as Sayles (1936a) and Di Peso (Di Peso et al. 1974a) have provided a working understanding of type

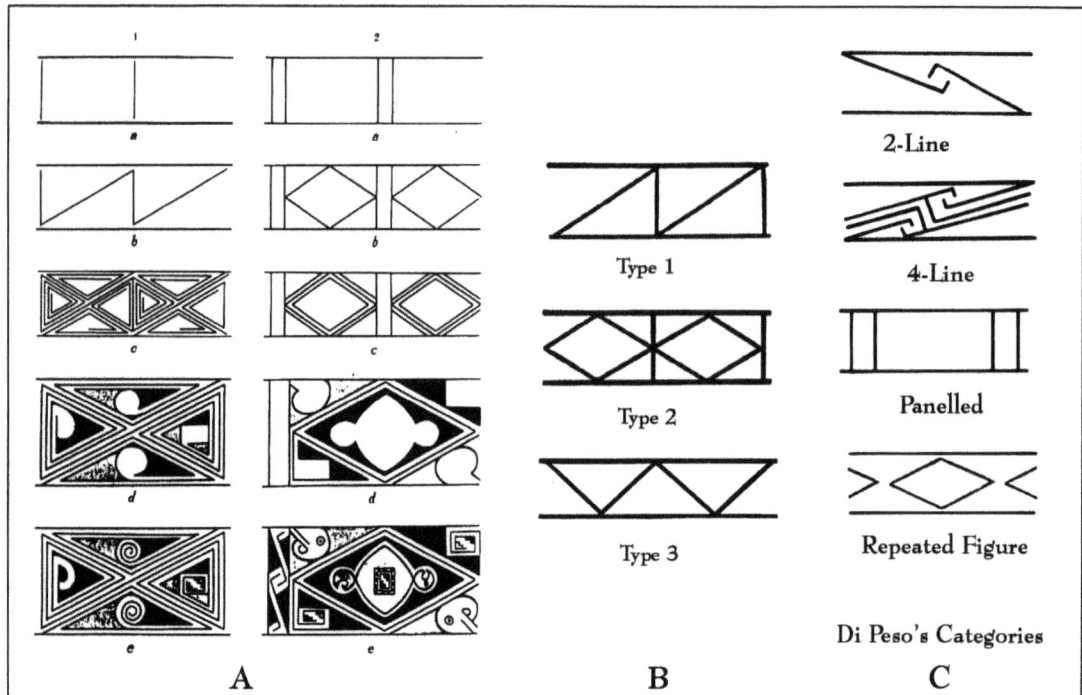

Figure 2.16a-c Sequence of decoration and layout classes identified by Kidder (A-B) and Di Peso (C) (from Kidder 1916:pl. IV, 261-262; Di Peso et al. 1974:7-14)

differences and bonds shared within the tradition, these are not explicitly outlined in the body of their research.

Interpretation

Ultimately, archaeologists seek not only patterning but also a better understanding of the prehistoric meaning behind the symbols represented in material culture. Until recently, interpretation of design on Chihuahuan polychromes has focussed on recording design patterns and placing them within the structure of a typology. The broader issues that have been discussed in the literature can be grouped into those that deal with the symbolic origins of the Chihuahuan tradition or the search for meaning.

Is the Decoration Southwestern, Mesoamerican or Local?

As with most archaeological data, the interpretation of decorative meaning in the Medio period ceramics is hindered by the absence of direct ethnographic correlates for comparison. To compensate for this lack of data, investigations on the subject of decorative origins have relied heavily on Southwestern or Mesoamerican analogies. For instance, Pueblo-like designs identified in the Chihuahuan tradition, such as the double staircase and forked line, have been interpreted according to Southwest ethnographic examples as symbolizing clouds or lightning (Bandelier 1890:29). Chapman (1922), albeit from a more art historical approach, also argued that the Chihuahuan zoomorph motifs fit within the basic forms used in US Southwestern styles. While connections with

the Southwest are undeniable, direct transfer of meaning does not provide a clear understanding of the prehistoric purpose of decoration in the Chihuahuan tradition.

Di Peso (1974: 548-569) formulated the most elaborate explanation of Paquimian iconography, but was interested in showing its relationship to the socio-religious iconography of the Quetzalcoatl, Tlaloc, and Xipe Totec cults originating from Mesoamerica. The problems with Di Peso's hypothesis, as illustrated above in discussing the role of effigy vessels, are its reliance on questionable evidence of decoration as well as the wide temporal gaps between Chihuahuan and Toltec and Aztec cultures in the Mesoamerican core. As mentioned previously, the recent suggestion by Nelson (1992) that the Mesoamerican cultures on the northern periphery flourished during this 'middle' period provides credence to the continued examination into the nature of southern contact with Chihuahua. Ultimately, the problem with ascribing a sudden Mesoamerican migration to the rise of Paquimé rejects any formal continuity in the Chihuahuan ceramic tradition. Di Peso himself offers contradictory statements about the continuity of these ceramics, by suggesting that there is little to bind the Viejo and Medio ceramics based on design trends (Di Peso et al. 1974a:99), but then states that there is also evidence to support continuity throughout the entire tradition (Ibid.:3-4). At present, there is no doubt that southern influences are found in the Medio period, however, the level of interaction suggested by the material culture does not support the replication of the elaborate southern symbolic system suggested by Di

Peso. More importantly, the direction of this influence is not necessarily of southern origins. Thompson's (1999) study of the Mesoamerican designs in Mimbres pottery again represents a possible precursor of the stylized iconographic content present in the Chihuahuan tradition. Further comparison of combinations of decorative traits is required if we wish to clarify the origins of the Chihuahuan tradition, be they northern, southern, or indigenous.

The only other attempts at tackling meaning in Chihuahuan decoration from a non-Mesoamerican point of view were undertaken by Brooks (1973) and Mann (1980). Brooks sought, "to reconstruct, bit-by-bit, the perceptual activity of these particular people" through an examination of decorative traits in a loosely formed structural framework (1973:11). Her paper detailed some basic patterning of specific motifs such as the hooked triangle, bull's eye and plumed serpent but did little to compare the relative frequency of each or their relationship to one another. Mann's (1980) discussion of whole vessels from the University of Texas compared the colors, motifs, and number of design repetitions in Chihuahuan decoration with the mythical imagery of the Egyptian, Christian, and Indian religions. Neither study represents an in-depth, critical evaluation of meaning within the Chihuahuan tradition; instead they provide broad art historical perspectives on a few painted designs. The gap in research aimed at understanding symbolic meaning is slowly being filled through recent studies of Chihuahuan decoration by numerous graduate students. This research represents an exciting array of archaeologically-based interpretations of symbolism that will greatly expand our understanding of this decorative system.

PROBLEMS WITHIN THE CHIHUAHUAN TRADITION

The previous discussion of the role of ceramics in Chihuahuan research has provided not only a backdrop of the general research trends but also outlined the shortcomings in our knowledge. Perhaps the most critical point to be made is that we must become more introspective in our research design and begin to develop new questions regarding the polychrome types. For instance, do we understand the social implications behind the physical and decorative properties of types that we use for field and laboratory analysis? Reviewing the literature, it becomes apparent that many issues and research questions either were not or could not be examined within the past archaeological paradigms. Given the aid of history and changes to method and theory, the same excuses cannot be made for present research. As a result, we must adopt a more encompassing perspective to tap into the potential of our expansive data set.

From the summary presented above, three main problems can be identified that need to be addressed in the Chihuahuan tradition: 1) the significance of trait overlap between polychrome types; 2) time, the question of type development and temporal differences between the polychrome types; and 3) space, defining the geographical distribution of the polychrome types. Addressing these important and fundamentally culture historical concerns will also facilitate the investigations of meaning within the Chihuahuan tradition as well as to better define its role in the Greater Southwest culture area.

Trait Overlap

Any study incorporating ceramics will ultimately impact on the regional classification. Rather than reflecting a lack of temporal or spatial data, trait overlap discovered between ceramic types is a methodological problem that must be studied in the lab rather than the field. Ford (1954) noted the problem of blending or smearing of mutually exclusive traits in a classification. While trait overlap arguably pervades each ceramic tradition to some degree, it is most commonly associated with situations where the archaeologist is faced with an overabundance of data (Lyman et al. 1997:156). More succinctly, the problem stems from the desire to take into consideration as many traits as possible in the creation of type descriptions. A critical issue of the Chihuahuan typology is demonstrated through two statements made by Di Peso and colleagues in their analysis of the material recovered from Paquimé,

> Though each painted type had traits setting it off from the others, all showed relationships in one or more characteristics, binding them into one school – in some cases, in fact, it was difficult to type sherds or even whole vessels because of this. Further, as far as the designs were concerned, the variants of some types had less similarity to each other than to one or more variants of another type,

> As far as elements and motifs were concerned, Dublan Poly had the least variation and Escondida and Ramos the most...Ramos Poly Standard Variant was the classic type of the period. It was made of a light-colored, hard, compact paste, symmetrically formed into a number of shapes which were embellished with the fine-line designs laid on with precision, control, and balance. However, Babícora Poly shared a larger series of characteristics with the rest of the school than any other single pottery type. This tendency for the types to blend into one another was characteristic throughout the Casas Grandes historical continuum, (Di Peso et al. 1974a:2).

These comments present a problematic situation to the archaeologist concerned with interpreting and applying the Chihuahuan typology to an excavated or museum-based assemblage. On the one hand, the first statement presents an argument that unites the different types into a tradition, as defined here, or a school, as described by Di Peso (Di Peso et al. 1974a:1). For example, variants of both Babícora and Villa Ahumada have been identified that conform to the established parameters of decoration in Ramos but are distinguished from it through the presence of dark paste or white slip (Ibid.:183, 299). The typology is riddled with overlapping traits that make it difficult to discern whether a sherd or pot can be placed confidently within a particular category. On the other hand, the second statement leaves the reader with the impression that there are distinct, diagnostic traits that can be used to define particular types, both in the relative quantity or kind of characteristics on each vessel. Neither of these statements is unique to this classification system, as any typology of merit contains numerous diagnostic traits for each type, and all detailed typologies suffer from attribute overlap, "creep", or type "fuzziness" (Ford 1954:52).

It is possible to argue that one of the most important factors affecting the clarity of the Chihuahuan typology is that it was formed through a process of accretion, rather than as a single classificatory event. However, when the results from a single site are examined it becomes obvious that there is more happening in this tradition than we expected. With recent interest and advances in understanding the regional archaeology, the research climate in Chihuahua has reached the point where these gaps need to be investigated and, hopefully, filled.

Temporal Differences
Two theoretical camps have been established to explain the temporal development of the Chihuahuan tradition. In the first group are those who favour a developmental sequence where particular types represent predecessors (Babícora) of later types (Ramos) (Amsden 1928; Sayles 1936a; Carlson 1982:213). Put into perspective, we must realize that the approximate 250-year span of the Medio period is equated to roughly half the duration of the Roman Empire, a time period which saw massive changes in material culture that are easily recognizable through art styles and written documents. While the Chihuahuan culture lacks the written word, the elaborate decorative tradition represents an ample and commonly used dataset for archaeologists to examine changes through time. Comparable studies have already produced definitive temporal markers of decorative variation within the Mimbres wares (Shafer and Brewington 1995). The major fault of the hypothetical sequences proposed by Sayles and Carlson is their reliance on artistic feel, lack of metholodogical rigour, and, most importantly, the need for contextual evidence from a properly seriated site to support their claims. Even today an internally divided Medio period ceramic sequence has eluded researchers working in and around the site of Paquimé (Michael Whalen, personal communication 1999).

The second camp follows the belief that the types appeared simultaneously and were produced throughout the Medio period. Utilizing the deep deposits from Paquimé, Di Peso attempted to produce the seriation missing from the premise of ceramic development, but instead found each of the polychrome types at the lowest levels of excavation. Di Peso concluded (Di Peso et al. 1974a:80), therefore, that there was no developmental sequence for the polychrome types. It is entirely possible that complex site formation processes at Paquimé may be obscuring any recognizable sequence. A re-evaluation of this ceramic data by Whalen and Minnis (1996) appears to have identified an early and late phase based on the frequency of types across the site. Using discriminant analysis, they combined architectural seriation and ceramic stratigraphic position from Paquimé with their survey data from the areas surrounding the site to identify what they called early Medio and late Medio period groups. Unfortunately, this data has not yet been extended to a comparison of individual decorative characteristics within these proposed phases.

It is counter-intuitive, in light of the success in locating temporally sensitive markers in decorative traits within Mimbres pottery, to think that the polychrome types were produced simultaneously and remained unchanged over the duration of the Medio period. Through the rigorous analysis of decorative traits from museum collections and with inclusion of knowledge presented by the Chihuahuan literature, it will be possible to construct testable models of temporal development.

Geographical Distribution
Little is known about production centers or distribution of the individual polychrome types across the Chihuahuan landscape. The pioneering work completed by Lumholtz (1902), Brand (1933), Sayles (1936a; 1936b), and Lister (1946) suggested that each type was centered in a particular region. Babícora is associated with sites found along the headwaters of Rio Santa Maria and Babícora Basin. Ramos is primarily located along the Rio Casas Grandes, and Villa Ahumada, which appears at its eponymous type site but also in the area straddling the Santa Maria at Galeana and continues into the Rio Casas Grandes area (Sayles 1936a:17, 20, 53-54; Robert Leonard, personal communication, June 1999). As these basic distributions suggest, the geographical extent for each type is very broad and frequently overlaps with others across the culture area.

Recent investigation has not significantly altered our knowledge of production areas for the polychrome types. Instead, studies of geographical distribution have established the spread and production of Ramos polychrome on the northern frontier (Woosley and Olinger 1993) and defined the southern boundaries of Chihuahuan culture (Kelley et al. 1999a). Broad-scale comparison of polychrome types is therefore needed to assess whether there is a differential use of decoration within Chihuahua. The identification of regional styles will aid in understanding the relationship between primary sites, like Paquimé, Galeana, and more distant centers such as Villa Ahumada, Raspadura on the Río Santa María, and El Zurdo in the Babícora basin.

Summary
Excluding the issue of trait overlap, the problems plaguing Chihuahuan ceramic research can and will be addressed through future field research and excavation. With the logistical constraints in undertaking large-scale research projects, the museum collection represents an excellent data set for the analysis of decorative traits to explicitly describe the polychrome types and formulate models of temporal or spatial variation. For example, there has yet to be a concise definition and quantification of decorative traits that define a type as Babícora or Ramos and even the tradition as Chihuahuan. Expressly defining the layouts and motifs and their relative frequencies within these scaled categories will provide a crucial benchmark for future researchers to apply to recently excavated assemblages or re-discovered museum collections. This approach has the dual benefit of creating a solid base for intra-regional investigations and evaluating the origin of designs as being locally derived or borrowed from outside Chihuahua and incorporated in its symbolic system. In the end, interpretation of the variability in design from museum collections offers only a partial solution to these problems and must inevitably be tested in future fieldwork.

CHAPTER III

DESIGN ANALYSIS: THEORY, METHOD AND MODEL CONSTRUCTION

Rosencrantz: Fancy a game?
Guildenstern: We're spectators.
Rosencrantz: Do you want to play questions?
Guildenstern: How do you play that?
Rosencrantz: You have to ask questions.
Guildenstern: Statement! One-love.

Rosencrantz and Guildenstern are Dead
(Stoppard 1991:20)

This chapter will introduce design analysis as an approach that can usefully incorporate museum data to aid our understanding of the variation within the Chihuahuan ceramic tradition. Explanation of the design analysis will be presented in two parts. The first section will elaborate on the specific theoretical and methodological components to be used in this analysis and detail a range of potential models to explain any decorative patterning discovered. The second will focus on the application of design analysis to the data derived from the Chihuahuan polychrome jars housed at the ROM and WPM. Due to the restrictions of using material with no provenience, this study cannot produce direct explanations for the decorative variation in an assemblage, but it can propose new questions and extend our current conceptions of developments within the Medio period.

THE IMPORTANCE OF RAISING QUESTIONS

The museum study cannot be used to identify specific locations in time or space, nor to account directly for social explanations of decorative variation. Instead of concrete answers, the critical point of this process is that new questions must be generated and posited if we want to fill the gaps in our understanding of Chihuahuan prehistory. In her examination of variability and social boundaries in Puebloan ceramics, Hegmon (1998:278) suggested that, "if we ask enough 'why?' questions we will be able to develop a more comprehensive understanding of the relationship between material culture and social practices". Past research in Chihuahua has provided detailed descriptions of individual types, but has neglected to ask *why* these types occur and how they are related within the tradition. Using the design analysis presented above, we will ask questions such as: What is the range of design traits within the ceramic assemblage? How similar are the Chihuahuan polychrome types? Are these differences more prevalent within a particular level of decoration such as the element, motif or layout? Is there shared patterning between types? The second step in this process is to translate this information into questions that relate to cultural phenomenon and process,

rather than simply translating data of similarity or difference to the realm of typology. For instance: are the differences within the types indicative of temporal variation? Do the individual types represent regional variations of a shared ceramic heritage or symbolic system? Were the types used by different social classes within a single area? Raising new questions will spur ceramic research and provide a more diverse perspective of what forces may have played a role in the decorative variation present in the Chihuahuan tradition. Models constructed from the museum-based data can then be incorporated as heuristic devices to be tested with contextualized assemblages.

INTRODUCTION TO THE STUDY OF DESIGN IN CERAMICS

The study of design has a long and well-established history in the study of prehistoric and historic ceramics (e.g., Raymond et al. 1975; Plog 1980; Hodder 1982a; Steponaitis 1983; Hardin 1984; Hole 1984; Kintigh 1985; DeBoer 1990; Crown 1994; Hegmon 1995; Goodby 1998). Perhaps the greatest asset of design analysis lies in its versatility. For instance, painted, textured, and modelled decoration have each been measured, compared, and interpreted to address temporal distinctions (Raymond et al. 1975), social divisions (Hodder 1982a; Steponaitis 1983), and group interaction (Goodby 1998). The range of theoretical and methodological perspectives presented in the archaeological literature provides the foundation for explaining decorative variation in the museum sample. A further benefit of using design analysis, as Chilton (1998:146) points out, is that it facilitates investigation of variability within an assemblage and, therefore, avoids the need for extra-regional comparison to derive significant cultural information. As illustrated in Chapter II, introspective investigation has been largely missing from Chihuahuan research programmes. Both the range of potential questions and the ability to emphasize internal developments make design analysis an extremely valuable tool for evaluating decorative variation. Further discussion of the theoretical framework underlying this approach is presented in the proceeding sections.

Creation of an Appropriate Design Analysis

The design analysis developed for this thesis is directly linked to the following goals:

- to explicitly identify decorative trait frequencies for three Chihuahuan polychrome types
- to search for patterns of traits shared across the ceramic tradition; and
- to propose explanatory models for any decorative overlap discovered between types.

Based on these criteria, the approach devised for this study, summarized in Figure 3.1, emphasizes specific design levels that are selected and examined individually, in combination, and within the context of specific

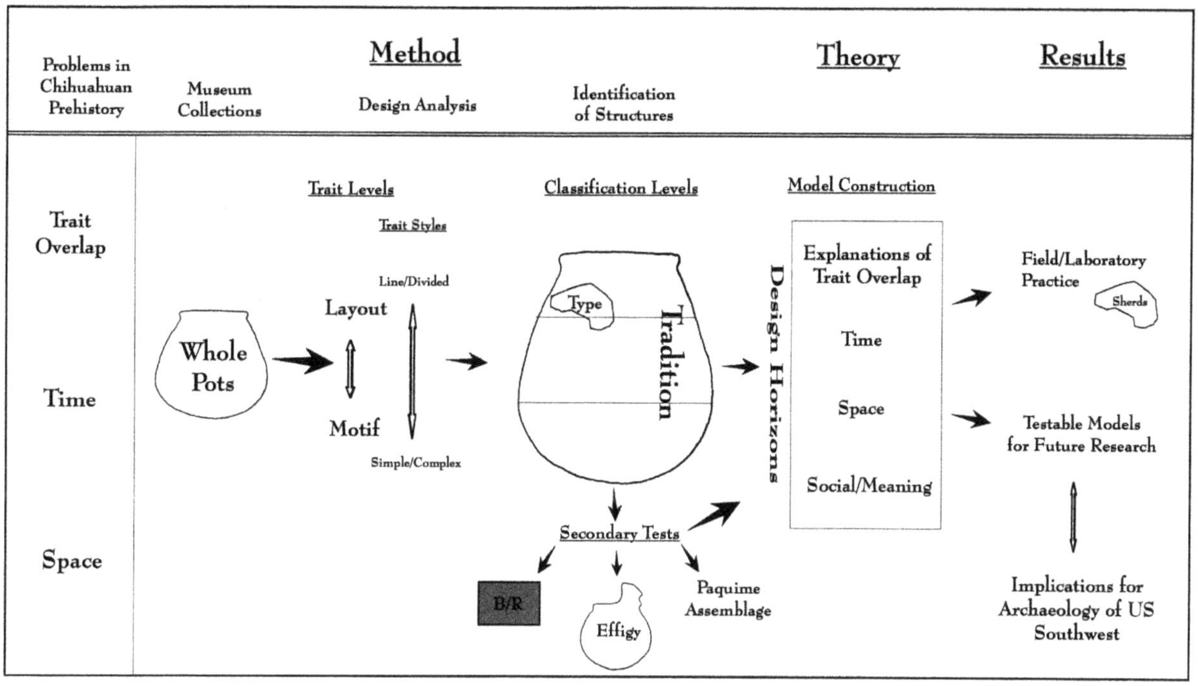

Figure 3.1 Methodological and theoretical trajectory for the analysis of Chihuahuan culture whole vessels from the ROM and WPM collections

classification levels and contrastive variables. The central concept is that recurring decorative patterns, or styles, reflect cultural structures shared by potters from a specific time, place, or group. Combinations of elements, motifs or layouts that are regularly shared between ceramic types, for instance, may be linked to interaction, while differences within a single type may reflect temporal change. In order to identify and model causation for such structures, traits are selected using the precepts of hierarchical relationships and then evaluated using a contrastive approach. In short, hierarchy provides the basis for trait selection by recognizing inherent relationships between levels of decoration (design levels). Contrast facilitates the identification of culturally significant relationships by examining the co-occurrence of specific traits within these design levels. The relationships that are derived from this investigation can be conceived within the idea of design horizons, which span the polychrome types. Once these design horizons are recognized, we can posit models of temporal, spatial or social variation for their occurrence in the ceramic assemblage. Before elaborating on the cultural implications of shared/differential patterning within the Chihuahuan tradition, more detailed background on the concepts of structure, hierarchy, and contrast must be provided.

The Search for Patterns

A pivotal claim in this analysis is that museum collections contain cultural information that has not been gleaned through previous research in Chihuahua or elsewhere in North America. Through the comparison of decorative traits, it is suggested that recurring interrelationships discovered in an assemblage reflect choices that are shared by the society being studied. The root of the structuralist perspective, in its formal anthropological sense, can be traced to ideas borrowed from mathematics and linguistics,

> just as no single element of a language system can be determined without its relationships to all other elements [within] the same system...and as every experience is reducible to a system of correlative elements... the meaning of such elements are thus relatively stated in terms of [their] relationships [to one another] (Broekman 1974:9-10).

Regularly occurring structures are produced through both deliberate and unconscious action and are recognized by anthropologists as being within kin or political groups (Leach 1954), myths (Levi-Strauss 1963), *habitus* (Bourdieu 1973), and in portable objects, such as Wola shield decoration (Sillitoe 1980). An underlying element of these structures is that they are passed on through the transmission of ideas or learning within a culture. Ideology and techniques are transmitted to younger generations by their elders, thereby sustaining a particular world view. Similar applications of structural theory are found in archaeology through the study of architectural and portable material remains. Examination of building form and layout from a structural perspective are understandably common since the relationship between the components of a house is not only integral to keep it standing, but also directly reflects the intentions and influences of the builder's cultural milieu. Glassie's (1975) work on 17th century Middle Virginian folk house forms represents the seminal example of how structural theory can be methodically employed to uncover deep-seated cultural patterns from material remains. The premise adopted by Glassie is framed within a rigorous scientific research programme,

> It begins with the recognition of a pattern of relationships at the phenomenal surface and leads through the search for explanations to the discovery of patterns in logic (structures) (Ibid.:160).

His study recognized a consistent geometric repertoire in the production of houses using the basic floor plan, the process of adding rooms, and the location and number of doors, windows, and chimneys on a building (Ibid.:19-40). Variations in construction (structures) were then interpreted according to natural (i.e., environment), economic (i.e. building materials), political (building shape), and cultural influences (i.e., ethnicity, individualism) present during this period (Ibid.:114-175). This data was then used to inform on the region's history, demonstrating the utility of material evidence to provide information to a discipline often reliant on the written word (Ibid.:176-193).

Pottery decoration similarly lends itself to structuralist investigation. Painted or textured designs have played an important role in understanding the structural aspects of overall composition (Hole 1984), decorative grammars (Hodder 1982a), design symmetry (Washburn 1983; Hegmon 1995), decorative sequence (Freidrich 1970; Hardin 1984; Van Keuren 1999), and dualism (Roe 1995:61). Each of these structuralist inquiries can be applied to the Chihuahuan polychrome tradition. However, before we turn our attention to specific details of motif symmetry or decorative syntax, we must account for the formal structure and record the different levels of design used to compose that structure. Following the model established by Glassie, the museum collections will be analyzed to recognize not only patterns, but also to identify recurring structures that are indicative of widespread cultural choices. Selection of appropriate traits and method of analysis, therefore, are critical components in realizing the structural relationships within a decorative tradition.

Reinforcing Decorative Structures: Perspective for Trait Selection and Analysis

Selection of related and comparable traits is extremely important in the search for structural patterning in material culture. The concepts of hierarchy and contrast are used in the analysis of the museum sample to bolster the recognition of such structural relationships.

Hierarchy

The hierarchical approach to trait selection views vessel decoration as being divisible into a series of inter-related maximal to minimal units (Colton and Hargrave 1937; Freidrich 1970; Hill 1985:374). Hardin (1984:576) identifies four design levels of pottery decoration within this sequence, which include, from 'largest' to 'smallest', whole vessel decoration, configuration (layout), motif, and element. Each decorative level represents one aspect of a scalar decorative sequence (Shepard 1956:267) that is enacted by a painter during the creation of a specific design. Study of these design levels in ceramics can reveal clues about the rules used to organize the designs and the prehistoric significance of this patterning (Hegmon 1995:160). The variables selected for this analysis will therefore include different design levels, each defined as a distinct unit in the hierarchical design process that can be examined individually or in combination with a 'higher' or 'lower' level of decoration.

General acceptance of hierarchical trait selection has been questioned on the grounds that it does not reflect the way potters think about the decorative process (see Jernigan 1986). However vehemently Jernigan protests this approach, there remains no acceptable alternative to the selection of traits and, as a result, hierarchy remains the most consistently used technique (Hegmon 1995:160). While this debate echoes that regarding the etic and emic conceptions of culture, we must remember that the majority of decorative analyses rely heavily on pre-established relationships of regional typologies, which are fundamentally archaeological constructs that combine etic and emic perspectives in undefined manners.

Contrast

Recovery of structural 'rules' from the Chihuahuan polychrome tradition requires the contrast, and not merely recording, of decorative traits and design levels. Following Van der Leeuw,

> the study of these correlations and contrasts is one of the major tools available for the reconstruction of the social, behavioural, technological, and other variables that are ultimately responsible for the pottery product as we find it (1991:23-24).

This approach affords the user the flexibility to address a wide range of potential archaeological investigations and cultural causes. In adopting this method to examine assemblage variability, Van der Leeuw also urges the researcher to,

> develop a contrastive approach that aims at seeing more and more dimensions of variability rather than fewer and fewer, and that may lead to proximal explanations involving individuals and individual phenomena rather than aggregates (Ibid. 1991:13-14).

This statement has three important implications within the context of this thesis. First, in order to realize the full potential of this technique, a contrastive approach should address as many different variable permutations as possible from the data. Second, comparison of the selected design levels must be multi-scalar and include broader archaeological constructs such as type and tradition. Last, Van der Leeuw raises the idea that we need to consider whether variation is related to group or individual choices. Glassie (1975:182-184) and Hill (1985:375-376) both recognized the importance of individual agency within their discussion of collective styles or structures and have attempted to explain the potential reasons for changes in material culture (see also Dobres and Hoffman 1994). Distinguishing the agency of material change in the museum collection context, however, is not the main focus of this analysis. Instead, the critical feature of contrast is the identification of more informative cultural patterns (or at least new and viable avenues of investigation) than are supplied solely through typological description and trait frequencies (Dietler and Herbich 1998:260-261).

Based on the review of Chihuahuan ceramic research in Chapter II, the contrastive approach represents an excellent tool to push the limits of our perceptions of decorative variation. Contrast can be applied to decorative variables individually and collectively, thereby facilitating the identification of regularly occurring structures. The greater number of aspects that are contrasted, the greater the chance that the appearance of regular decorative patterning represents some form of widely held cultural conception of design. A further benefit of using this approach is that it is not limited solely to decorative characteristics and can feasibly incorporate each component of variation on a whole vessel, including technique, material, or function. While the idea of contrast is implicit in most archaeological studies, it is critical in this study if we are to successfully use museum-based sources of data.

APPLICATION OF DESIGN ANALYSIS TO THE MUSEUM SAMPLE

The design analysis developed above can now be applied to the ceramic data from museum contexts. The three main components of this study are:
- design levels (layout and motif),
- design styles (layout and motif styles) and,
- classification levels (type and tradition)

Secondary tests of these variables are also included in this study to test the basic decorative parameters established for type and tradition. Included in this analysis are the presence of black borders around red motifs, the effigy sub-class of the jar form, and the excavated whole vessels from Paquimé.

Design Levels

The two levels of decoration chosen for this analysis are the layout (the structural lines that organize the design around the vessel surface) and the motif. These levels of design are chosen because they are hierarchically linked in the decorative sequence, (relatively) easy to distinguish and record, and both have been used in past studies of Chihuahuan decoration (see Chapter II).

Layout

The layout represents the basic framework of lines that serve to divide the decorative space on the surface of a vessel (see Figures 2.18, 2.19). In ceramic research the examination of layout is normally approached through either: 1) the sequence of construction, or 2) the characterization of the complete structure. The former approach relies on understanding the steps used in the production of the layout and is more commonly associated with ethnographic research (Freidrich 1970; Hardin 1984; 1991). New studies are showing that it is possible to determine the order of layout decoration from archeological data via the microscopic examination of the sequence of line painting (see Van Keuren 1999). The overall structure or 'footprint' view perspective (i.e. Hodder 1982a; Hole 1984) is selected here because it more easily facilitates the identification of relational patterns between hierarchical levels, such as layout and motif. It is argued that we must first understand the basic frequency differences of layouts before expanding our investigation to determine the actual order of line placement.

Examples of different layouts recorded from the museum collection are illustrated in Figure 3.2. The classification of layouts is based on the system developed by Di Peso (Di Peso et al. 1974a:7-14) and each layout class is defined in Chapter IV.

Motifs

Methods of identifying the primary units of design in archaeological analysis have proven quite variable in the archaeological literature. Differential emphasis has been placed on the element (the smallest, irreducible part of a design) or the motif (the combination of elements) as the most appropriate design level (see Raymond et al 1975; Plog 1980; Crown 1994; Hegmon 1995). Selection between these two levels is primarily determined by the nature of the questions being asked, but also by the complexity of the decorative tradition being studied. Shepard argues this point,

> Because of its greater complexity, the motif is necessarily more varied and distinctive than the element...The simpler the style, the greater probability that the element is the basic decorative unit, and the more significant it will be. The more complex the design, the greater the probability that the units of composition are combinations of elements (motifs) (1956:267).

The elaborate detail of Medio period artistry attests to the difficulty of examining anything other than the motif. Recognizing and quantifying the individual elements comprised within even one motif, while potentially useful, ignores the proverbial 'forest for the trees' and represents an arduous and less time-effective approach to establishing basic decorative relationships. This is not to say that an element analysis is an invalid exercise for the Chihuahuan tradition, but until we know how the 'larger' levels are related, further dissection of motifs may miss patterns that are critical to understanding variability in elements. Use of the motif is justified because it can be recognized on both whole vessels and sherds. Figure 3.3 illustrates a small sample of motifs recorded from the museum sample.

Design Styles

A further comparative level introduced into this study is the design style. Each style is an etic construct used to group motifs or layouts based on structural similarity or degree of elaboration. The utility of creating this secondary division within each design level is to look for broader stylistic patterns between types that may not be readily apparent due to the large number of motifs and layouts recorded in the assemblage.

Layout Style

The majority of layouts from the ROM and WPM jars fit within either the Continuous or Segmented style category. A Continuous layout (Figure 3.2a-b) is characterized by at least two lines that extend continuously and in patterns that repeat at least twice around the exterior of the vessel. Motifs are often appended to the central lines and interact with motifs attached to the upper and lower borderlines within the band. The Segmented style (Figure 3.2c-d) is distinguished by the presence of vertical lines (often connected to the upper and/or lower borderlines) that create distinct panels on the surface of a vessel. There are only two primary fields of design in the Segmented style.

Motif Style

Motifs are divided into the qualitative categories of 'Simple' and 'Complex' styles. A Simple motif (Figure 3.3a-d) is composed of a single primary line or basic shape that is often contains smaller elements appended to the basic shape, such as a triangle or hooked triangle. The majority of Simple motifs are based on right-angled triangles. Complex motifs (Figure 3.3e-g) contain at least two primary lines and have several smaller elements appended to the body of the motif (e.g., eyes, circles, ticks). A second class of Complex motif consists of unique composite shapes such as bird or animal figures (Figure 3.h).

Classification Levels

Because I am directly interested in explaining patterns shared within the Chihuahuan tradition, the concept of hierarchy is also extended to different levels of archaeological perception. The comparison of design levels and styles is examined according to individual polychrome types as well as patterns shared throughout the tradition.

The Type

The classification of artifact types is fundamental to the discipline of archaeology. Researchers enact classification by quantifying the number of shared characteristics within a given medium (e.g., ceramics) in an effort to create recognizable entities, or types. A ceramic type is therefore composed of a group of sherds/vessels that share a cluster of recognizable traits (i.e. paste, manufacturing technique, decoration). In

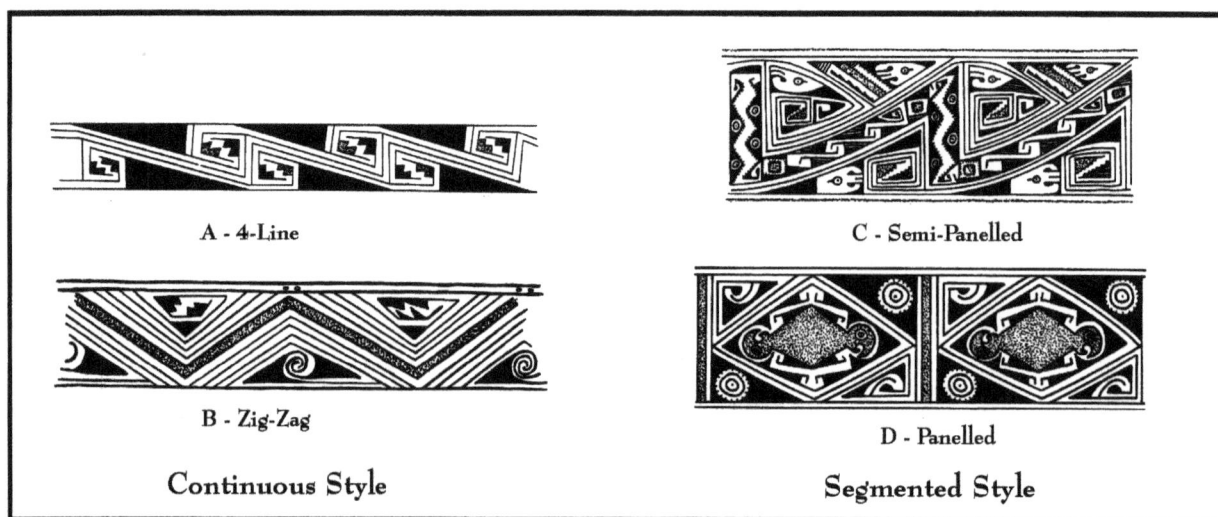

A - 4-Line

B - Zig-Zag

Continuous Style

C - Semi-Panelled

D - Panelled

Segmented Style

Figure 3.2a-d Layouts and Layout Styles recorded in the design analysis (from Di Peso et al. 1974; upper row – l to r - figure 345-6 [17], 290-6 [49] lower row - figure 345-6 [20], 290-6 [42])

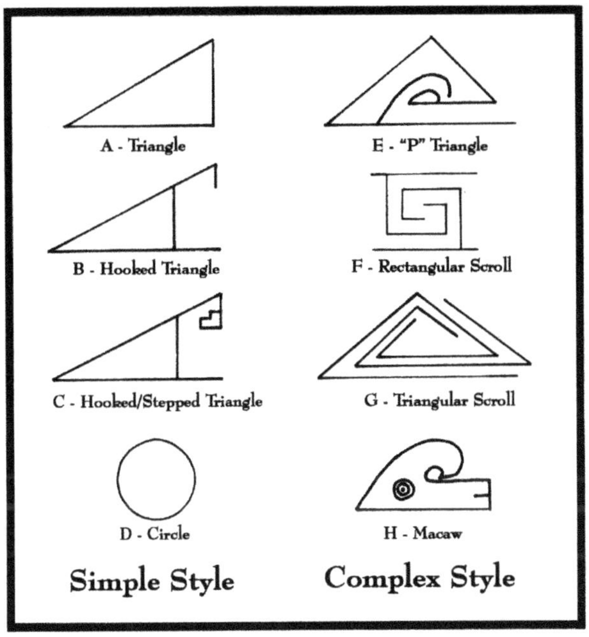

Figure 3.3a-h Examples of Motif and Motif Styles recorded in the design analysis

theory, a type is associated with mutually exclusive groups (some traits found within one type are not found in the others), but in practice these units often contain traits shared across established type boundaries (see Adams and Adams 1991).

Type represents one of the key building blocks for this investigation as the museum collections were not previously classified and the type is a critical construct in the comparison of different design levels. By examining how types vary internally we can begin to assess models to explain this variation, and then begin to consider the results from other type analyses and the tradition of which these are components.

The Tradition

Tradition is the over-arching concept that binds each of the types within a specific culture. Following Willey (1948), a pottery tradition also reflects long-time historical relationships. A ceramic tradition represents a body of interrelated traits that are found, but not necessarily shared ubiquitously, within a corpus of assemblages over a given period of time and space. Recognition of a Chihuahuan tradition occurred long before the establishment of a formal typology (Bandelier 1890; Kidder 1977:267; Chapman 1923; Harcum 1923), but it was Di Peso who formalized the idea through his detailed analysis of the Paquimé assemblage,

> though each painted type had traits setting it off from the others, all showed relationships in one or more characteristics, binding them into one school...(Di Peso et al. 1974a:2).

By contrast with type, patterns found throughout the tradition have often been ignored in favour of discussions of regional development and external interaction. In order to deal with issues such as trait overlap, it is necessary to examine the presence of traits that transcend the type concept indicated by the Di Peso's formation of type variants, and look at the broader tradition for a more holistic view of cultural developments.

Secondary Tests of the Museum Sample
The addition of secondary variables to this study is aimed at testing specific assumptions of typological or cultural significance within the tradition. Black-bordered red motifs (BoR), effigy vessels, and the Paquimé whole vessel collection are each selected to examine particular relationships within the Chihuahuan tradition.

Black-Bordered Red Motifs
The use of BoR was proposed by Di Peso (Di Peso et al. 1974a:254-256) and David Phillips (1999, personal communication) as having important stylistic implications within the Chihuahuan tradition, particularly in the identification of Ramos polychrome. While this is an intriguing notion, there has been no deliberate quantification of this trait within the ceramic collections. By testing the presence of BoR within the parameters of motif, layout, type and tradition, it will be possible to evaluate whether it is associated only with one specific type or if it transcends the type definition.

Effigy Vessels
The fundamental reason for analyzing the effigy class separately is based on the fact that these vessels represent an elaboration of the most common ceramic form, the jar. Given this familial similarity, it will be informative to determine whether effigy pots are merely elaborated forms of jars that share the same design structure, or if they are decorated with a particular style that differentiates them from normal jars. This latter scenario would provide further evidence that effigy vessels were imbued with different symbolic properties by Medio period potters.

Paquimé Assemblage
The final test to be conducted against the museum sample data is the comparison with the whole vessel assemblage exhumed by Di Peso from Paquimé (Di Peso et al. 1974a). While a portion of these jars originated from museums, Di Peso's collection provides a comparative sample with specific spatial context. Patterns produced by the ROM and WPM sample can be tested to see how closely they mirror the type frequencies and decorative structures from Paquimé. The excavated jars represent a more realistic representation of the frequency of type and effigy vessels than the museum sample; however, we must remember that it is somewhat biased by cultural (e.g., use of painted vessels in the past), taphonomic (e.g., site collapse, erosion), and modern (e.g., pothunters) processes.

PRODUCTS OF THE DESIGN ANALYSIS

The first goal of this design analysis is to produce an explicit list of decorative traits within the ceramic tradition and outline the frequency of design characteristics for the polychrome types in the sample. Hill refers to the corpus of these traits as a community's 'style unit pool', which he defines as, "the inventory of all the components of that style (not including combinatory rules)" (1985:375). For example, if there is a general similarity in decoration between the Chihuahuan polychrome types, we are presented with the basis for arguing the existence of a shared pool of designs used in different combinations by Medio period artisans. A more distant aim would extend the design pool concept to address whether or not a symbolic or conceptual reservoir exists (MacIntosh 1992) for the Chihuahuan culture. This reservoir represents the shared body of symbols in a culture, from which groups select particular elements and combinations to define their social unit. In effect, it is a conceptual framework that is used to account for similarities between related sub-groups (see MacEachern 1998). Unfortunately, to carry much weight these symbols must be recognized in more than the ceramic medium, as witnessed among the Shipibo-Conibo of Amazonian Peru (De Boer 1990; 1991) and Lake Baringo peoples of East Africa (Hodder 1982b). One factor that supports the adoption of this concept for the Chihuahuan tradition is the considerable time depth of the decorative suite, a period of at least 250 years. For now, we must be content with the identification of the pool of traits, but keep in mind the underlying implications of widespread use and interaction of symbols in the region.

The second product of this analysis is the recognition of shared decorative traits throughout the tradition that may reflect distinct design horizons or styles. The concept of the design horizon, according to Colton and Hargrave (1937), occurs when multi-levelled orders of elements and patterns are found on two or more pottery types. Examples of design horizons have been identified at a regional level in the Kayenta area (Plog 1980:127) and in the Salado phenomenon (Crown 1994:177-179), as well as within individual sites within the Mimbres area (Shafer and Brewington 1995). Crown (1994:78) suggests that the most significant benefit of the design horizon is that it allows movement beyond type and formalized spatial and temporal boundaries, and can possibly indicate interaction between regions. While this study focusses solely on local wares, this idea may have an impact on identifying localized design horizons, or style zones, within Chihuahua.

CONSTRUCTING EXPLANATORY MODELS FOR DECORATIVE VARIATION

The first step in the design analysis process will be to quantify the decorative traits in the museum collections and outline the basic motif and layout trends that characterize each polychrome type and the Chihuahuan tradition. Once this is established it will be possible to evaluate these characteristics according to the use of BoR, variability in decoration within effigy classes, and then compare the museum data to the results from Paquimé.

The second part of this study is the search for patterns, or design horizons, that transcend the type concept. A design horizon is defined by the regular occurrence of motifs and layout combinations within an assemblage. Michael Whalen (personal communication, June 1998) suggested that we begin to address the existence of horizon styles within the Chihuahuan ceramic assemblage, yet no one has attempted to locate any distinct patterning. The existence of variants within the polychrome types suggests that the design horizon concept may prove to be a useful marker for explaining similarities within the Chihuahuan tradition.

Both type differences and similarities observed on the museum jars are examined within the context of several explanatory models. The following sections will propose hypotheses of temporal, spatial, and in relation to cultural developments to explain these trends and provide models that can be tested through future research with excavated or museum-based data.

Temporal Change in the Polychrome Ceramics

Temporal change in the Chihuahuan tradition is the most important issue in this discussion, and stems from the lack of a proper stylistic sequence. As a result, archaeologists are faced with two choices: 1) the types were produced from the beginning of the Medio period, or 2) the types appeared at different stages.

Support for the contemporaneous appearance and production of the Chihuahuan polychrome tradition is championed by Di Peso. His research at Paquimé convinced Di Peso that the decorative similarity found throughout the ceramic assemblage provided evidence for 'eighteen generations' of consistent ceramic production (Di Peso et al. 1974:2). It is argued here that this fluid sequence is attributed to Di Peso's inability to reconstruct a chronological sequence from the complex formation processes at the site. As a result, Di Peso argued that each of the polychrome types appeared at the beginning of the Medio period (~A.D.1060 [1200]) and continued unchanged until the collapse of the Chihuahuan culture (A.D. 1340 [1450]). Certainly this scenario is possible, however, with nearly two hundred and fifty years of production, the chance of temporal variation *not* occurring is highly unlikely. By contrast, studies in the Anasazi area have noted important changes over a period of only 100 years (Plog 1980:24), a significantly shorter duration than the Chihuahuan Medio period. Whether Di Peso was unable to order the ceramic diversity chronologically, or simply could not manage the enormous quantity of material from Paquimé, painted designs still remain a significant indicator of temporal change. With the lack of a well-seriated assemblage to assess these differences we must turn to an in-depth examination of decoration. The issue we face is how to coax time out of this elaborate painting tradition.

The first mention of temporal differences in the Chihuahuan ceramics was made rather off-handedly Kidder, who encountered difficulties in making concise type descriptions from the Peabody museum collection: "the problem with museum collections is that they probably contain both late and early specimens, and we have no way of determining which is which" (1916:264). Later research by Sayles (1936), and then Carlson (1982), further suggested a developmental sequence of the ceramics (see Figure 2.9), however, neither study attempted to test these inferences through the rigorous investigation of the data set or to posit reasons for such differences.

One solution to this problem is to turn to some basic theoretical conceptions of how objects change through time. In Clarke's (1968:167) discussion of time pattern regularities, he suggests that temporal change can be measured by comparing both the attributes and the number of attributes found within each artifact. The changing degree of elaborateness and overall sophistication within an artifact form is therefore seen as an important marker of shifts through time. If we find significant differences in the use or quantity of traits between types or design horizons, this may be our first clue in identifying temporal markers in the ceramic assemblage. Using the museum data, we can compare the range and number of motifs used to decorate a collection of ceramics as an indicator of change through time. A second point raised by McGuire provides the approach for recognizing the orientation of material differences: "to understand a qualitative transformation we should initiate our study at a point prior to that transformation and carry through past the transformation" (1992:100). Following these arguments, temporal differences can be distinguished by comparing the decorative patterns of the period in question with the patterns of an earlier stage.

For the purposes of this study, our point of reference for temporal change is the Viejo period painted wares, which are commonly represented by monochrome vessels, geometric designs with a small range of motifs, and relatively crude execution. Comparable traits located within the Medio assemblage are, by extension, more likely related to this earlier style.

A second, though less tenable, reference point for the opposite end of the temporal scale is to compare the museum ceramics with those recovered from Paquimé. This argument follows the inference that the complete vessels excavated by Di Peso represent the end of the Medio period. Several logical explanations can be provided to justify this claim. First, if the site was occupied for over 200 years, the chance that a large proportion of 'early' vessels remained unbroken is highly unlikely. Second, Di Peso (1974) argues that the site was suddenly sacked and abandoned shortly afterwards, a process in which many vessels may have been left behind or buried in the rubble. Potential problems with this argument lie in the number of jars found in burials and the possibility that well-painted vessels were curated over several generations. Ultimately, neither Di Peso (Di Peso et al. 1974b) nor Ravesloot (1989) were successful in distinguishing a definitive temporal sequence from the burial data either. If the analysis of layout and type in the Paquimé assemblage provides a distinct pattern we can begin to challenge Di Peso's assumption that all the polychrome types were produced at the beginning of the Medio period.

Spatial Variation
Positing hypotheses of spatial distribution for un-provenienced artifacts is extremely difficult, if not impossible. The utility of Chihuahuan museum data to address spatial concerns has also been understandably bleak. Brand argued that,

> Practically none of the…collection material is of value for a study of the areal distribution of pottery types, since the pottery was commonly purchased in large groups lacking specific identification of provenience (1933:60).

Regardless of the inherent limitations of museum data, we must ask the question, if decorative variation is not the result of temporal change, what other cause could account for such differences? Despite the obvious restrictions of this data set, spatial variation is one possibility that must be considered. Two lines of evidence can be combined to posit spatial explanations for the patterns found in the museum sample: 1) the archaeological database presented in Chapter II, and 2) the adoption of interaction theory.

The archaeological literature provides both a basic knowledge of the distribution of types across this vast area coupled with a series of extensive type descriptions. Unfortunately, the problem is that these types are also frequently found to co-occur throughout the region and, following Di Peso's identification of variants, often share the same decorative structure. If we accept that the polychrome types were produced simultaneously and continuously throughout the Medio period, the artisans responsible for each type must be seen as drawing different combinations of traits or style units from the same pool. Since each type represents a part of the same tradition, it is not merely the association of individual motifs but the combination of traits that may reflect spatial patterning. The basic premise of interaction theory, while normally aimed at the study of different cultures, seeks to identify the direction, degree and impact of this overlap with strong interaction occurring when larger combinations of traits are found between two assemblages.

To provide a contextual reference point for this study, the museum sample will be tested against the layout and type data derived from the Paquimé collection. The utility of including excavated material is that it comes from a known location in space; therefore, common patterns uncovered in the museum sample may indicate that they originated from the same area. However, this process may be complicated when type and type distribution are considered. More specific comparisons will also be undertaken by looking for commonalities within the BoR and effigy variables.

Cultural Implications of Decorative Variation

A final aspect of this thesis is to extend the temporal and spatial frameworks of decorative variation to specific cultural causes. The majority of studies that seek to explain why this variation occurs have the luxury of knowing at least when or where the vessels originated and as a result can more easily discuss such factors as individual agency, class difference, or territoriality.

Two concepts that will be examined in relation to social causes are increased complexity (i.e. increases in number of traits, composite motifs, combinations of design levels) and standardization (i.e. regular use of design traits and combination of design levels). Each of these will be examined from the perspective of temporal and spatial importance, and may be the result of interaction (i.e. new ideas and symbols), economic change (i.e. craft specialization), or the development of socio-political constructs (i.e. class formation).

One component of social variability that can be addressed in more detail is whether jars and the related effigy subset share the same decorative structures. If effigy vessels are found to share the same combination of motif and layout combinations as regular jars, then the putative importance of these vessels must lie in the form and not the painted elements. On the other hand, if the effigies are found with different decorative structures, we may conclude that they contain a separate body of symbolic information from their unappended cousins. A deeper evaluation of the importance of the individual design levels would then be required.

Summary of the Design Analysis Approach

A discussion of the specific cultural causes and implications of decorative patterning obviously requires consideration of the entire archaeological assemblage, and not just ceramics. Given that this thesis cannot address *all* possible cultural permutations, these hypotheses are presented to question the previous ceramic interpretations and promote new ideas of explaining the decorative diversity in the Chihuahuan tradition.

CHAPTER IV
DATA COLLECTION AND METHODOLOGY

HISTORY OF THE COLLECTIONS
A brief summary of the acquisition of the collections used in this study is presented to provide at least some historical context for these whole vessels.

Royal Ontario Museum (ROM)
The ROM collection represents the largest known assemblage of Chihuahuan whole vessels in Canada. Obtained in 1921, from a joint purchase of a portion of the Ledwidge collection with the National Museum of Natural History in Washington D.C. and the State Museum of New Mexico in Santa Fe. The ROM collection contains a total of several hundred ceramic pieces, divided between plain, textured, and painted styles. With the exception of Harcum's (1923) brief report heralding the arrival of the collection there has been no published analysis of the pottery since its acquisition eighty years ago. None of the jars have any information about provenience other than the fact that they were recovered from northern Mexico.

Wilderness Park Museum (WPM)
The WPM acquisitions are also largely composed of vessels purchased from the Ledwidge family, in this case through a separate sale that took place in 1959 to the city of El Paso. In the years between 1978 and 1993, seventeen additional vessels were added to the collection included here (i.e., 1978 [1], 1981 [4], 1983 [3], 1985 [5], 1992 [3], and 1993 [1]). Of the 666 pieces in this collection, which include polychrome, textured, and plain wares in the form of bottles, bowls, as well as jars, there are no records of provenience for any of the collection. Interestingly, several pots still had prices written on their bases ranging from $5-15. Whether these values were placed on the vessels during the sale from Ledwidge to El Paso or at some later date is undetermined. Unlike the ROM collection, the WPM holdings are used with more regularity and are included in the dissertation research of Christine Van Pool (personal communication, September 2000) of the University of New Mexico and Patricia Lee (Christine Van Pool, personal communication, November 2000).

At the broadest level, the pots included from these museums represent only the jars that could be classified as Ramos, Babícora, or Villa Ahumada. Since these vessels were by far the most abundant form the focus of this investigation could not include the different vessel forms (e.g., bowls, bottles, etc.) or types (e.g., painted, textured, plain) that constitute the remaining portion of both the ROM and WPM collections.

DATA RECORDING
The study of the ROM collection took place over a week in January 1999 with the permission of Mima Kapches, head curator for North American Archaeology at the museum. Examination of the WPM collection occurred during five days in August 1999 with authorization of the City of El Paso and Dr. Marc Thompson, curator of the museum. From these short excursions, 361 polychrome jars (including effigies), 161 from the ROM and 200 from the WPM, were selected for this study. This total does not represent the entire collection of polychrome vessels from these museums since only three type categories (Babícora, Ramos, Villa Ahumada) were included in the design analysis. One caveat that must be examined in greater detail is the possibility that jars within both the ROM and WPM collections include more recent copies of prehistoric wares. This problem will be discussed in greater detail in Chapter VI.

Classification of the Museum Sample
As neither the ROM nor the WPM vessels were classified, the initial step in this study was to assign them to polychrome type categories. The characteristics used for making these type associations were based on Di Peso's dense descriptions published in the Casas Grandes Ceramic volume (see Table 2.2). This study produced 108 Babícora, 160 Ramos, and 93 Villa Ahumada jars respectively. The classification process followed the sequence outlined in Figure 2.5: presence of a white slip (Villa Ahumada) or paste colour (brown – Babícora, white – Ramos), coupled with the extensive list of decorative traits described for Ramos (i.e. BoR, fine execution, macaw motifs) (see Di Peso et al. 1974:254-286). A problem that slowed the type process, however, is Di Peso's identification of the Paquimé variant of Babícora, which for all intents and purposes, is a Ramos vessel made with a darker clay. Vessels from both the ROM and WPM collections were found to fit within this nebulous category through the combination of brown paste/surface colour and finely executed and elaborate decoration. Ultimately, if the decorative characteristics were the same, the defining factor was paste/surface colour. During this process it was discovered, not surprisingly, that the application of the Di Pesoan typology is highly individualized, and variation in final results or type justification is a recognized occurrence in research focussing on the Chihuahuan tradition (Hendrickson, in press). It is hoped that this thesis will, at the very least, clarify overlaps in decoration between types and posit an explanation for shared characteristics between our defined ceramic classes.

Size and Shape
The physical dimensions of each pot were measured following the variables used in the Casas Grandes Ceramic volume (Di Peso et al. 1974:6). Figure 4.1 illustrates the various physical dimensions (height, vertical tangency, maximum body and mouth diameters) recorded for the museum sample. Measurements were taken using an osteometric board at the ROM and a set of large tree calipers at the WPM.

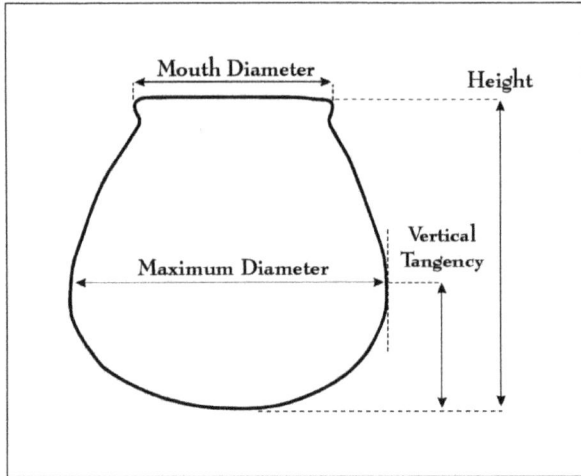

Figure 4.1 Physical dimensions recorded for each vessel from the ROM and WPM

Classification of jar shape similarly relied on the categories published by DiPeso, Fenner and Rinaldo (Di Peso et al. 1974:6). Each of the shape, effigy, orifice type, vertical section, neck form, rim type, and horizontal section classes used in this thesis are illustrated in Figure 4.2. Of these categories, estimation of vertical section and neck proved to be the most difficult to determine because the differences between, for example, ovoid, spheroid, and ellipsoid were not based on quantitative parameters (i.e. ovoid equates with greater height versus diameter, ellipsoid has greater diameter versus height). Instead, the recording standards presented in the Casas Grandes

volumes evidenced some degree of 'eye-balling' in order to determine the vertical section of a vessel. A comparable practice was adopted for the study of ROM and WPM collections. Perforations and suspension holes found under the lip of many jars or in lugs appended to the side of the vessel were also recorded.

Vessel condition in both museum collections was considerably varied presenting several interesting examples of re-use and reconstruction techniques. A number of jars had reworked edges, presumably after being broken, to facilitate continued use by prehistoric Chihuahuans, while others represent modern reconstruction. Figure 4.3 displays two notable examples from the WPM. The vessel on the left retains only the chin portion of the 'hood' (visible on the neck of the jar), while the jar on the right was reconstructed using a sherd that was not part of the original vessel. Many jars also displayed evidence of fire-clouding and sooting, the latter potentially indicating previous use for cooking.

These characteristics were not directly examined in the analysis of the museum sample, but are presented with the decorative information in Appendix A for future research.

Photographs

The original goal of this study involved the use of a panoramic camera to create roll-out photos of the complete layout for each pot. Due to the prohibitive cost of purchasing or renting this equipment, layout was

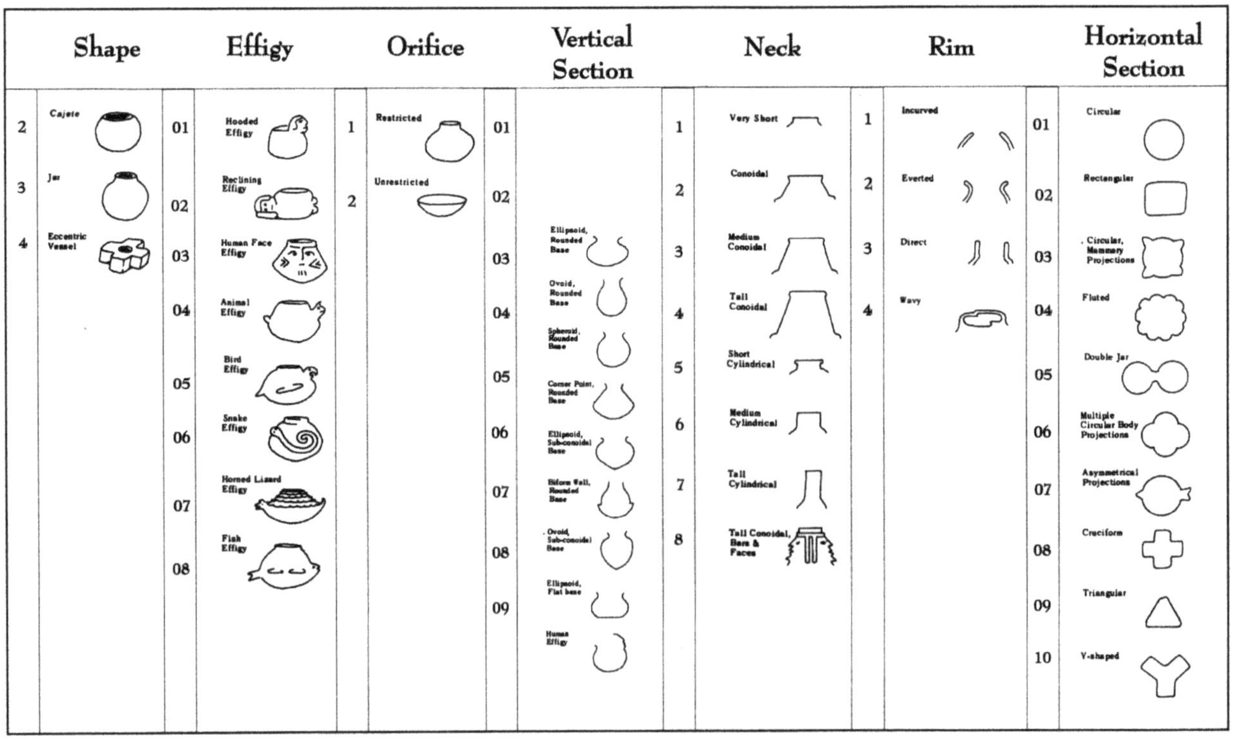

Figure 4.2 Shape characteristics recorded for each vessel from the ROM and WPM collections (based on categories in Di Peso et al. 1974:18-19)

Figure 4.3 Examples of altered and reconstructed jars from the WPM collection
(left - chin of effigy vessel [W599249], right - foreign sherd used to patch hole
in snake effigy vessel [EL47])

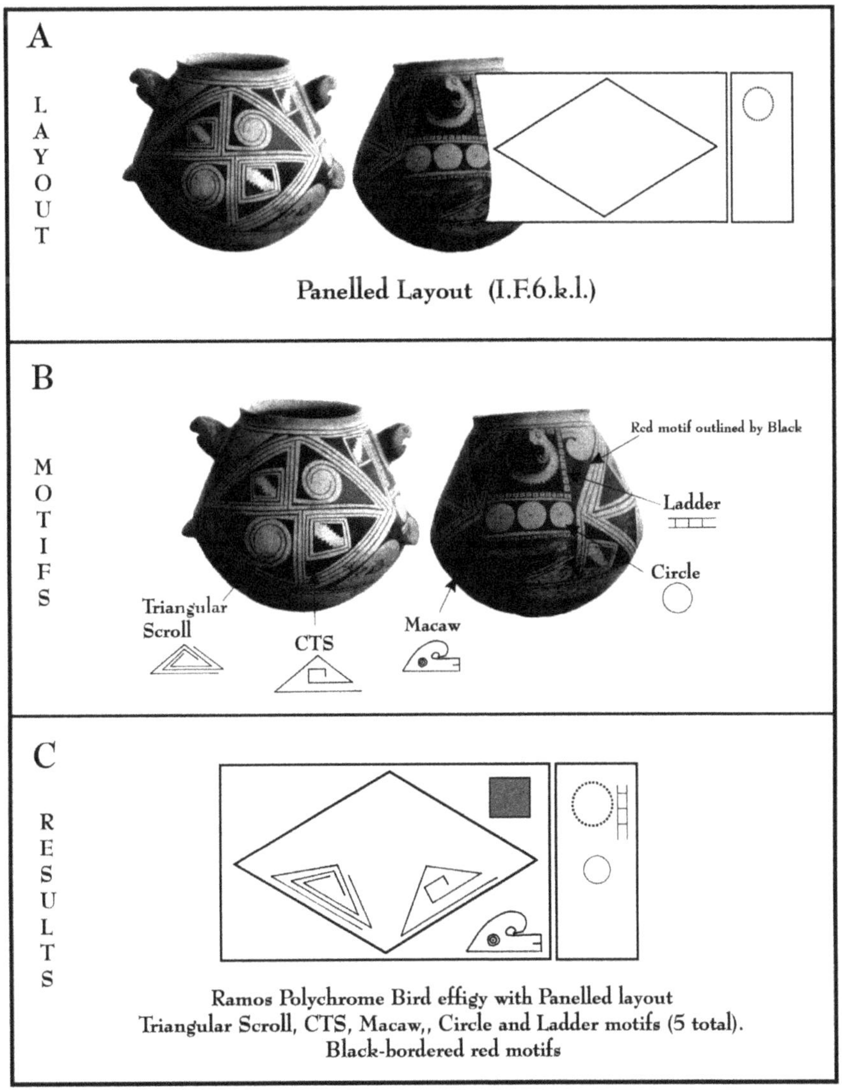

Figure 4.4a-c Decorative decoding process used in the design analysis
(bird effigy from collection of Mr. Harold Naylor)

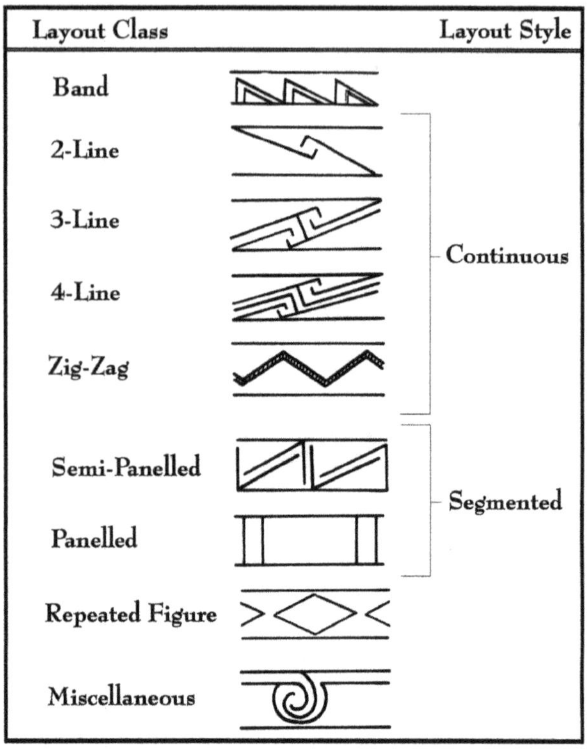

Layout Class		Layout Style
Band		
2-Line		
3-Line		Continuous
4-Line		
Zig-Zag		
Semi-Panelled		
Panelled		Segmented
Repeated Figure		
Miscellaneous		

Figure 4.5 Layout classes and styles recorded for the ROM and WPM collections (adapted from Di Peso et al. 1974:7-10)

documented through a series of photos taken with a Tamron 90mm lens mounted on a Pentax ME Super camera body with Konica 200 ASA film. Each pot was photographed at 90° intervals against a velvet background (red at the ROM, crème at the WPM) to provide a portable record for the analysis of motifs and layout. A professional light table equipped with halogen lights was provided to take the photographs at the ROM. Photographs of the jars from the WPM were taken on a small portable stand with incandescent spot-lights.

Decorative Traits
Layout
A layout is defined by the number of lines and the manner in which these lines separate the band into distinct design fields. The categories used to classify the layout on whole vessels are based on Di Peso's scheme developed for the Paquimé assemblage (Di Peso et al.:7-10). Even with this benchmark for comparison, determining the origin and orientation of lines was extremely difficult and required several weeks of constant examination to complete the analysis of each vessel layout. Figure 4.4a illustrates the decoding process for a vessel decorated with a Panelled layout. Figure 4.5 illustrates each of the layout classes that are defined as follows,

Basic - A band filled with repeated motifs

2-Line - Layout composed of lines extending from the upper and lower borderlines that repeat around the band

3-Line - Layout composed of lines extending from the upper and lower borderlines that interact with a third line running continuously around the vessel

4-Line - Layout composed of lines extending from the upper and lower borderlines that interact with a third and fourth line running continuously around the vessel

Zig-Zag - Layout composed of central band or pair of lines that form a zig-zag pattern running continuously around the vessel; band or lines do not interact with lines extending from the borderlines

Semi-Panelled - Layout subdivided by vertical lines into rectangular panels; vertical lines do not necessarily touch upper and lower borderlines

Panelled - Layout is divided by vertical lines into separate rectangular panels; vertical lines attached to upper and lower borderlines

Repeated Figure - Layout demarcated by the presence of large repeated figures

Miscellaneous - Layout does not correspond to any of the parameters established for other layouts

Each of the vessels examined from the ROM and WPM fit within one of these nine layout classes. It should be noted that sixty-one jars in the museum sample were recorded with more than one layout on their exterior. These jars frequently utilized the same layout, however, in cases where different layouts were recorded on a single jar the central, or primary layout, was selected for comparison.

Di Peso (Di Peso et al. 1974:7-10) further divided the layout classes into multiple variants. As many as twenty-six variations were identified within the Panelled layout from the museum sample (see Appendix A), illustrating the significant variation that exists within a single layout class. However, as with Di Peso's type descriptions, the layout variants were found to overlap layout classes, specifically examples associated with 3-Line and Semi-Panelled formats (see Figure 4.6). The determining factor in this situation was based on how the overall design field was used on the vessel (i.e. separate panels versus continuing line-motif interactions). Layout variants were originally incorporated in this study to enable a more specific comparison of trends between the two museum samples and the Paquimé collection. However, upon completing the analysis of layout, it was determined that the immense diversity and uneven distribution of layout

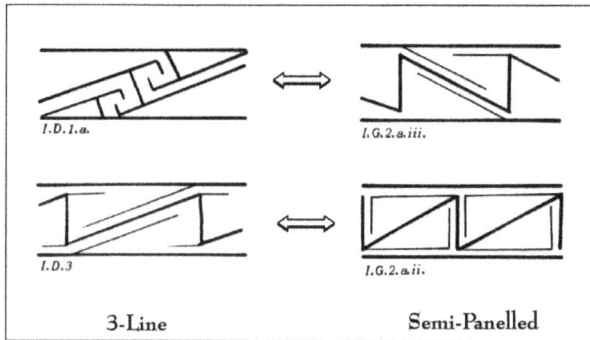

3-Line   Semi-Panelled

Figure 4.6 Potential overlap in layout categories identified from the Casas Grandes classification scheme (taken from Di Peso et al. 1974:7,9)

variants would prove too difficult to incorporate at this stage.

Layout Style

As discussed in Chapter III, the majority of layout classes can be associated with either the Continuous or Segmented style. Figure 4.5 illustrates the breakdown of layout class by style used in this study. Due to the variable representation of Basic, Repeated Figure, and Miscellaneous layouts these classes were not included within the two style categories used in this study. For the purpose of comparing layout styles, these vessels are not considered in the final discussion.

Motif

To date, no concise record of the range of different motifs exists for the Chihuahuan tradition. Labels have been given to particular motifs, such as the opposed stepped figure, club-shaped element, scrolls, and triangle with crooked appendage (Kidder 1916:262-264), or key, and tri-pointed flag (Sayles 1936:50-51). However, these represent only a portion of the entire decorative assemblage. A basic aim of this study, therefore, is to provide a standardized inventory of motifs for future use.

One of the most critical decisions in identifying and naming motifs is whether the focus is placed on the actual painted decoration or the result of this decoration (i.e. negative space created by the addition of lines). This study relies on the actual painted lines, rather than the spaces in between. The only instance where the negative perspective is recorded is in the regular depiction of circles. Figure 4.4b illustrates how motifs are recorded from the ROM and WPM samples. Nineteen different motifs were recorded from the museum collections based on a presence/absence basis for each vessel (Figures 4.7 and 4.8). As with layout classes, each motif is also placed into either a Simple or Complex style category. The individual motifs are defined as follows:

Triangle – three-sided form, normally filled/hatched (Figure 4.7a)

Hooked Triangle – triangle with line extending along one edge; secondary vertical element appended to end (Figure 4.7b)

Hooked/Stepped Triangle – triangle with line extending along one edge; secondary vertical/horizontal elements appended and contain two small opposed squares or steps (Figure 4.7c)

Stepped Triangle – triangle with line extending along one edge; line contains several small triangles arranged in stepped pattern (Figure 4.7d)

Scrolled Triangle – triangle with line extending along one edge; line curves inwards in a spiral shape (Figure 4.7e)

Barbed – similar to basic triangle shape; open end consists of pair of short acute angles, or barbs (Figure 4.7f)

Ladder – continuous parallel lines with vertical subdivisions creating a contiguous set of boxes, used as an elaboration of other motifs (Figure 4.7g)

Checkerboard – series of continuous parallel lines with vertical subdivisions; every second box is filled with paint creating regular pattern (Figure 4.7h)

Circle – circular form created by positive or negative painting technique (Figure 4.7i)

Diamond – four-sided vertically oriented design (Figure 4.7j)

Spirals – broad, inward curving lines (Figure 4.7k)

Miscellaneous – any design that did not occur more than once and is not similar to the remaining designs

Macaw – bird shaped figure with characteristic hooked beak and eye pattern (Figure 4.8a)

Feathers – triangular design with tripartite division on long edge and vertical cross-banding, often contains dots at the broad edge (Figure 4.8b)

Zoomorph – undetermined animal or human figure; includes plumed serpent, distinguished by forward curving plume or horn attached to head, toothed mouth, tail, and eye pattern (Figure 4.8c)

Rectangular Scrolls – two lines extending from upper and lower border lines, interlocking in a rectangular pattern in the center of the design (Figure 4.8d)

"P"-shaped Triangles – single line forming incomplete triangle with interior end terminating

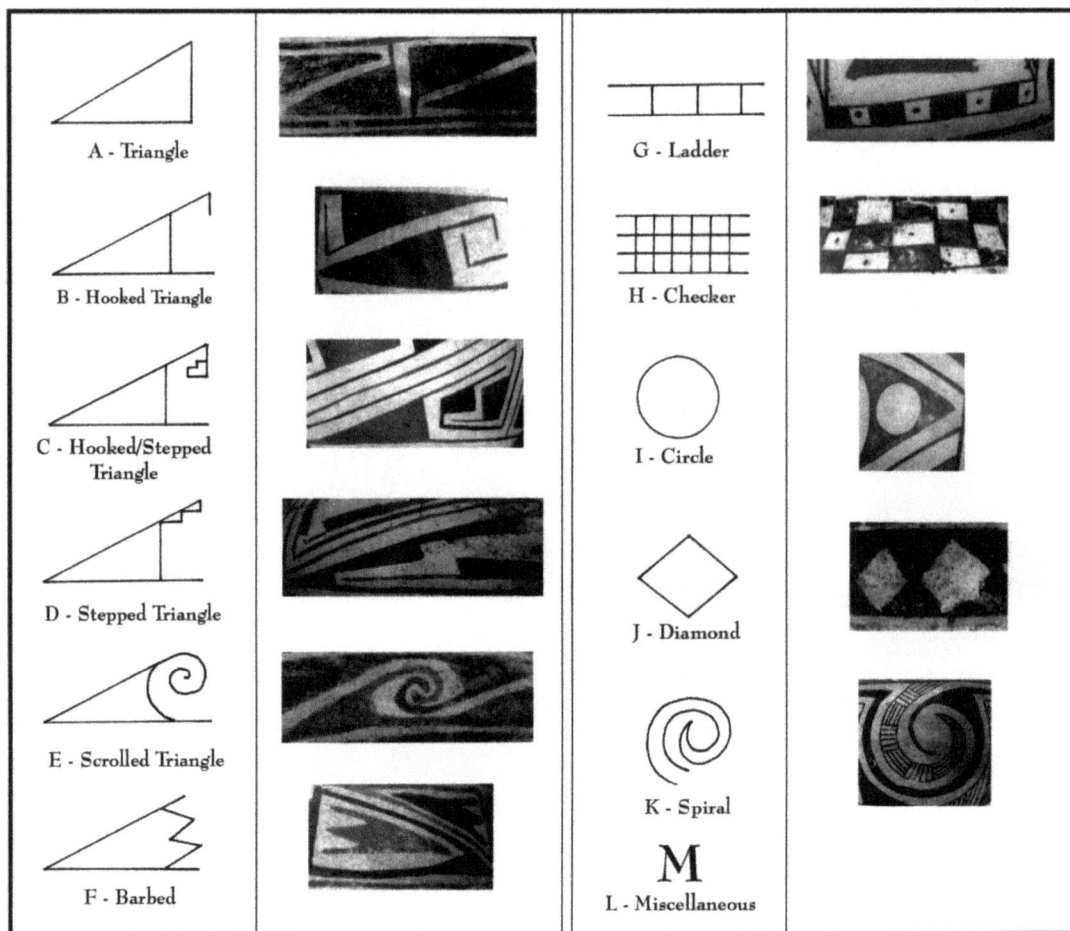

Figure 4.7a-l Simple style motifs recorded in the design analysis

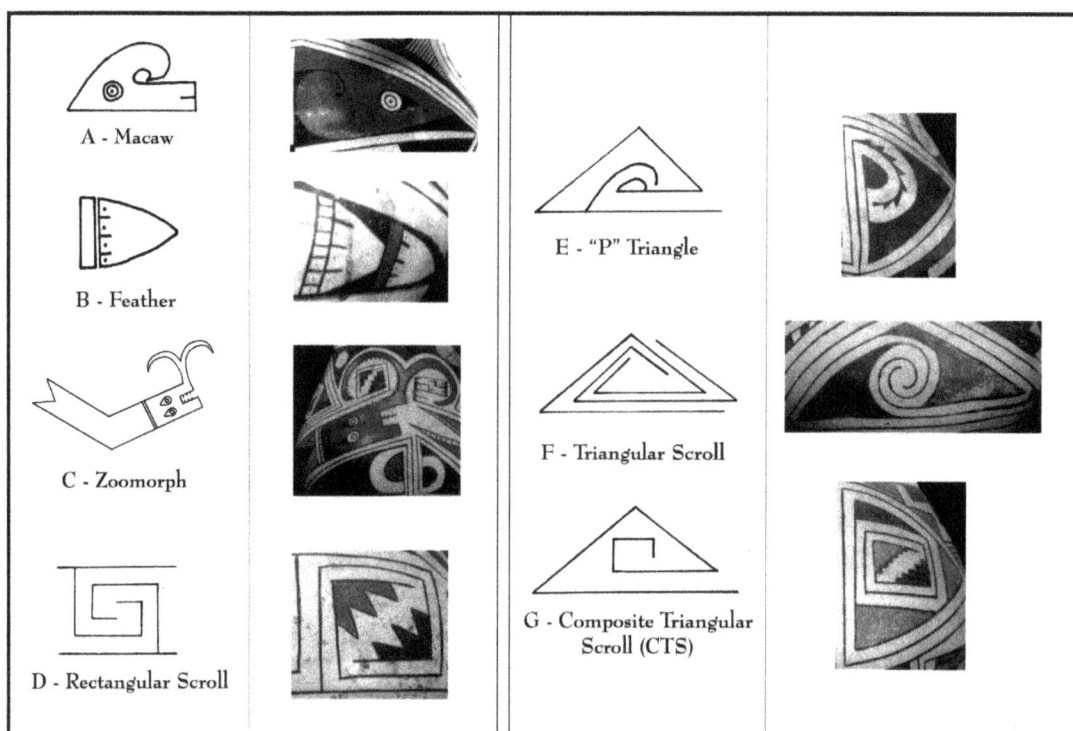

Figure 4.8a-g   Complex style motifs recorded in the design analysis

Figure 4.9 Examples of black-bordered red motifs from the WPM collection
(l to r WPM #181, #184, #89)

in half spade element; secondary line extends from base overtop half spade element producing a distinct "P" shape. Sometimes referred to as a stylized macaw (see Di Peso et al. 1974a:283) (Figure 4.8e)

Triangular Scrolls – two lines opposed and interlocked by central scroll in a triangular shape (Figure 4.8f)

Composite Triangular Scrolls (CTS) – similar to "P" triangle with inside line terminating in a single rectangular scroll which is filled with opposed, rectilinear steps (Figure 4.8g)

Each motif was recorded on a presence/absence basis, regardless of the number of times it appeared on a jar. Other categories that were included in the analysis were the colour of the motif (black, red, negative), presence of hatching, and the addition of secondary elements such as ticking or dots. Due to the number of basic motifs and diversity within the sample, none of these secondary characteristics are evaluated in the discussion of decorative patterning.

Secondary Variables
Black-bordered Red Motifs
This contrastive variable is recorded for a jar that contains at least one red motif that is outlined in black (Figure 4.9). The presence of BoR in individual motifs

was also noted in the initial study (Appendix A) but is not considered in the final analysis.

Effigy
The effigy classes to be compared against the trait level data of the museum sample have been previously defined in Chapter II, and are illustrated in Figure 4.2. In addition to motifs used on the body of the jar, any comparable motifs present on appendages (e.g., hoods, arms, and legs) were also recorded. The reason for including these extra-layout designs is to test the number and association of motifs between the jar and effigy forms.

The Paquimé Sample
A total of 146 jars with type and layout information were incorporated from the 306 vessels (jars, bowls, other shapes) excavated from the site (Di Peso et al. 1974). The frequency of each polychrome type was very different from the museum sample, with Ramos polychrome (106) being significantly better represented than either Babícora (23) or Villa Ahumada (13). That the relative proportion of these complete vessels is mirrored in the sherd counts (Ramos 11.6%, Babícora 1.5%, Villa Ahumada 1.3%) suggests that the ratio of complete vessels is an adequate representation of the Paquimé assemblage.

Vessel Decoding
An example of the recording process of layout, motif and secondary characteristics is illustrated in Figure 4.4c. The results of the analysis from the ROM and WPM using this method are presented in Chapter V.

CHAPTER V

DATA PRESENTATION

TERMINOLOGY AND RESEARCH FOCUS

Before examining the data for motif and layout frequencies, a brief discussion of the terminology and statistical approach used in this chapter is merited. Since the jars included in this study represent only a portion of the entire collection housed at the ROM and WPM, the body of data examined in this analysis will be referred to as the *museum sample*. Both museum data sets are included within this collective term and only a brief comparison of the two museum subsamples will be presented following the analysis of the combined collections. The reason for disregarding the modern 'provenience' is that, while each collection may represent a specific 'looting' phase from a particular region, we know little of the history surrounding these vessels prior to their accession into either museum. Further reason for combining both data sets into one sample is that most, if not all, of both the ROM and WPM holdings were obtained from the Ledwige family in El Paso. Because of this shared secondary provenience, these two assemblages may be inherently 'more related' than would vessels from two different collectors.

The design analysis presented below will emphasize statistical measures of relative frequency and percentages of decorative traits. By establishing hypotheses and relationships the next logical step will be to examine the statistical validity of models derived by the naked eye.

The use of type and tradition (here represented by the museum sample) perspectives is incorporated to explain decorative similarities or differences found within both classification levels. The type concept is applied to the body of museum data to hypothesize reasons for the appearance of specific motifs or layouts. The museum sample (here representing the 'tradition') provides the basic patterns shared across the types and represents the initial impetus for recognizing a design horizon within the ceramic assemblage.

DESIGN ANALYSIS

The data recorded from the ROM and WPM collections is examined through the design analysis developed in Chapters III and IV. Analysis of the decorative traits within the 361 Chihuahuan polychrome jars will progress through several stages outlined in Figure 5.1. The examination of layout includes a discussion of layout class and layout style, while motifs are analyzed according to motif class, motif style, and number of motifs per jar. Both design levels are then examined together within both classification levels. The last section compares the information of layout and motif against the number of jars with black borders around red motifs (BoR), between the effigy classes, and in contrast to the

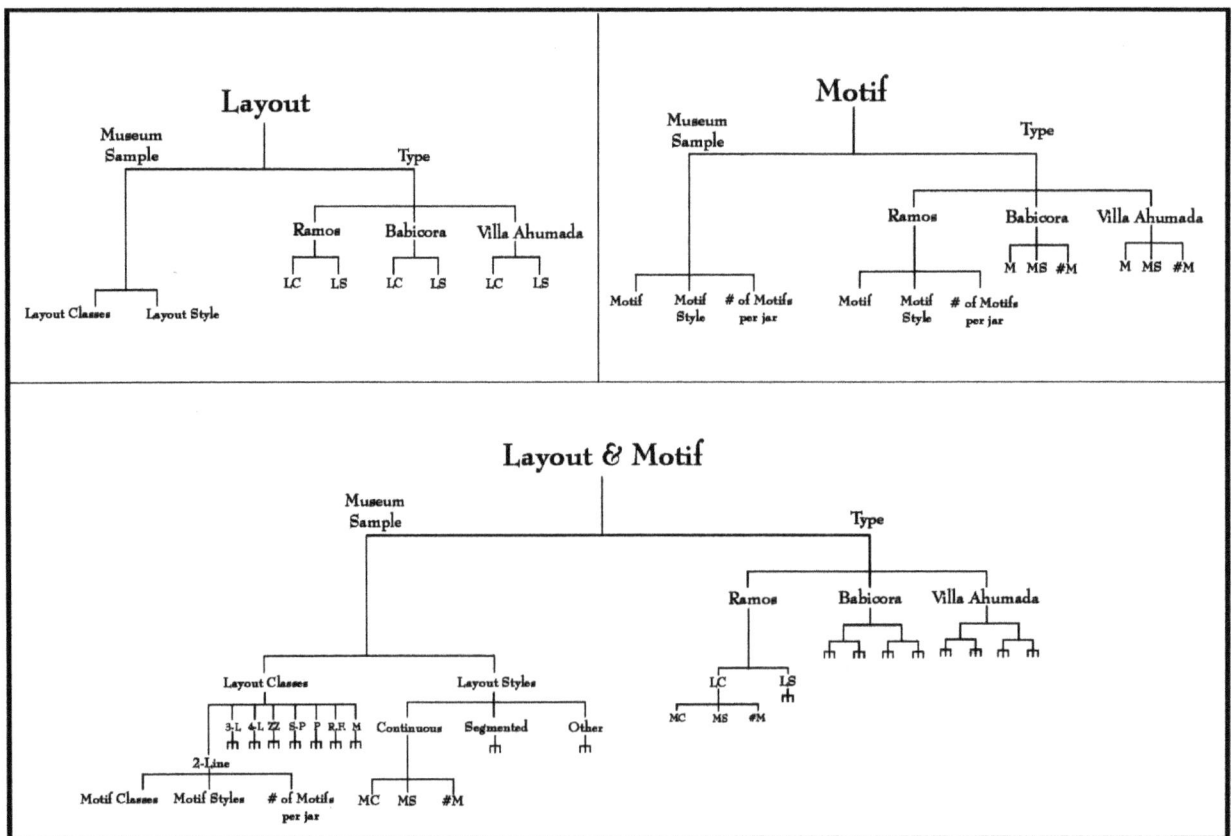

Figure 5.1 Levels of design analysis for the museum sample

44

Style	Layout	Ramos N=160	Babicora N=108	Villa Ahumada N=93	Museum Sample N=361
Continuous	Basic	0	2	0	2
	2-Line	1	26	36	63
	3-Line	6	15	12	33
	4-Line	3	20	19	42
	Zig-Zag	19	5	8	32
Segmented	Semi-Panelled	30	10	3	43
	Panelled	89	24	11	124
Other	Repeated Figure	7	3	3	13
	Miscellaneous	5	3	1	9
Style	Continuous	29	66	75	170
	Segmented	119	34	14	167
	Other	12	8	4	24

Table 5.1 Relative frequency of layouts by polychrome type and museum sample (ROM and WPM

Style	Motif	Ramos N=160	Babicora N=108	Villa Ahumada N=93	Museum Sample N=361
Simple	Triangle	60	24	15	99
	Hooked Triangle	49	27	27	103
	Hooked/Stepped Triangle	21	36	19	87
	Stepped Triangle	2	15	7	24
	Scrolled Triangle	11	23	25	59
	Barbed	13	22	12	47
	Ladder	21	5	3	29
	Checker	9	4	4	17
	Circles	39	10	12	61
	Diamond	4	4	2	10
	Spirals	6	0	1	7
	Miscellaneous	17	7	7	31
Complex	Macaw	24	5	7	36
	Feather	12	1	3	16
	Zoomorph	19	3	1	23
	Rectangular Scroll	8	4	28	40
	"P" Triangle	82	19	12	113
	Triangular Scroll	45	11	10	66
	Composite Triangular Scroll	89	22	9	120
	Total Appearances of Motifs	542	242	204	988
	Average # of Motifs/Jar	3.4	2.2	2.2	2.7
	Simple	263	177	134	574
	Complex	279	65	70	414

Table 5.2 Relative frequency of motifs by polychrome type and museum sample

results of the whole vessels recovered from Paquimé.

Layout

Layouts recorded in this discussion are evaluated according to the distribution of layout classes and styles (i.e., Continuous, Segmented) for the three polychrome types and the entire museum sample. The discussion is based on the data presented in Table 5.1.

Ramos Polychrome

Ramos polychrome is the most common type in the museum sample (160 of 361 vessels). Over half of these jars are decorated with Panelled layouts and, when combined with the Semi-Panelled examples, the Segmented style accounts for 75% of this type. With the exception of Zig-Zag layouts, Continuous classes are relatively infrequent.

Babícora Polychrome

The sample of 108 Babícora jars presents an eclectic range of layouts, several of which (i.e., 2-Line, 4-Line, and Panelled) are found on 19% or more of the assemblage (see Table 5.1). The Continuous style represents 61% of the entire assemblage of Babícora polychrome. Even with the high proportion of Panelled layouts, the Segmented style only constitutes 31% of the entire assemblage.

Villa Ahumada Polychrome

Villa Ahumada is the least common type found in the ROM and WPM collections. The overall style of this type is heavily reliant on Continuous structures, which comprise 81% of the decoration on these jars with the most common examples being the 2-Line and 4-Line classes. Panelled layouts are also evident but represent a less frequent class in the Villa Ahumada sample.

Museum Sample

The museum sample is dominated by Panelled (34%) and 2-Line (17%) layouts, while the remaining classes appear in smaller quantities. Basic, Repeated Figure, and Miscellaneous layouts represent the most infrequent classes. Overall, there is little difference in the relative frequency between Continuous (47%) and Segmented (46%) layout styles.

Summary: Comparison of Layout

Figure 5.2 illustrates the rank order of the five most commonly occurring layouts in each polychrome type and in the museum sample. The overall impression for the museum sample is one of heterogeneity; however, further examination of layout frequency by type shows considerable internal differences. This is most evident between Ramos polychrome and both Babícora and Villa Ahumada. While each layout class is represented within the Ramos sample, this type is decorated mostly with Segmented styles (74%) and this accounts for the high proportion of Segmented (i.e., Panelled) layouts in the

museum sample. In clear contrast, Villa Ahumada has few examples of the Segmented style (15%) and is mainly decorated with Continuous forms (81%). Babícora appears to bridge the gap between these two extremes through the frequent appearance of Panelled or Segmented style layouts (31%) within an overall majority of Continuous vessels (61%).

Motif

The examination of motifs present on the polychrome types and museum sample includes discussion of the frequency of individual motifs, the number of different motifs appearing on a vessel, and the distribution of design styles (i.e. Simple and Complex). Each motif is recorded as being present or absent on a jar; the number of times it occurred on the same vessel is not considered.

The frequency of each motif is determined through the following equation:

$$\frac{\text{total number of jars in the sample that display a particular motif}}{\text{total number of jars (i.e., type or museum sample)}}$$

For example, a motif that is found on 56 jars in a sample of 200 (56/200 x 100) would have a motif frequency of 28%.

The average number of different motifs for a given type is recorded using the following process:

$$\frac{\text{total appearances of motifs}}{\text{total number of jars (i.e., type or museum sample)}}$$

If a particular type contains a total of 378 motifs from a sample of 65 jars, the average number of different motifs for that type is 5.8 per jar.

Finally, the comparison of motif styles is accomplished by dividing the number of Simple or Complex motifs by the total appearances of motifs from a given type or museum sample. For example, a type with 164 motifs (56 Simple, 108 Complex) will have a ratio of 34% Simple (56/164 x 100) and 66% Complex (108/164 x 100).

Ramos Polychrome

Ramos jars (see Table 5.2) are most often found decorated with a trio of motifs that include the CTS, "P" Triangles (both occurring on over half of the assemblage) and Triangles. Other common motifs that appear on this type are the Hooked Triangle, Triangular Scroll, Circle, and Hooked/Stepped Triangle. Given the large proportion of Ramos jars with CTS (Composite Triangular Scroll) and "P" Triangles, it is striking that a significant number of the remaining motif classes are found on less than 10% of the type (i.e., Barbed, Feather, Scrolled Triangle). It is evident that Ramos polychrome is decorated with a diverse range of motifs but the focus is heavily oriented towards a specific set of designs.

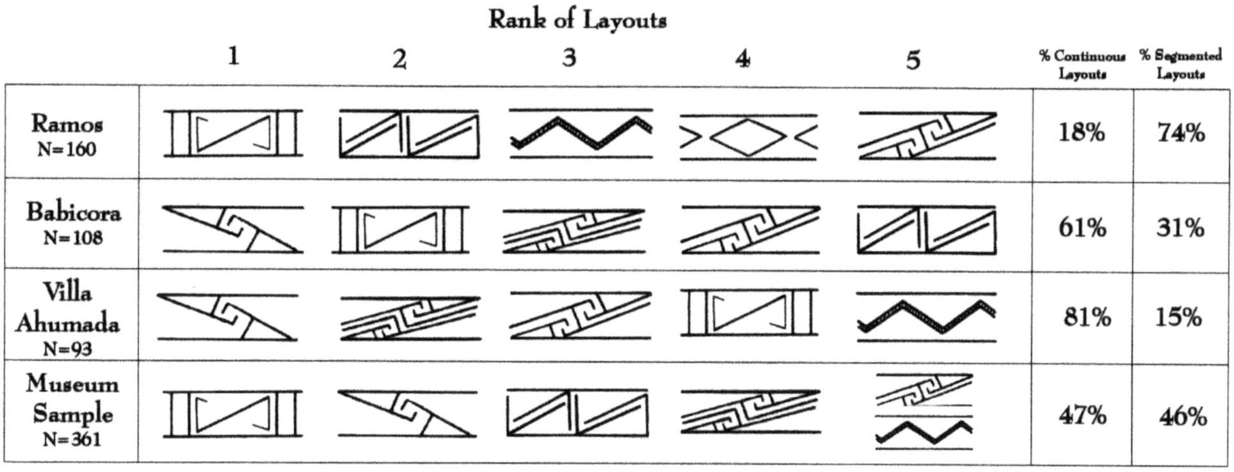

Rank of Layouts

	1	2	3	4	5	% Continuous Layouts	% Segmented Layouts
Ramos N=160						18%	74%
Babicora N=108						61%	31%
Villa Ahumada N=93						81%	15%
Museum Sample N=361						47%	46%

Figure 5.2 Summary of layouts recorded on each polychrome type and the museum sample

# of Motifs	Ramos N=160	Babicora N=108	Villa Ahumada N=93	Museum Sample N=361
zero	1	1	2	4
one	15	28	26	69
two	26	42	32	100
three	50	23	22	95
four	39	11	7	57
five	16	2	4	22
six	6	0	0	6
seven	4	1	0	5
eight	2	0	0	2
nine	1	0	0	1

Table 5.3 Number of different motifs per jar by polychrome type and museum sample

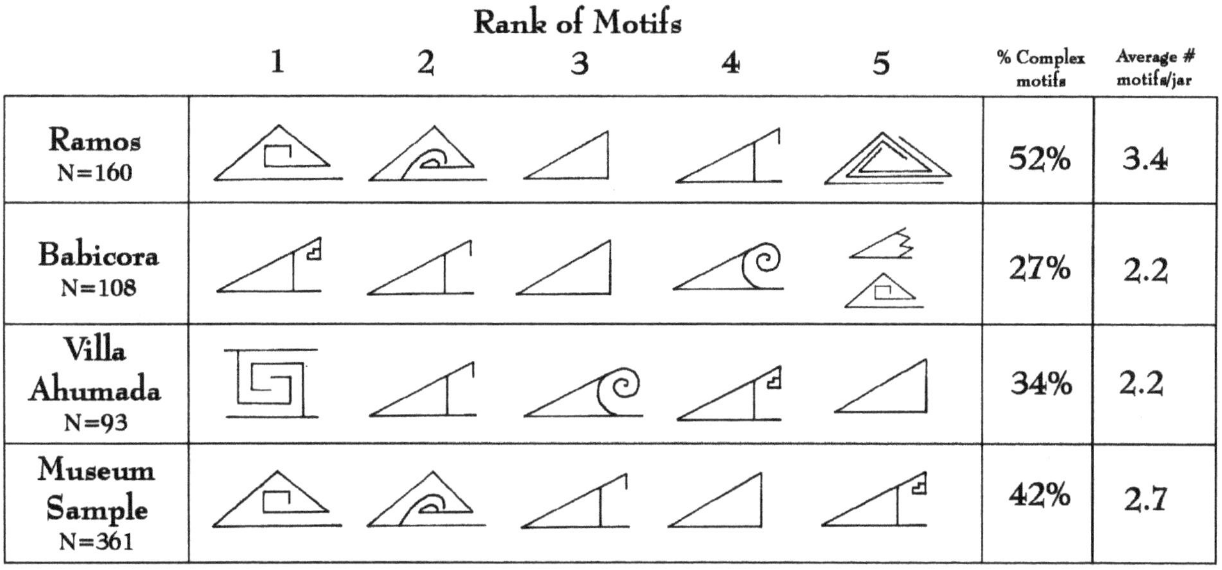

Rank of Motifs

	1	2	3	4	5	% Complex motifs	Average # motifs/jar
Ramos N=160						52%	3.4
Babicora N=108						27%	2.2
Villa Ahumada N=93						34%	2.2
Museum Sample N=361						42%	2.7

Figure 5.3 Summary of Motifs present in each polychrome type and the museum sample

Ramos jars (see Table 5.3) are decorated with as many as nine different motifs on a single vessel, however, the type is dominated by vessels with three (31%) or four (24%) motifs. On average there are 3.4 motifs per vessel.

Simple and Complex motifs are equally distributed in this type (Table 5.2). Three of the most common designs are from the Complex style (CTS, "P" Triangle, and Triangular Scroll), however, simple motifs play an important role in Ramos decoration and are typically represented by triangle-based motifs (i.e., Triangles, Hooked Triangles), Circles, or Ladders. The rarest motif recorded from the museum sample is the Spiral, while both Diamond and Stepped Triangle are absent.

Babícora Polychrome
The frequency of motifs on Babícora jars can be partitioned into five hierarchical categories (see Table 5.2). Overall, the Hooked/Stepped Triangle is the most commonly employed motif, appearing on 33% of the sample. While this may be the most frequent, there is a suite of secondary motifs (e.g., Hooked Triangles, Triangles, Scrolled Triangles, Barbed, CTS, and "P" Triangles) that appear on at least 19% of the Babícora jars in this analysis. This variety indicates that this type is fairly heterogeneous at the level of motif. Nearly half of Babícora jars are decorated with at least two different motifs (see Table 5.3) resulting in an average number of 2.2 motifs per jar.

Simple motifs dominate the decoration found on Babícora pots (73%). The Complex style (27%) normally appears in the form of CTS, "P" Triangle, and Triangular Scroll designs, while each of the remaining Complex motifs are found on less than 4% of the sample each.

Villa Ahumada Polychrome
The most commonly occurring motif in Villa Ahumada (Table 5.2) is the Rectangular Scroll (30% of all jars), followed closely by the Hooked Triangle (29%) and Scrolled Triangle (27%). The Hooked/Stepped Triangle and Triangle motifs are less prominent in the overall total but appear with some regularity.

Villa Ahumada (see Table 5.3) displays the most limited range of motifs per vessel, with the vast majority containing one to three different motifs. The average number of motifs for this type is 2.2 per vessel.

With the exception of Rectangular Scrolls, Simple motifs are the norm in Villa Ahumada painting schemes and occupy 66% of the type sample. The greater quantity of Simple style designs are specifically bolstered by the abundance of Hooked Triangles, Scrolled Triangles, Triangles, and Barbed motifs. With the exception of the Rectangular Scroll, the remaining Complex motifs (e.g., "P" Triangles, Triangular Scrolls, CTS, and Macaws) are recorded on less than ten jars. Other Life-based designs (i.e. Feathers and Zoomorphs), as well as Diamonds and

Spirals are infrequent.

Museum Sample
Three groups of motifs can be identified from the museum data set based on their relative frequency (Table 5.2). The most abundant motifs are found on over 25% of the vessels analyzed and include Complex Triangular Scrolls (CTS), "P" Triangles, Hooked triangles, Triangles, and Hooked/Stepped Triangles. The majority of motifs are present on 10 to 25% of the assemblage, and the most infrequent (<10%) are Checkers, Feathers, Diamonds, and Spirals.

In the absolute frequency of different motifs per vessel (Table 5.3), 54% are found to have two or three motifs decorated on the vessel surface. At the extreme ends of this range, pots decorated with zero and more than six motifs are encountered but are quite rare. The average for the museum sample is 2.7 motifs/jar.

Two Complex motifs, CTS (33%) and "P" Triangles (31%), are the most abundant individual motifs for the museum sample. On the other hand, Simple style motifs, such as Hooked Triangle, Triangle, and Hooked/Stepped Triangle, constitute 58% of the total assemblage. Other non-triangle shaped motifs that occur commonly in the museum sample are the Circle and Ladder.

Summary: Comparison of Motifs
Figure 5.3 summarizes the basic trends of motifs recorded for the individual types and the museum sample. The most evident discrepancy between the three types is found in the ratio of Complex motifs and the number of motifs per vessel. Overall, Ramos contains a much higher proportion of Complex motifs and number of designs painted on a single jar than the other types. By comparison, Babícora and Villa Ahumada share a comparable ratio in both categories. This distinction is also evident through the comparison of motif rank order. While all three polychrome types present a high frequency of Hooked Triangles and Triangles, both Babícora and Villa Ahumada share a high frequency of Hooked/Stepped Triangles and Scrolled Triangles. There is, however, a significant difference between these two types manifest in the regular occurrence of CTS motifs on Babícora jars. Another point that distinguishes Villa Ahumada from Babícora is the re-curring appearance of Rectangular Scrolls in the former. It is evident, simply from this basic comparison, that there are some obvious distinctions between each of the three polychrome types.

Layout and Motif
Following the analytical framework presented in Figure 5.1 the frequency of motifs in each layout class is evaluated by each polychrome type and the museum sample. General patterns will be assessed for each type in relation to individual motif frequencies, number of different motifs per jar, and according to layout and motif

styles.

The discussion of design levels between the three polychrome types is based on the data presented in Table 5.4 (motif frequencies), Table 5.5 (number of different motifs per vessel), and Table 5.6 (motif and layout styles). Because only associated with Babícora polychrome shows evidence of Basic layouts, this class is not included in the comparison of type and tradition.

Ramos Polychrome

The museum sample of Ramos jars is heavily oriented towards vessels decorated with Panelled, Semi-Panelled, and Zig-Zag layouts (Table 5.4a). The motifs present in these classes are similarly distributed by rank order (see Figure 5.4), and a few of these 'typical' designs are also found in other layouts. For example, "P" Triangles appear in every layout and CTS are absent in only two of the eight recorded layout classes. If we look at the actual frequency of "P" Triangles, regardless of the actual number of jars per class, this motif appears between 33% and 63% of the time. This is not to suggest that each class contains the same suite of motifs, as evidenced by the lack of Circles, Triangles, and Triangular Scrolls in 2-Line and 4-Line jars. However, the motifs that typify Ramos vessels (i.e., CTS, "P" Triangle, Triangular Scroll, Triangle, and Circle) extend beyond the confines of Panelled and Semi-Panelled layouts. Comparison of the percentage of Complex motifs in each layout confirms the general bias towards this style of motif in all but the Miscellaneous layout classes.

The number of different motifs present in the Ramos layout classes presents the only statistic that may distinguish different structural characteristics of the type. One group, consisting of 2-Line, 3-Line, 4-Line, and Miscellaneous jars, has an average of less than two different motifs, while Zig-Zag, Semi-Panelled, Panelled, and Repeated Figure each display over three designs per vessel. Looking at the actual count of motifs (see Table 5.5a) illustrates that, with the exception of Repeated Figure, the latter group of layouts can be decorated with as many as nine different motifs. By contrast, the Miscellaneous class is the only example that displays four designs.

Ramos polychrome is predominated by vessels using the Segmented layout style (Table 5.6). These jars are decorated with a specific suite of motifs that include both Simple and Complex motifs (i.e., CTS, "P" Triangles, Triangles, Hooked Triangles, Triangular Scrolls, and Circles). Interestingly, the few vessels decorated in the Continuous style are decorated with a higher proportion of Complex motifs than are the Segmented Ramos jars. The average number of different motifs (2.9 to 3.6) also suggests a fairly widespread homogeneity within the type, regardless of layout style. One point that requires mentioning is the difference in motif characteristics between Zig-Zag and the Continuous layouts. Each of the categories in Figure 5.4 illustrates that Zig-Zag layouts actually share much more in common with the motif trends of the Segmented style.

Babícora Polychrome

This type contains fairly equal numbers of 2-Line, 4-Line, and Panelled layouts (see Table 5.4b) but the frequency of motifs in the latter class is markedly different (i.e., Hooked/Stepped Triangle, Barbed figure, Scrolled Triangle; Triangle, CTS, "P" Triangle) (Figure 5.5). A similar trend is also evident in the less common layouts (i.e., 3-Line; Zig-Zag and Semi-Panelled). The result is a noticeable break within the layout classes in the general rank order of motifs and the percentage of Complex motifs. In one group are the 2-Line, 3-Line, 4-Line, Repeated Figure, and Miscellaneous layouts, while the other is composed of Zig-Zag, Semi-Panelled, and Panelled. Such groups are only broadly defined and there are several internal differences that correspond to the heterogeneous character of this type. For instance, 80% of 3-Line layouts contain Hooked/Stepped Triangles but these motifs are only found on 55% and 23% of 4-Line and 2-Line classes. A more divergent result is the frequency of Triangles in Semi-Panelled (10%) and Panelled (50%) jars.

Comparison of the average number of motifs per jar in each layout class is a less definitive marker for Babícora. Smaller differences are noted from the sample of this type, with vessels normally containing slightly less or more than two motifs; the only possible exceptions are the Semi-Panelled and Panelled examples, whose average is closer to three motifs per jar. This separation is somewhat justified by the actual count of motifs by layout presented in Table 5.5b, since these layout classes contain as many as seven different designs on an individual pot. If we disregard these anomalies, the majority of layout classes have several examples with three or four motifs.

Continuous style layouts outnumber Segmented jars two to one in the Babícora assemblage (Table 5.6). The Continuous style appears to emphasize a suite of motifs dominated by Simple motifs (e.g., Hooked/Stepped Triangles, Scrolled Triangles, Barbed Figures, and Stepped Triangles). A few Complex motifs, such as the "P" Triangle, CTS, and Triangular Scroll do appear but are much less common. Segmented Babícora jars incorporate a larger proportion of these Complex motifs but these designs are still less frequent than Simple style designs. The average number of motifs between these two styles indicates that Segmented jars are populated with slightly more motifs than are their Continuous cousins. As discovered in the presentation of Ramos polychrome, many of the Complex motifs (32%) in the Continuous Babícora jars are derived from Zig-Zag layouts, which appear to have more in common with the Segmented style.

49

5.4a Ramos

Style	Motif	2-Line N=1	3-Line N=6	4-Line N=3	Zig-Zag N=19	Semi-Panelled N=30	Panelled N=89	Repeated Figure N=7	Miscellaneous N=5
Simple	Triangle	0	0	0	3	9	46	0	2
	Hooked Triangle	0	0	0	1	3	43	2	0
	Hooked/Stepped Triangle	0	3	2	3	6	17	1	0
	Stepped Triangle	0	0	0	0	0	2	0	0
	Scrolled Triangle	0	0	0	2	1	7	0	1
	Barbed	0	0	0	3	1	8	1	0
	Ladder	0	0	0	2	2	14	2	1
	Checker	0	1	0	1	5	2	0	0
	Circles	0	0	0	6	8	25	0	0
	Diamond	0	0	0	1	0	1	2	0
	Spiral	0	0	0	0	0	2	1	3
	Miscellaneous	0	0	0	1	3	10	1	2
Complex	Macaw	0	1	0	5	7	8	3	0
	Feather	0	0	1	2	3	5	1	0
	Zoomorph	0	1	0	6	4	7	1	0
	Rectangular Scroll	0	1	0	0	2	4	1	0
	"P" Triangle	1	2	1	12	14	49	3	0
	Triangular Scroll	0	0	0	5	8	28	4	0
	Composite Triangular Scroll	0	1	1	15	19	53	0	0
	Total Appearances of Motifs	1	10	5	68	95	331	23	9
	Simple	0	4	2	23	38	177	10	9
	Complex	1	6	3	45	57	154	13	0

5.4b Babicora

Style	Motif	2-Line N=26	3-Line N=15	4-Line N=20	Zig-Zag N=5	Semi-Panelled N=10	Panelled N=24	Repeated Figure N=3	Miscellaneous N=3
Simple	Triangle	7	0	1	0	1	12	2	0
	Hooked Triangle	6	5	3	0	1	10	0	1
	Hooked/Stepped Triangle	6	12	11	2	1	3	1	0
	Stepped Triangle	6	2	7	0	0	0	0	0
	Scrolled Triangle	11	2	3	0	1	3	1	1
	Barbed	10	3	3	0	1	2	0	3
	Ladder	0	1	1	0	1	2	0	0
	Checker	2	0	0	1	0	1	0	0
	Circles	2	1	0	1	2	4	0	0
	Diamond	0	0	0	1	2	0	1	0
	Spiral	0	0	0	0	0	0	0	0
	Miscellaneous	2	0	1	1	0	2	1	0
Complex	Macaw	1	1	0	0	0	3	0	0
	Feather	0	1	1	0	0	0	0	0
	Zoomorph	0	0	0	1	1	1	0	0
	Rectangular Scroll	3	0	0	0	1	0	0	0
	"P" Triangle	2	0	1	1	4	9	1	0
	Triangular Scroll	0	0	1	2	4	4	0	0
	Composite Triangular Scroll	0	1	1	2	7	11	0	0
	Total Appearances of Motifs	58	29	34	12	27	67	7	5
	Simple	52	26	30	6	10	39	6	5
	Complex	6	3	4	6	17	28	1	0

5.4c Villa Ahumada

Style	Motif	2-Line N=36	3-Line N=12	4-Line N=19	Zig-Zag N=8	Semi-Panelled N=3	Panelled N=11	Repeated Figure N=3	Miscellaneous N=1
Simple	Triangle	6	1	2	0	2	3	0	1
	Hooked Triangle	10	3	2	3	1	6	1	1
	Hooked/Stepped Triangle	3	7	7	0	1	1	0	0
	Stepped Triangle	1	0	5	0	0	0	1	0
	Scrolled Triangle	16	2	5	1	0	0	0	1
	Barbed	4	1	5	1	0	0	1	0
	Ladder	1	0	0	0	0	1	0	1
	Checker	2	1	2	0	0	0	0	0
	Circles	4	2	0	0	0	6	0	0
	Diamond	1	0	0	1	0	0	0	0
	Spiral	0	0	0	0	0	1	0	0
	Miscellaneous	1	1	1	3	0	1	0	0
Complex	Macaw	1	0	0	2	1	2	0	0
	Feather	0	0	1	1	1	0	0	0
	Zoomorph	1	0	0	0	0	0	0	0
	Rectangular Scroll	15	3	3	1	0	4	2	1
	"P" Triangle	0	1	1	4	1	5	0	0
	Triangular Scroll	0	2	3	2	1	1	0	0
	Composite Triangular Scroll	0	1	2	0	0	5	1	0
	Total Appearances of Motifs	66	25	39	19	8	36	6	5
	Simple	49	18	29	9	4	19	3	4
	Complex	17	7	10	10	4	17	3	1

5.4d Museum Sample

Style	Motif	2-Line N=63	3-Line N=33	4-Line N=42	Zig-Zag N=32	Semi-Panelled N=43	Panelled N=124	Repeated Figure N=13	Miscellaneous N=9
Simple	Triangles	13	1	3	3	12	61	2	3
	Hooked Triangles	16	8	5	4	5	59	3	2
	Hooked/Stepped Triangles	9	22	20	5	8	21	2	0
	Stepped Triangles	7	2	12	0	0	2	1	0
	Scrolled Triangles	27	4	8	3	2	10	1	3
	Barbed	14	4	8	4	2	10	2	3
	Ladder	1	1	1	2	3	17	2	2
	Checker	4	2	1	2	5	3	0	0
	Circles	6	3	0	7	10	35	0	0
	Diamonds	1	0	0	3	2	1	3	0
	Spirals	0	0	0	0	0	3	1	3
	Miscellaneous	3	1	2	5	3	13	2	2
Complex	Macaws	2	2	1	7	8	13	3	0
	Feather	0	0	3	3	4	5	1	0
	Zoomorphs	1	1	0	7	5	8	1	0
	Rectangular Scrolls	18	4	2	1	3	8	3	1
	"P" Triangles	3	4	3	17	19	63	4	0
	Triangular Scrolls	0	2	5	9	13	33	4	0
	CTS	0	3	4	17	26	69	1	0
	Total Appearances of Motifs	125	64	78	99	130	434	36	19
	Simple	101	48	60	38	52	235	19	18
	Complex	24	16	18	61	78	199	17	1

Table 5.4a-d Frequency of motifs by layout for each polychrome type and the museum sample

Table 5.5a Ramos

# of Motifs	Basic N=0	2-Line N=1	3-Line N=6	4-Line N=3	Zig-Zag N=19	Semi-Panelled N=30	Panelled N=89	Repeated Figure N=7	Miscellaneous N=5
0	0	0	0	0	0	0	0	0	1
1	0	1	3	2	3	2	2	1	1
2	0	0	2	0	4	5	13	0	2
3	0	0	1	1	4	13	28	3	0
4	0	0	0	0	2	7	27	2	1
5	0	0	0	0	3	2	10	1	0
6	0	0	0	0	1	1	4	0	0
7	0	0	0	0	0	0	4	0	0
8	0	0	0	0	2	0	0	0	0
9	0	0	0	0	0	0	1	0	0
Total	0	1	6	3	19	30	89	7	5

Table 5.5b Babicora

# of Motifs	Basic N=2	2-Line N=26	3-Line N=15	4-Line N=20	Zig-Zag N=5	Semi-Panelled N=10	Panelled N=24	Repeated Figure N=3	Miscellaneous N=3
0	1	0	0	0	0	0	0	0	0
1	0	6	6	8	1	2	4	0	1
2	0	10	6	10	2	4	6	2	2
3	1	8	1	2	1	2	7	1	0
4	0	2	2	0	1	1	5	0	0
5	0	0	0	0	0	0	2	0	0
6	0	0	0	0	0	0	0	0	0
7	0	0	0	0	0	1	0	0	0
Total	2	26	15	20	5	10	24	3	3

Table 5.5c Villa Ahumada

# of Motifs	Basic N=0	2-Line N=36	3-Line N=12	4-Line N=19	Zig-Zag N=8	Semi-Panelled N=3	Panelled N=11	Repeated Figure N=3	Miscellaneous N=1
0	0	2	0	0	0	0	0	0	0
1	0	11	5	6	2	0	1	1	0
2	0	16	3	7	3	1	1	1	0
3	0	6	2	5	2	2	4	1	0
4	0	0	2	1	0	0	4	0	0
5	0	1	0	0	1	0	1	0	1
Total	0	36	12	19	8	3	11	3	1

Table 5.5d Museum Sample

# of Motifs	Basic N=2	2-Line N=63	3-Line N=33	4-Line N=42	Zig-Zag N=32	Semi-Panelled N=43	Panelled N=124	Repeated Figure N=13	Miscellaneous N=9
0	1	2	0	0	0	0	0	0	1
1	0	18	14	16	6	4	7	2	2
2	0	26	13	14	9	10	20	3	4
3	1	14	2	10	7	17	39	5	0
4	0	3	3	1	3	8	36	2	1
5	0	0	1	1	4	2	13	1	1
6	0	0	0	0	1	1	4	0	0
7	0	0	0	0	0	1	4	0	0
8	0	0	0	0	2	0	0	0	0
9	0	0	0	0	0	0	1	0	0
Total	2	63	33	42	32	43	124	13	9

Tables 5.5a-d Actual count of the number of different motifs recorded by layout class in each polychrome type and entire museum sample

Style	Motif	Ramos Continuous N=29	Ramos Segmented N=119	Babicora Continuous N=66	Babicora Segmented N=34	Villa Ahumada Continuous N=75	Villa Ahumada Segmented N=14	Museum Sample Continuous N=170	Museum Sample Segmented N=167
Simple	Triangle	3	55	8	13	9	5	20	73
	Hooked Triangle	1	46	14	11	18	7	33	64
	Hooked/Stepped Triangle	8	23	31	4	17	2	56	29
	Stepped Triangle	0	2	15	0	6	0	21	2
	Scrolled Triangle	2	8	16	4	24	0	42	12
	Barbed	3	9	16	3	11	0	30	12
	Ladder	2	16	2	3	1	1	5	20
	Checker	2	7	3	1	4	0	9	8
	Circles	7	33	4	6	5	6	16	45
	Diamond	1	1	1	2	3	0	5	3
	Spiral	0	2	0	0	0	1	0	3
	Miscellaneous	1	13	4	2	6	1	11	16
Complex	Macaw	6	15	2	3	4	3	12	21
	Feather	3	8	2	0	2	1	7	6
	Zoomorph	7	11	1	2	1	0	9	13
	Rectangular Scroll	1	6	3	1	21	4	25	11
	"P" Triangle	16	63	4	13	7	6	27	82
	Triangular Scroll	5	36	3	8	8	2	16	56
	Composite Triangular Scroll	17	72	4	18	3	5	24	95
	Total Appearance of Motifs	85	426	133	94	150	44	348	571
	Average # of Motifs per Jar	2.9	3.6	2	2.8	2	3.1	2.2	3.4
	Simple	30	215	114	49	104	23	248	287
	Complex	55	211	19	45	46	21	120	284

Table 5.6 Comparative frequency of motifs between Continuous and Segmented layouts for each polychrome type and the museum sample

Ramos

Layout	Rank of Motifs 1	2	3	4	5	% of Complex Motifs	# of Motifs per Jar
2-Line N=1						100%	1.0
3-Line N=6						60%	1.7
4-Line N=3						60%	1.7
Zig-Zag N=19						66%	3.6
Semi-Panelled N=30						53%	3.2
Panelled N=89						47%	3.7
Repeated Figure N=7						57%	3.3
Miscellaneous N=5						0%	1.8

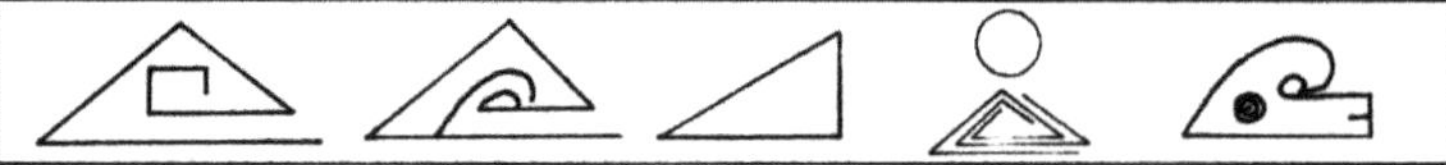

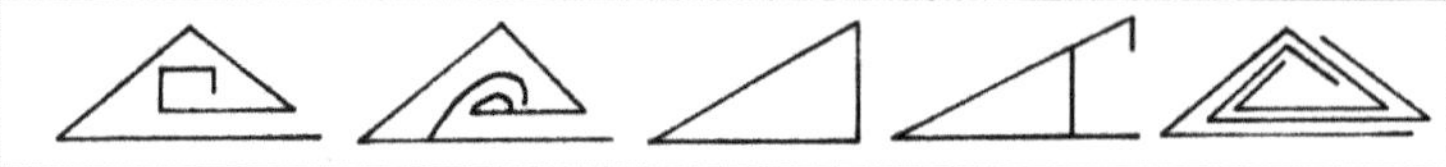

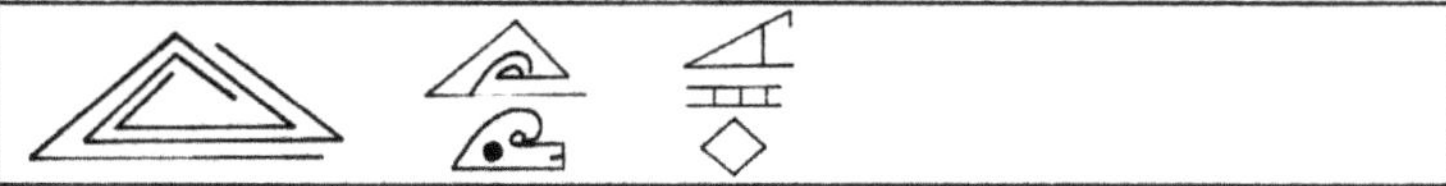

Figure 5.4   Summary of motif frequency by layout for Ramos polychrome
Note - spaces indicate lack of motifs occurring on more than one pot

Babicora

Layout	Rank of Motifs 1	2	3	4	5	% of Complex Motifs	# of Motifs per Jar
2-Line N=26						10%	2.2
3-Line N=15						10%	1.9
4-Line N=20						13%	1.7
Zig-Zag N=5						50%	2.4
Semi-Panelled N=10						57%	2.7
Panelled N=24						42%	2.8
Repeated Figure N=3						14%	2.3
Miscellaneous N=3						0%	1.8

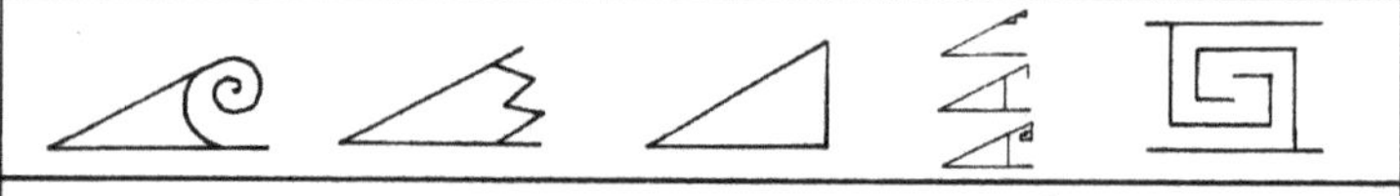

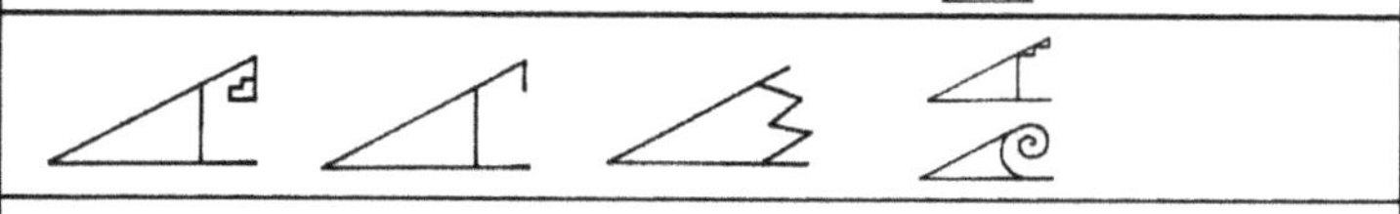

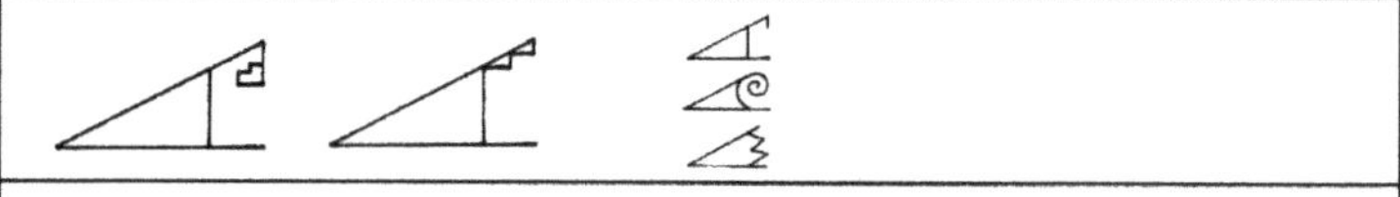

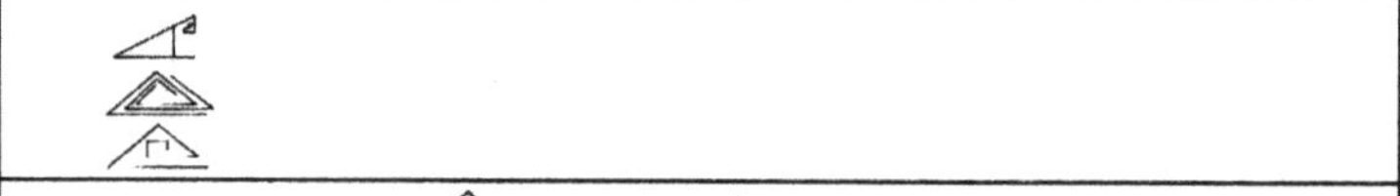

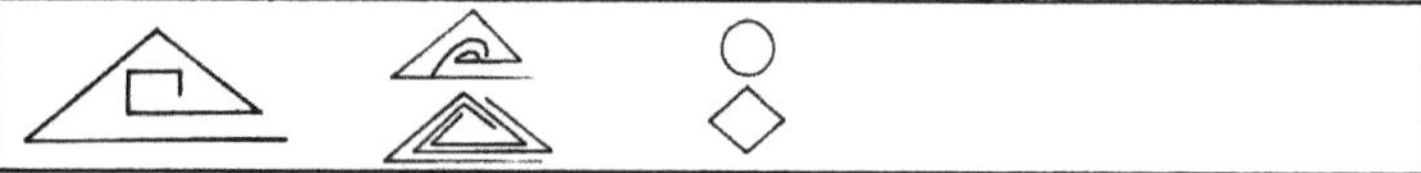

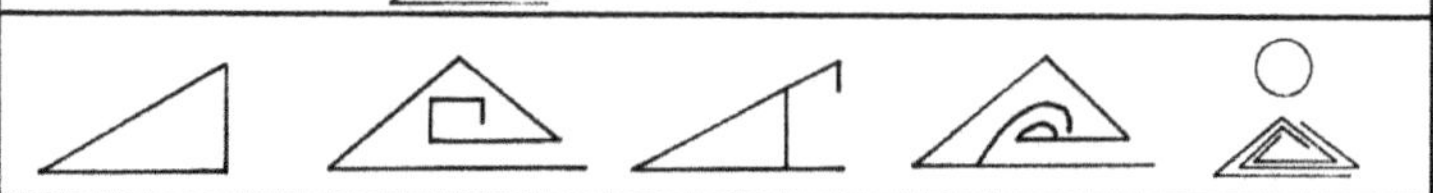

Figure 5.5 Summary of motif frequency by layout for Babicora Polychrome
Note - spaces indicate lack of motifs occurring on more than one pot.

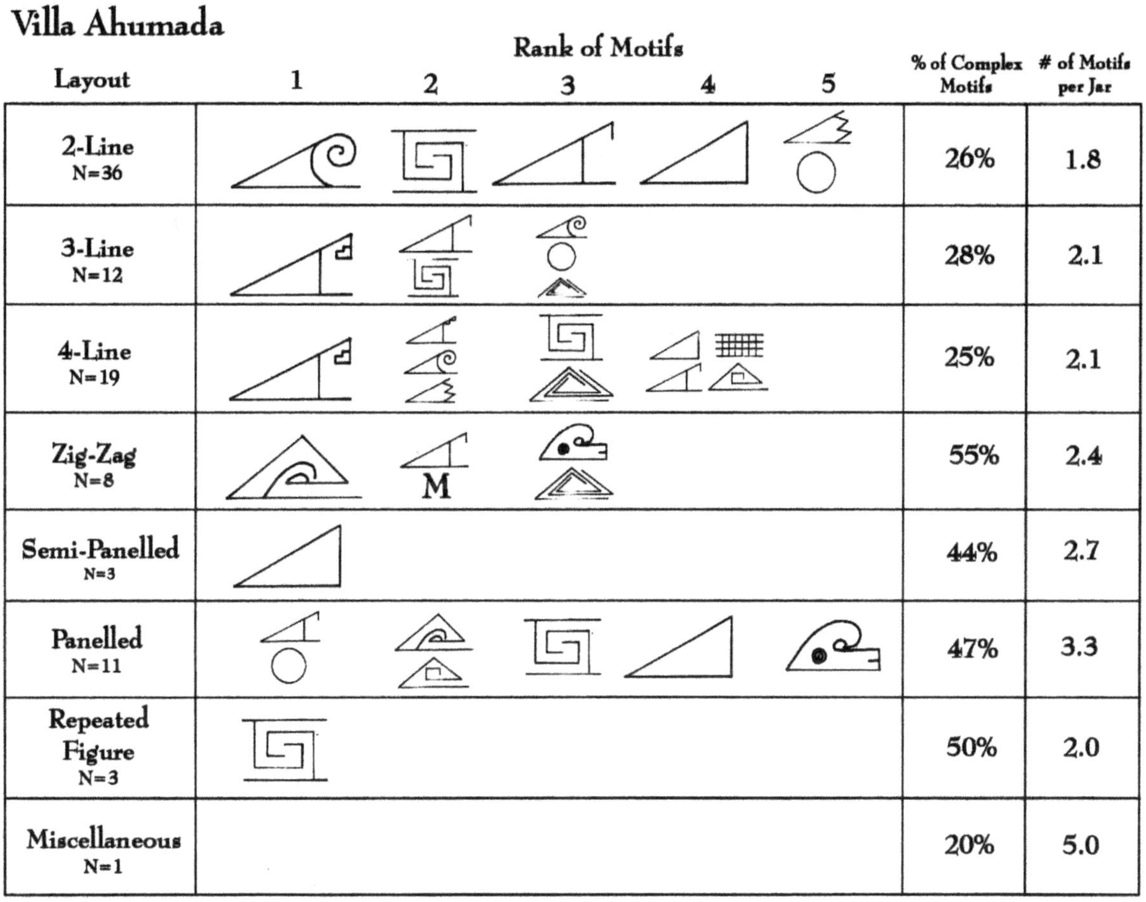

Villa Ahumada

Layout	Rank of Motifs					% of Complex Motifs	# of Motifs per Jar
	1	2	3	4	5		
2-Line N=36						26%	1.8
3-Line N=12						28%	2.1
4-Line N=19						25%	2.1
Zig-Zag N=8						55%	2.4
Semi-Panelled N=3						44%	2.7
Panelled N=11						47%	3.3
Repeated Figure N=3						50%	2.0
Miscellaneous N=1						20%	5.0

Figure 5.6 Summary of motif frequency by layout for Villa Ahumada Polychrome
Note - spaces indicate lack of motifs occurring on more than one pot.

Villa Ahumada Polychrome

The line-based layouts constitute the most common classes in Villa Ahumada, with specific emphasis on the 2-Line forms (Table 5.4c). Panelled layouts are frequent, but the differences in motif representation from these Line-based classes are quite striking (Figure 5.6). For example, 2-Line layouts are characterized by a range of triangle-based motifs, while the Panelled class is typified by such motifs as Circles, CTS, and "P" Triangles. The small sample of Zig-Zag suggests that it is normally decorated in a similar fashion as Panelled. A broader association of layouts is recognized in the average number of complex motifs used in each class. This statistic would separate 2-Line, 3-Line, 4-Line, and Miscellaneous layouts from the jars containing Zig-Zag, Semi-Panelled, Panelled and Repeated Figure structures. Regardless of these differences, the key variable that seems to link each of the layouts is the use of Rectangular Scrolls. Only the Semi-Panelled class (which occurs only three times in the museum sample) lacks this motif. The frequency of motifs across the layout classes in Villa Ahumada suggests a very heterogeneous use of design, yet the heavy reliance on Simple triangle-based motifs or CTS and "P" Triangles suggests a degree of standardization.

With the exception of Miscellaneous layouts, the number of motifs recorded on each Villa Ahumada jar is quite varied (see Figure 5.6). The only obvious difference is found in the Panelled layouts, as the remaining classes indicate a range slightly above or below two motifs per jar. A lack of patterning is apparent in the actual count of motifs per jar by layout (see Table 5.5c), as most classes have at least one vessel with four or more different motifs.

Continuous style layouts are overwhelmingly common in the Villa Ahumada sample (Table 5.6). These vessels are decorated with a combination of Simple motifs and a single Complex design, the Rectangular Scroll. Some overlap is evident with the common motifs used on rare examples of Segmented styles such as CTS, "P" Triangle, and Circles. When we look at the source of these motifs, however, 47% of the Complex designs in Continuous layouts are attributed to Zig-Zag layouts. Comparing the ratio of Simple and Complex motifs by layout style, there is a remarkable difference between Continuous (52% to 48%) and Segmented (69% to 31%) jars in this type. A comparable situation is also present in number of different motifs used to fill each of these layout styles.

Museum Sample

Panelled layouts are twice as abundant as the next common class (2-Line) in the museum sample (Table 5.4d). The remaining layout classes are much less frequent by comparison. Looking at the rank order of motifs, each class appears to have its own distinct characteristics (Figure 5.7). In the broader picture, each class does share some basic commonalities with at least two other layouts. For instance, the rank order of Semi-Panelled and Panelled jars is nearly identical, and both are very similar to that presented by the Zig-Zag class. A second example is that Hooked/Stepped Triangles occur on over 50% of both 3-Line and 4-Line layouts and generally share a predisposition towards triangle-based designs illustrated in the 2-Line jars. The most indistinct motif patterns are associated with the Repeated Figure and Miscellaneous classes.

Comparing the frequency of Complex motifs within these layout classes, two coherent patterns can be identified. One group consists of layouts with very few Complex designs, including 2-Line, 3-Line, 4-Line, and Miscellaneous, while Zig-Zag, Semi-Panelled, Panelled, and Repeated Figure classes contain either a more equal balance between motif styles or greater reliance on Complex. A comparable grouping is present when the number of different motifs depicted on each jar is considered. Looking at the actual count of motifs per jar

(see Table 5.5d) there is an increase in the maximum number of motifs from the 2-Line to Panelled classes, with the largest jump occurring between 4-Line and Semi-Panelled layouts.

The frequency of Continuous and Segmented layouts in the museum sample is comparable and the range of motifs used in each style is similarly quite diverse (Table 5.6). Closer inspection of the actual proportions of motifs indicates that Continuous vessels are more broadly reliant on triangle-shaped motifs (i.e., Hooked/Stepped Triangles, Scrolled Triangles, Hooked Triangles, Barbed Figures), whereas Segmented jars focus on a specific suite of motifs (i.e., CTS, "P" Triangle, Triangle, Hooked Triangle, Triangular Scroll, Circle). Comparison of the number of motifs per jar and the ratio of motif styles also indicates that there is a significant difference between the decorative strategy used on jars decorated with Continuous or Segmented layouts.

Two other points that must be addressed from the examination of layout style. First, both layout styles from the museum sample demonstrate the infrequent incorporation of life-designs (e.g., Feathers and Zoomorphs), Diamonds, and Spirals. Second, as with the earlier discussions for the polychrome types, is that the frequency of CTS, "P" Triangle, Triangle, and life-based designs in Continuous layouts is attributed to the Zig-Zag

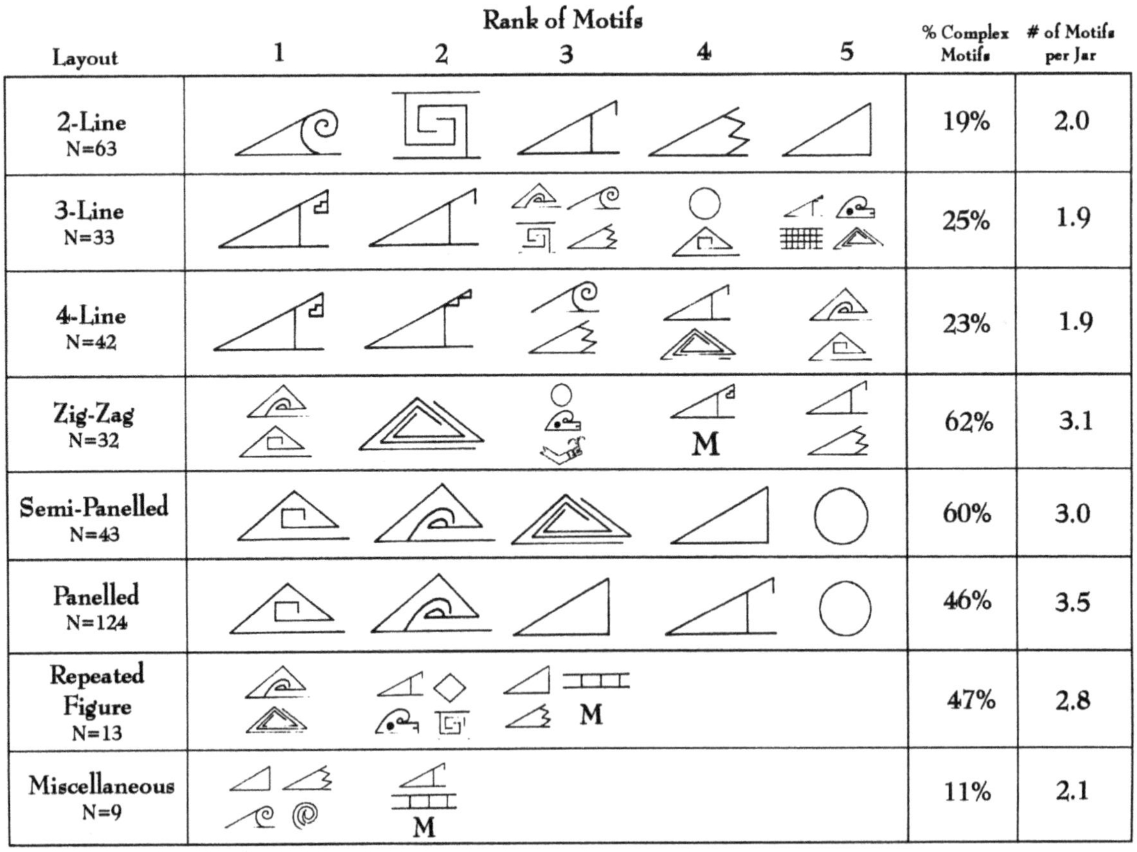

Layout	Rank of Motifs					% Complex Motifs	# of Motifs per Jar
	1	2	3	4	5		
2-Line N=63						19%	2.0
3-Line N=33						25%	1.9
4-Line N=42						23%	1.9
Zig-Zag N=32				M		62%	3.1
Semi-Panelled N=43						60%	3.0
Panelled N=124						46%	3.5
Repeated Figure N=13			M			47%	2.8
Miscellaneous N=9		M				11%	2.1

Figure 5.7   Summary of motif frequency by layouts for the museum sample
Note - spaces indicate lack of motifs occurring on more than one jar.

layout. Of these motifs, 71% of CTS, 63% of "P" Triangles, and 56% of Triangular Scrolls in the Continuous style are presented on the Zig-Zag layouts. Further discussion of the association of Zig-Zag layouts with the Continuous style is merited before summarizing the patterns for layout and type.

The Zig-Zag Problem

Zig-Zag layouts were originally categorized as part of Continuous style in the original analysis. The reason for incorporating Zig-Zag with 2-Line and other line-based layouts is that it is constructed of a secondary band that runs continuously around the design field and, for the most part, does not contain vertical boundaries. Comparing the frequency of motifs for each of the Continuous and Segmented layouts the placement of the Zig-Zag layout in the former style is somewhat problematic (Figure 5.8). Jars decorated with a Zig-Zag design structure tend to display the combination of "P" Triangle, CTS, Triangular Scroll, and Circle commonly affiliated with Semi-Panelled or Panelled layouts as opposed to the Simple motifs used in Continuous layouts. A further test to clarify this relationship was to compare the motif percentages when Zig-Zag layouts are moved from Continuous to Segmented style (Figure 5.9a-b). First, Continuous layouts (Figure 5.9a) increase in each of the motifs commonly associated with this style (i.e., Triangles, Hooked Triangles, Hooked/Stepped Triangles, Stepped Triangles, Scrolled Triangles, Barbed and Rectangular Scrolls) while they decrease in each of the Complex motifs and Circles. Second, the results for the Segmented style layouts (Figure 5.9b) change very little, with small fluctuations in Triangles and Hooked Triangles, as well as minor motifs such as Ladders, Checkers, and Spirals. Zoomorph is the only motif that increases through the alteration of layout style categories.

Because the definition of layout follows the dichotomy of vertical division and continual bands, the Zig-Zag layout will remain part of the Continuous style. However, it is pertinent to note the significant differences in motif frequencies between this layout and others within the Continuous style.

Summary: Comparison of Layout and Motif

The frequency of motifs in each layout class (see Figures 5.10-5.15) suggests that some basic structural similarities can be identified for the individual polychrome types and across the Chihuahuan ceramic tradition. Due to the small number of Basic, Repeated Figure, and Miscellaneous layouts in each type, these classes are not included in the comparison of motif characteristics.

Vessels decorated with 2-Line, 3-Line, and 4-Line layouts share the same basic suite of triangle-shaped motifs. Even when the classes are divided into type categories, the kind and rank order of motifs is comparable. Generally, there is a substantial reliance on Simple motifs, such as Scrolled Triangles, Hooked

Stepped Triangles, Hooked Triangles or Stepped Triangles, and most vessels are composed of two different designs. Babícora and Villa Ahumada are greatly responsible for this pattern. The only significant contrast are the results for Ramos which have at least 60% of the motifs being Complex in style. Overall, the kind of motifs in 2-Line, 3-Line, and 4-Line layouts appears to be determined by the type on which they occur; while the standardized results for the number of different motifs appears to be a function of the layout itself.

A second cluster of layout classes is comprised of the Zig-Zag, Semi-Panelled, and Panelled jars (Figures 5.13-5.15). The actual rank order of motifs displayed by the polychrome types and museum sample is quite varied, however, these layouts share a core of motifs, that include the CTS, "P" Triangles, Triangular Scrolls, Triangles, Macaws, and Circles. Other similarities are noted in the greater reliance on Complex motifs and, though somewhat less apparent, in the number of different motifs depicted per jar. The most obvious differences are found between the polychrome types in each class, specifically between Ramos and Babícora /Villa Ahumada. For instance, the number of different motifs for Ramos is much higher than the other types for both the Zig-Zag (3.6 to 2.4) and Semi-Panelled (3.2 to 2.7). Interestingly, the Babícora jars are much less elaborate than either Ramos or Villa Ahumada in the Panelled class (Figure 5.15). Beyond this statistic, each of the polychrome types corresponds to the basic parameters of the layout class. The most standardized layout of this group is the Panelled class. With the exception of Rectangular Scrolls and Triangular Scrolls, the most common motifs in Ramos (and the museum sample) are present in the top five designs.

When we compare the frequency of motifs in the Continuous and Segmented layout styles (Figure 5.16), a coherent picture of type decoration emerges from the data. The frequency of motifs, motif styles, and number of different motifs changes dramatically for both Babícora and Villa Ahumada. By contrast, Ramos polychrome maintains a core of motifs and motif styles between the Continuous and Segmented layouts. This may be a factor of the significantly smaller number of Continuous Ramos jars, however, in the face of the difference illustrated by Segmented Babícora and Villa Ahumada, this trend likely reflects a strong type association with a specific decorative style.

The patterns of motif and layout will be presented in a type description within Chapter VI. In order to flesh-out the existing patterns and contribute to a more distinct definition of the decoration within Ramos, Babícora, and Villa Ahumada, the design levels presented above are subjected to three secondary comparative tests: the presence of black borders around red motifs (BoR), effigy jars, and the excavated whole vessels from Paquimé.

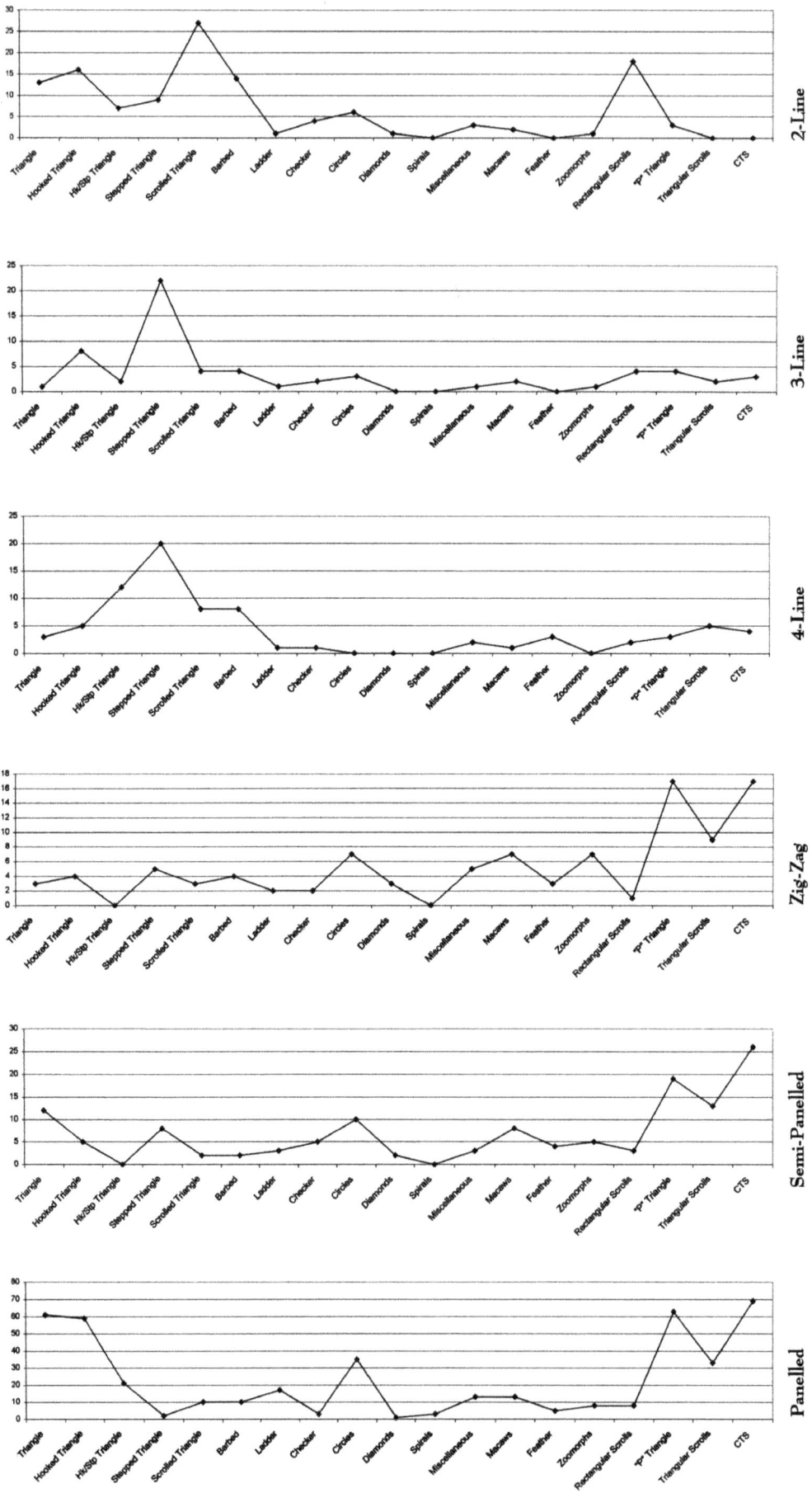

Figure 5.8 Relative frequency of motifs by layout class

56

5.9a Continuous Layout

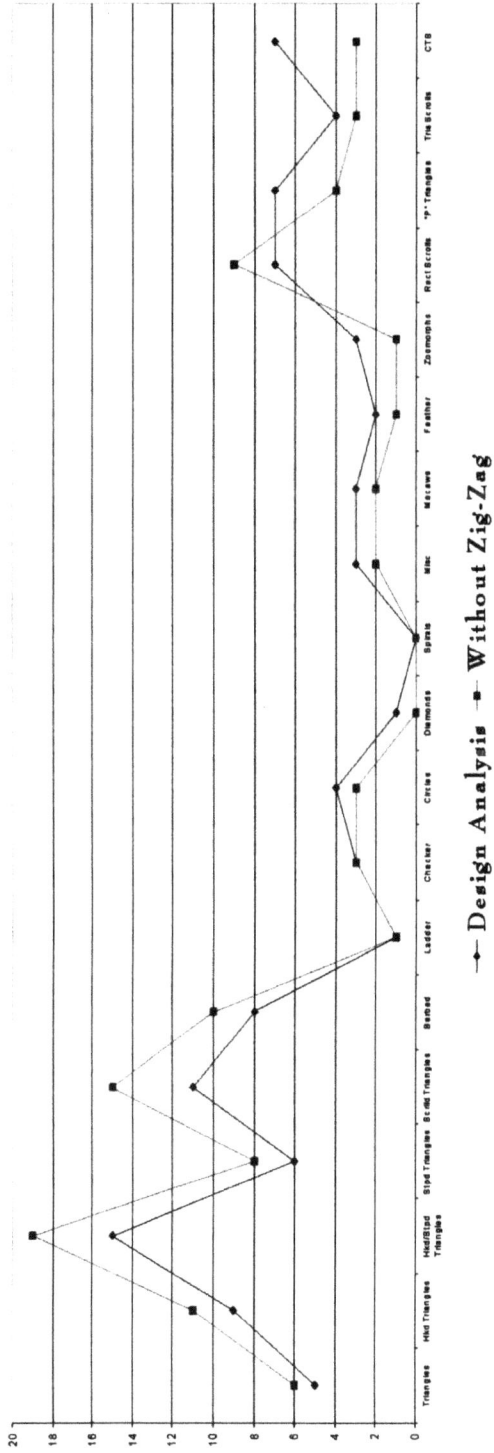

← Design Analysis ■ Without Zig-Zag

5.9b Segmented Layout

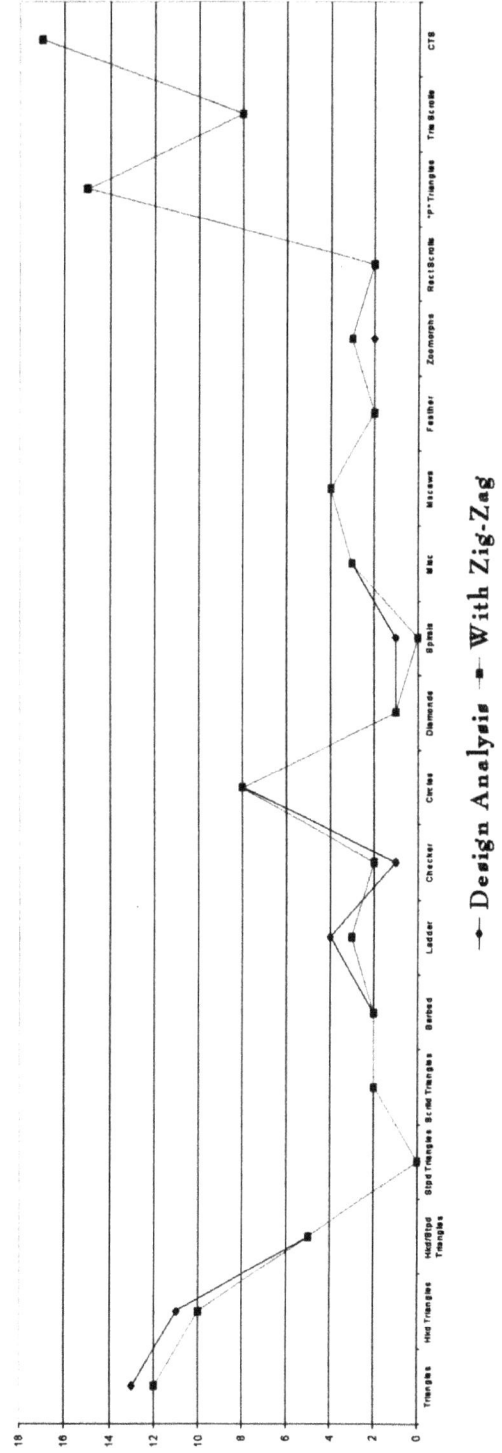

← Design Analysis ■ With Zig-Zag

Figure 5.9a-b Comparison of relative motif frequencies for each layout style with and without the Zig-Zag class
(note - where it appears that only one graph line is present, both motif frequencies are the same)

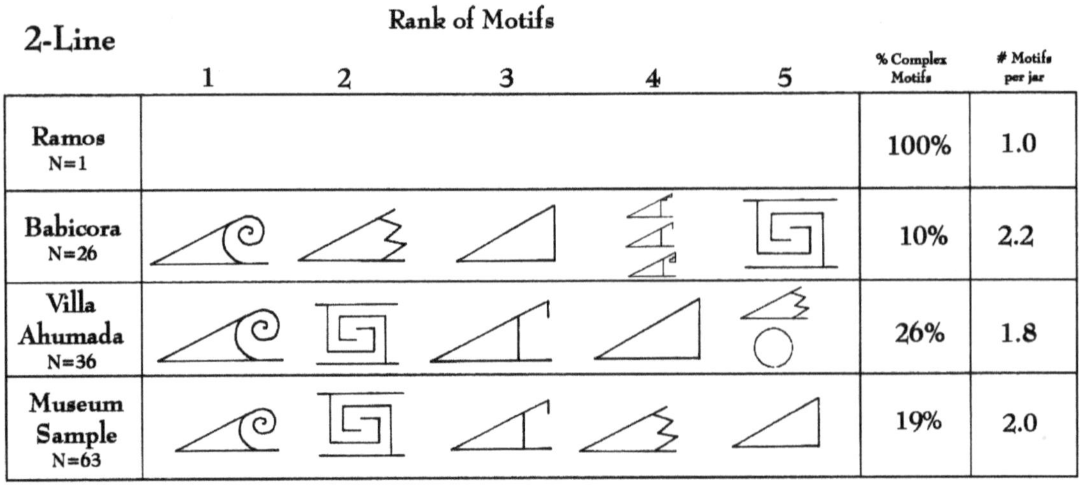

2-Line

Rank of Motifs

	1	2	3	4	5	% Complex Motifs	# Motifs per jar
Ramos N=1						100%	1.0
Babicora N=26						10%	2.2
Villa Ahumada N=36						26%	1.8
Museum Sample N=63						19%	2.0

Figure 5.10 Summary of motif frequency by polychrome type and museum sample with 2-Line layouts. Note - spaces indicate lack of motifs occurring on more than one jar

3-Line

Rank of Motifs

	1	2	3	4	5	% Complex Motifs	# Motifs per jar
Ramos N=6						60%	1.7
Babicora N=15						10%	1.9
Villa Ahumada N=12						28%	2.1
Museum Sample N=33						25%	1.9

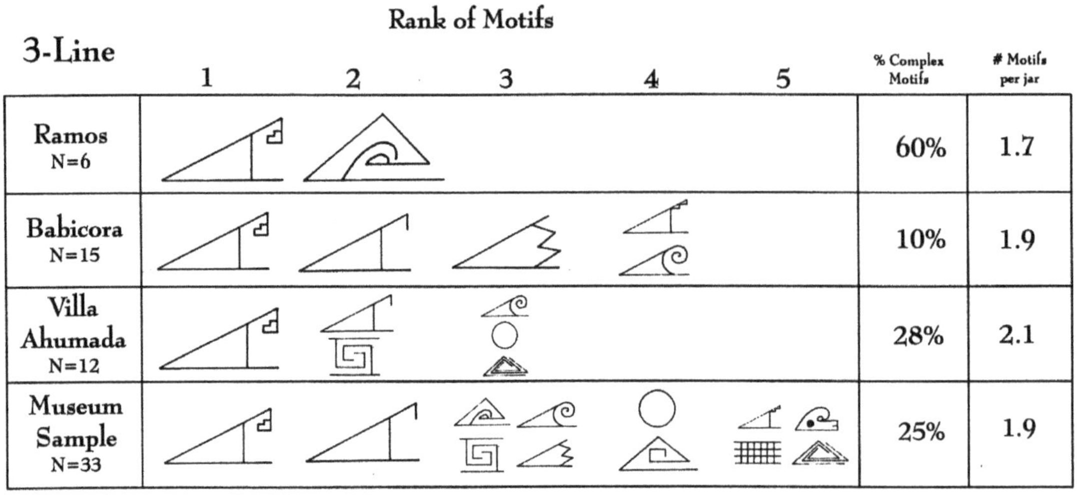

Figure 5.11 Summary of motif frequency by polychrome type and museum sample with 3-Line layouts. Note -spaces indicate lack of motifs occurring on more than one jar

4-Line

Rank of Motifs

	1	2	3	4	5	% Complex Motifs	# Motifs per jar
Ramos N=3						60%	1.7
Babicora N=20						13%	1.7
Villa Ahumada N=19						25%	2.1
Museum Sample N=42						23%	1.9

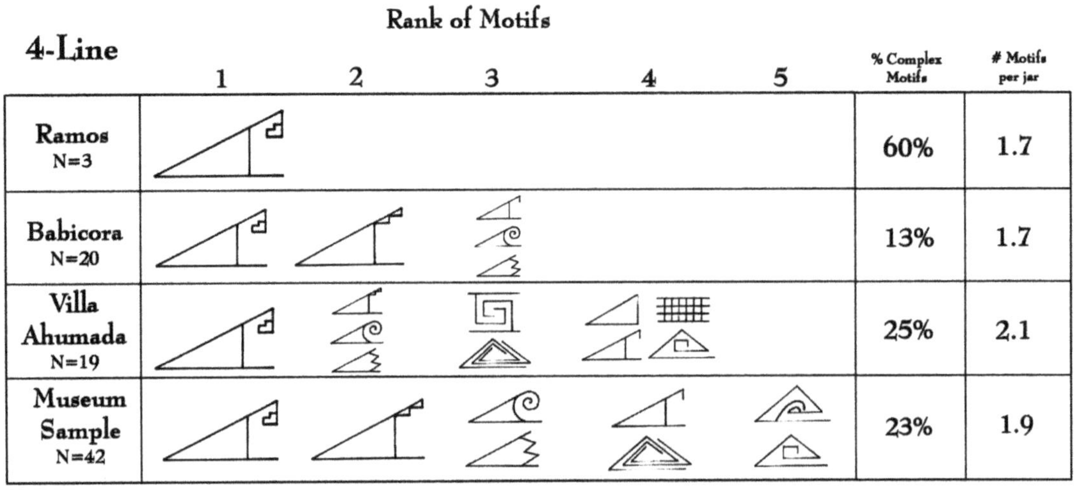

Figure 5.12 Summary of motif frequency by polychrome types and museum sample with 4-Line layouts. Note - spaces indicate lack of motifs occurring on more than one jar

58

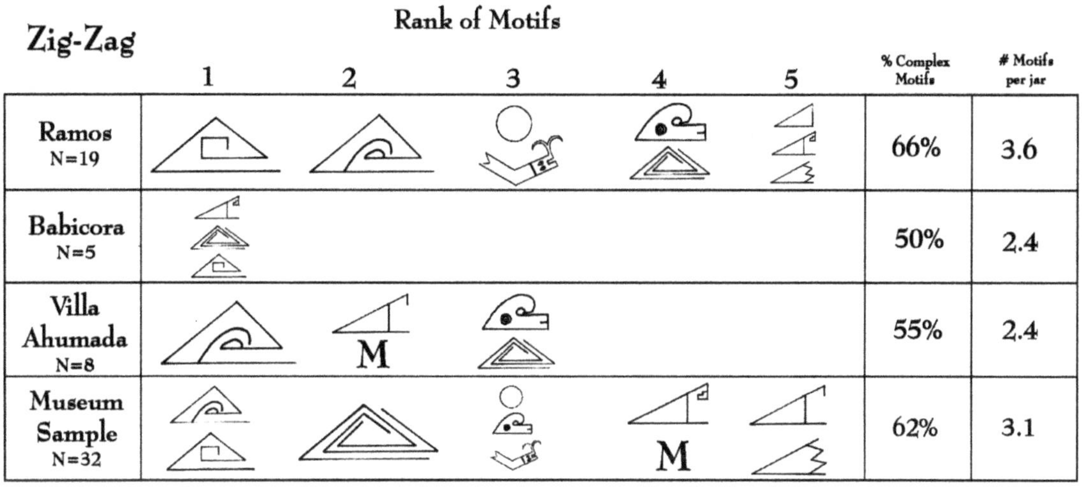

Zig-Zag

	1	2	3	4	5	% Complex Motifs	# Motifs per jar
Ramos N=19						66%	3.6
Babicora N=5						50%	2.4
Villa Ahumada N=8		M				55%	2.4
Museum Sample N=32				M		62%	3.1

Rank of Motifs

Figure 5.13 Summary of motif frequency by polychrome types and museum sample with Zig-Zag layouts. Note - spaces indicate lack of motifs occurring on more than one jar

Semi-Panelled

	1	2	3	4	5	% Complex Motifs	# Motifs per jar
Ramos N=30						53%	3.2
Babicora N=24						57%	2.7
Villa Ahumada N=3						44%	2.7
Museum Sample N=43						60%	3.0

Rank of Motifs

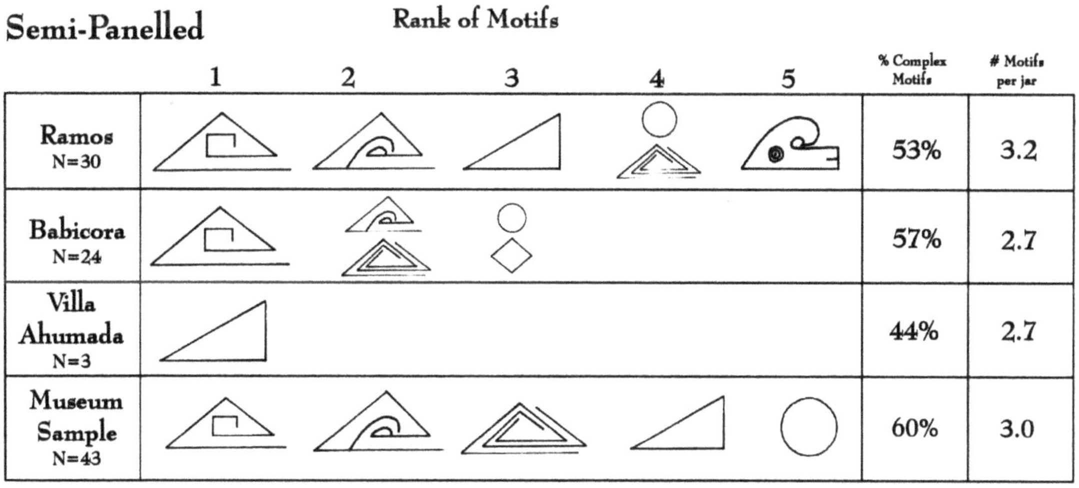

Figure 5.14 Summary of motif frequency by polychrome types and museum sample with Semi-Panelled layouts. Note - spaces indicate lack of motifs occurring on more than one jar

Panelled

	1	2	3	4	5	% Complex Motifs	# Motifs per jar
Ramos N=89						47%	3.7
Babicora N=24						42%	2.8
Villa Ahumada N=11						47%	3.3
Museum Sample N=124						46%	3.5

Rank of Motifs

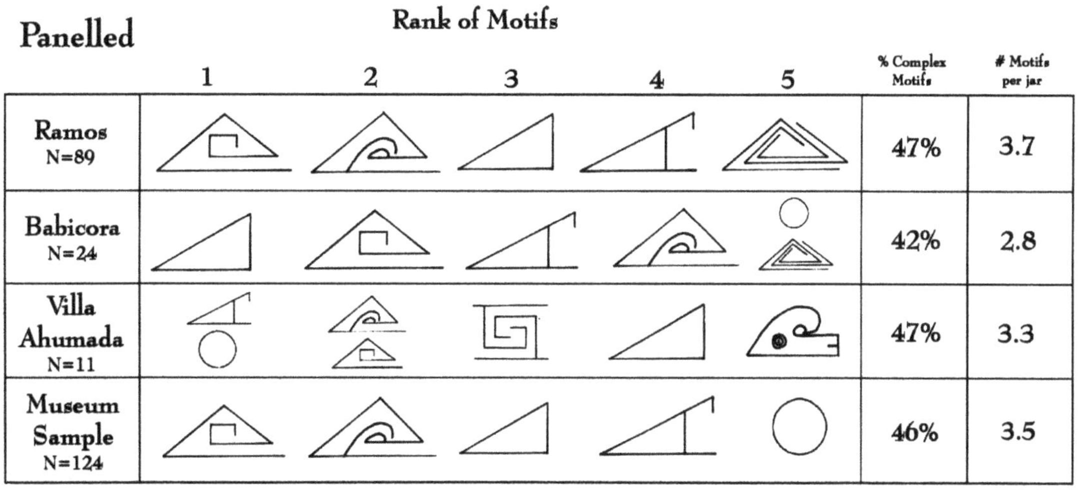

Figure 5.15 Summary of motif frequency by polychrome types and museum sample with Panelled layouts. Note - spaces indicate lack of motifs occurring on more than one jar

59

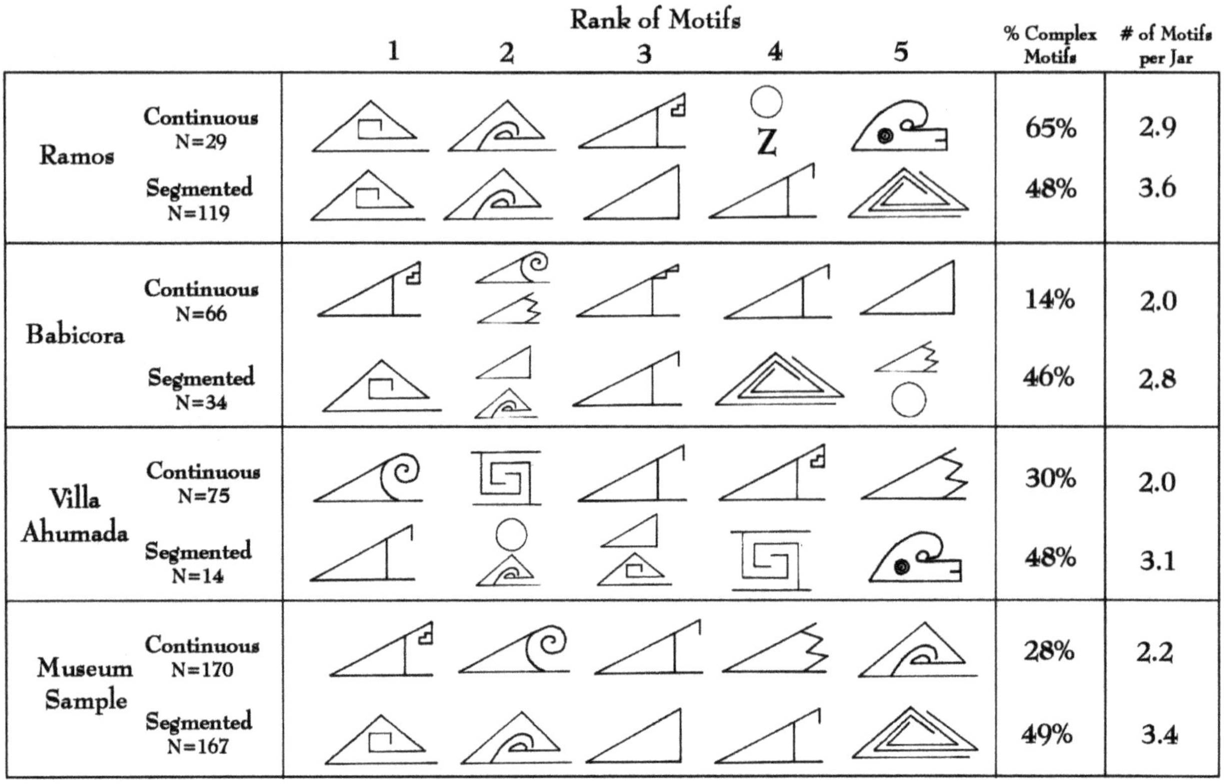

		Rank of Motifs					% Complex Motifs	# of Motifs per Jar
		1	2	3	4	5		
Ramos	Continuous N=29						65%	2.9
	Segmented N=119						48%	3.6
Babicora	Continuous N=66						14%	2.0
	Segmented N=34						46%	2.8
Villa Ahumada	Continuous N=75						30%	2.0
	Segmented N=14						48%	3.1
Museum Sample	Continuous N=170						28%	2.2
	Segmented N=167						49%	3.4

Figure 5.16 Summary of motif frequency by layout style for the polychrome types and museum sample

SECONDARY COMPARATIVE TESTS

The design analysis data presented above will now be subjected to three separate tests to clarify or expand the information potential of specific design levels or patterns in the museum sample. First, the presence of red motifs outlined by black (BoR) on these jars is compared against the design information provided for the entire sample. Second, the decorative patterns on effigy vessels are discussed individually and then in contrast to the results for all polychrome jars. Last, the museum data is compared according to layout and type with the collection of whole vessels recovered by Di Peso at Paquimé. In order to expand the contrastive value of this exercise, each successive test will include the previous variable in its discussion (i.e., effigy vessels are examined according to BoR, Paquimé according to BoR and effigy).

Black-Bordered Red Motifs

Each vessel in this study is classified according to the presence of Black-bordered Red motifs (BoR) or absence (NoBoR) of this trait on its exterior. Any motif that displays this trait on a jar is considered part of the BoR category. This trait is examined within the context of the individual polychrome types and the museum sample, and in association with the design levels and styles examined above. Due to the extensive list of layouts and motifs, the focus of this investigation is on identifying broader patterns of motif and layout style rather than individual characteristics of each design level.

Distribution of BoR

The frequency of pots with BoR is slightly greater (55%) than vessels that do not utilize this decorative feature (Table 5.7). When the museum sample is divided into the respective type categories, both Babícora (36%) and Villa Ahumada (15%) contain relatively few BoR vessels, however, nearly all Ramos polychrome jars incorporate at least one motif with BoR (91%). While Ramos and Villa Ahumada are diametrically opposed in the frequency of this trait, the results for Babícora suggests that this type may bridge the gap between these disparate styles.

Layout Style and Type

Division of the sample into polychrome types (see Table 5.7) produces stylistic patterns that appear frequently throughout this design analysis. First, Babicora and Villa Ahumada are found to share comparable ratios of BoR in each of the layout styles: Continuous layouts are clearly associated with the NoBoR trait (86% and 90%), and BoR is related to Segmented style structures (76% and 64%). While the results for Ramos polychrome mirror the pattern for BoR, those vessels without this trait are also dominated by Segmented style layouts. Another potentially significant difference present in the Ramos sample is the high number of Zig-Zag layouts in the BoR category. From this information we must again consider the implications of such patterning within this Continuous layout category. Further discussion of this subject will be considered in Chapter VI. Overall, comparison of layout and type with the BoR trait again suggests that Ramos vessels are more elaborate and standardized in decoration than either Babícora or Villa Ahumada.

Layout Style and Museum Sample
The frequency of each layout class for the museum sample presents a basic dichotomy between vessels in the NoBoR and BoR categories (Table 5.7). Vessels lacking BoR are commonly associated with Continous layouts (i.e., 2-, 3-, 4-Line) while those that do incorporate this trait are found in the Segmented style, and specifically in Panelled layouts (57% of all BoR layouts).

Motif Style and Type
Explaining the patterns of motif and motif style for the museum sample is aided by the data presented by each polychrome type (see Table 5.8). The most consistent results are found in the NoBoR vessels, as the results for Babícora, Ramos, and Villa Ahumada each display a greater emphasis towards Simple motifs. Even with the small sample size, the Ramos jars still contain one more motif per vessel than either Babícora or Villa Ahuamda. This homogeneity contrasts with the results for the BoR category, where only Ramos and Villa Ahumada have a greater proportion of Complex motifs. Babícora jars, which are much more common than Villa Ahumada, contain significantly more Simple motifs and have a slightly reduced average number of motifs per vessel.

Motif Style and Museum Sample
The relative frequency of motifs, both individual and by style, for BoR and NoBoR classes is presented in Table 5.8. It should be noted that this tally does not represent actual motifs decorated with BoR but the number of motifs that are found to co-occur on pots decorated using this technique.

The absence or presence of BoR in the museum sample corresponds to one of two ranges or suites of motifs. Those vessels that lack BoR rely on Hooked/Stepped Triangles, Scrolled Triangles, Hooked Triangles, Barbed figures, Rectangular Scrolls and Triangles and display a fairly low number of motifs per individual jar. It is not surprising that Simple motifs should therefore represent the great majority of motifs (77%) recorded on NoBoR vessels. By contrast, jars that contain the BoR trait are associated with CTS, "P" Triangles, Triangles, Hooked Triangles, Triangular Scrolls, and Circles and an average vessel is decorated by at least 3 different motifs. In total, however, Complex motifs are just slightly (52%) more abundant than the Simple (48%) style designs.

Layout and Motif Styles
The large amount of data presented in Table 5.9 is summarized according to basic patterns found in each

polychrome type and the museum sample. Due to the small number of Basic, Repeated Figure and Miscellaneous layouts the following discussion is restricted to those vessels which correspond to Continuous and Segmented formats.

Ramos
The abundance of BoR Segmented vessels and the distinctive motif characteristics present in that category suggests that this decorative patterning is a reliable characteristic for identifying Ramos polychrome jars (Table 5.9). In comparing these results with the rest of the Ramos assemblage, at least one of the characteristics that define BoR Segmented vessels (i.e., greater number of different motifs per jar, increased reliance on Complex motifs) are also found in each category. Even the NoBoR Segmented vessels, which display a greater ratio of Simple motifs (60%), contain as many different motifs per vessel as the BoR Segmented vessels. This data further supports the argument that Ramos polychrome is the most consistent of the three types examined in this study.

Babícora
Jars with NoBoR Continuous and BoR Segmented are also the most common categories for Babícora polychrome (Table 5.9). While these two categories produce comparable patterns to the entire sample, the results from the less common variants are more closely related to the NoBoR Continuous vessels in the number of motifs per jar (1.6 and 2.3) and predominance of Simple motifs (88% and 75%).

Villa Ahumada
Comparison of the motif characteristics within Villa Ahumada by BoR and layout style presents a melange of results that reveal similarities with both Babícora and Ramos polychrome (Table 5.9). Unlike the heterogeneity of Babícora, and in direct contrast to Ramos polychrome, the majority of Villa Ahumada jars are NoBoR Continuous. The motif data, however, is similar to that found in the Babícora examples (i.e., few different motifs per vessel, reliance on Simple motifs). By contrast, the remaining categories that are poorly represented show more consistencies with Ramos polychrome. It is worth noting that the Rectangular Scroll appears most often in NoBoR Continuous contexts, however, it is also used on 33% of the BoR Segmented vessels.

Museum Sample
The frequency of each BoR category and layout style provides the primary division for examining the patterns of motif style. At the broadest level, the NoBoR Continuous and BoR Segmented categories represent the majority of vessels from the museum sample, while BoR Continuous and NoBoR Segmented are much less common. When these categories are compared according to specific motif and style data some vital information becomes apparent, and a definite break exists between the

Effigy Class	Museum Sample N=58	Babicora N=15	Ramos N=24	Villa Ahumada N=19
Hooded	29	9	12	8
Reclining	3	1	0	2
Human Face	6	1	4	1
Animal	6	0	3	3
Bird	9	2	4	3
Snake	3	1	1	1
Fish	2	1	0	1

Table 5.10 Distribution of effigy classes by polychrome type and museum sample

NoBoR and BoR jars. NoBoR is decorated with Continous layouts, Simple motifs, and an average of one or two motifs depicted on each vessel, while BoR contains Segmented layouts, a greater reliance on Complex motifs, and at least three different motifs per jar. This dichotomy is also present in the use of individual motifs, as NoBoR emphasize Hooked/Stepped Triangles, Scrolled Triangles, Hooked Triangles, and BoR are more commonly decorated with CTS, "P" Triangles, Triangles, and Circles.

The association between these two 'styles' is somewhat blurred by the results from the remaining vessels of NoBoR Segmented and BoR Continuous. Unlike their more frequent counterparts, these categories share a similar average number of motifs per vessel and a reliance on several individual motifs (i.e., CTS, Hooked/Stepped Triangle, Circles, "P" Triangles). While this information suggests a similar decorative scheme to that used in the BoR Segmented jars, the NoBoR Segmented examples still rely more heavily on Simple motifs.

Summary of BoR

Figure 5.17 illustrates the basic differences within the museum sample through the comparison of motif, layout, and type when considering presence of Black-bordered red motifs. In general, the fundamental distinctions recorded in the NoBoR and BoR jars for the museum sample mirror the results found for the design styles identified in the initial design analysis discussed above. NoBoR vessels with Simple motifs have fewer motifs per vessel and are normally associated with Continuous layouts, while BoR emphasize Complex motifs, contain more motifs per jar, and have Segmented layouts. With the exception of Ramos polychrome, the individual types produce a comparable dichotomy between motif and layout frequencies when compared according to presence of black-bordered red designs. Ramos is by far the most distinct type, as it has very standardized frequencies of motifs (i.e. CTS, "P" Triangle and Triangle), motifs per vessel, and jars decorated in Segmented style in both NoBoR or BoR classes.

Effigy Vessels

A second test in this design analysis is to examine the decorative patterning found on effigy vessels, which are a subset of the jars incorporated in the museum sample. The importance of this test is to determine whether the artisans employed the same decorative strategies in both jar forms. Decorative traits are discussed according to

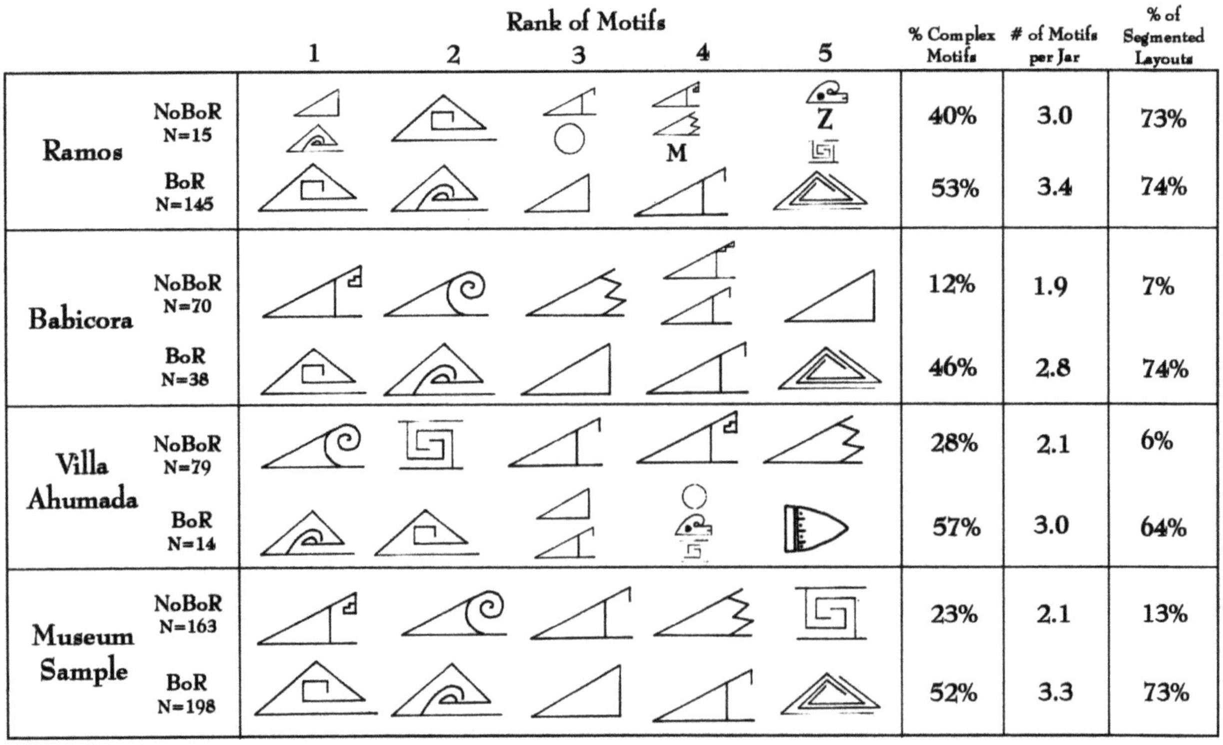

Figure 5.17 Summary of motif frequency for the polychrome types and museum sample categorized according to presence/absence of black borders around red motifs

design levels, design styles, and between polychrome types, as well as in relation to the frequency of these traits in the context of black-bordered red motifs. As discussed previously, effigy jars are represented by several distinct classes however, due to the small sample size of most classes, the depth of this investigation is often restricted to broader associations of type and tradition.

Distribution of Effigy Classes

The most common effigy classes from the museum sample are the Hooded (50%), Bird (16%), Animal and Human Face (10%) (Table 5.10). Few examples of Reclining, Snake and Fish effigy classes are present and there are no Horned Lizard effigies for Babícora, Ramos, or Villa Ahumada. As a result, these classes cannot contribute to the discussion of patterns that are delimited to or transcend polychrome types. Instead, they are included to act as reference points for outlining trends within the entire tradition.

Effigy Class and Type

Ramos polychrome is the most common type representing 41% of the effigy sample (see Table 5.10), while the number of Villa Ahumada jars exceeds the Babícora type. The distribution of each effigy class within these types is fairly similar as Hooded vessels are by far the most common class. Animal, Bird and Human Face are also present in each polychrome type, however, only Ramos contains multiple examples of all three classes. Reclining and Fish effigies are restricted to Babícora and Villa Ahumada.

Layout and Layout Style

Effigy jars are predominantly decorated with Panelled layouts (41%), however the overall ratio of Segmented (47%) to Continuous (43%) style is more or less equal (see Table 5.11). Based on the data from the entire museum sample it is not surprising that Babícora and Villa Ahumada show a greater reliance on Continuous layouts while nearly all Ramos effigies have a Segmented structure.

Even though few individual effigy classes are found in great quantities, the distribution of layouts suggests some fairly distinct patterning. Hooded jars, the most common class, are decorated more often with Panelled layouts but the overall ratio of Continuous to Segmented styles is nearly identical. An equal ratio of layout styles is also characteristic of Human Face effigies, although the Segmented pots display more Semi-Panelled layouts. In contrast to the equal representation of these classes, two groups of effigies appear to favour one layout style. Bird, followed by Animal and Human Face effigies are more commonly associated with Segmented layouts (i.e., Panelled). The Reclining Figure, Snake, and Fish classes are restricted to the Continuous style or, in rare instances, found decorated with Repeated Figure or Miscellaneous layouts.

Motif and Motif Style

The distribution of motifs for the effigy collection and by effigy class is presented in Table 5.12. At the level of the museum sample, the most commonly occurring motifs are Hooked Triangle (33%), Hooked/Stepped Triangle (31%), Triangle and "P" Triangle (28%), and Rectangular Scroll (26%). At the other end of the scale, the Zoomorph, Feather, Macaw, Diamond, and Spiral motifs are among the rarest motifs used to decorate these effigy jars. The absence painted life forms is intriguing given that the vessel shape represents an animal or human. Another distinguishing feature of the effigy collection is that even though the ratio of motif styles is skewed towards Simple designs (66%), the number of different motifs used to decorate each vessel is quite high. Consideration of type differences offers some explanation for this markedly greater average. Babícora and Villa Ahumada rely on Simple motifs almost exclusively and display a comparable number of different motifs. Ramos also incorporates a larger proportion of Simple motifs, however, significantly more motifs are used to decorate each effigy. Given that Ramos examples outnumber the remaining types, this partially explains the anomalous association of Simple style and increased elaborateness of the effigy collection.

Comparison of motifs by effigy class presents more individualized results. Hooded effigies are predisposed towards Hooked/Stepped Triangles, Triangles, and Hooked Triangles, yet several pots are also decorated with "P" Triangles, Triangular Scrolls, and Composite Triangular Scrolls. Even with the frequent use of these Complex motifs, Simple style designs (62%) are more common in the Hooded effigy class. Human Face vessels also contain a wide array of Simple, triangle-shaped motifs but no single motif appears on more than two jars. A quite different range of motifs is present within the Animal effigies, specifically with the incorporation of Circles or Diamonds, and the general absence of most Simple, triangle-based motifs. Bird effigies are the most densely decorated class with nine different motifs appearing on at least three jars. Again, Simple motifs predominate this effigy class (66%). The only motif missing from the entire inventory of this sub-class of Bird effigies is the Spiral.

With the exception of Bird effigies, the number of motifs per vessel is consistent between the respective effigy classes. Hooded, Reclining, Animal, Snake, and Fish effigies share a comparable average ranging between 2.5-2.8 motifs/jar and the results for Human Face jars, while greater than the bulk of effigies examined here, are not nearly as elaborate as the Bird effigy class.

Layout and Motif Styles

The data for layout and layout style compared against motifs is presented in Table 5.13. Even with the small representation of layouts, the motif frequency in each class produces similar results to that associated with the

Style	Layout	Museum Sample N=58	Babicora N=15	Ramos N=24	Villa Ah N=19	Effigy Class Hooded N=29	Reclining N=3	H. Face N=6	Animal N=6	Bird N=9	Snake N=3	Fish N=2
	Band	1	1	0	0	1	0	0	0	0	0	0
Continuous	2-line	11	6	0	6	5	2	1	1	0	1	2
	3-line	5	1	3	1	4	0	1	0	0	0	0
	4-line	6	3	0	3	4	0	1	1	0	0	0
	Zig-zag	3	0	1	2	2	0	0	0	1	0	0
Segmented	Semi-Panelled	3	0	3	0	1	0	2	0	0	0	0
	Panelled	24	3	16	4	12	0	1	4	6	0	0
	Repeated Figure	3	1	0	2	0	1	0	0	2	0	0
	Miscellaneous	2	0	1	1	0	0	0	0	0	2	0
	Continuous	25	10	4	12	15	2	3	2	1	1	2
	Segmented	27	3	19	4	13	0	3	4	6	0	0

Table 5.11 Frequency of layout classes and style for effigy jars by polychrome type, museum sample and effigy class

Style	Motif	Type Ramos N=24	Babicora N=15	Villa Ah N=19	Museum Sample N=58	Effigy Class Hooded N=29	Reclining N=3	H. Face N=6	Animal N=6	Bird N=9	Snake N=3	Fish N=2
Simple	Triangle	10	3	3	16	9	0	2	0	3	2	0
	Hooked Triangle	10	4	5	19	8	2	2	0	4	1	2
	Hooked/Stepped Triangle	12	3	3	18	12	0	1	2	3	0	0
	Stepped Triangle	1	5	2	8	3	1	2	1	1	0	0
	Scrolled Triangle	2	4	6	12	7	0	2	0	1	1	1
	Barbed	0	4	4	8	1	2	2	1	2	0	0
	Ladder	5	0	1	6	1	0	1	0	3	1	0
	Checker	2	3	0	5	1	1	1	0	1	0	1
	Circles	6	0	1	7	1	0	0	2	4	0	0
	Diamond	0	1	2	3	0	0	0	1	2	0	0
	Spiral	1	0	0	1	0	0	0	1	0	0	0
	Miscellaneous	3	2	3	8	2	0	0	1	3	2	0
Complex	Macaw	2	0	0	2	2	0	0	0	0	0	0
	Feather	3	0	0	3	2	0	1	0	0	0	0
	Zoomorph	3	0	0	3	1	0	1	1	0	0	0
	Rectangular Scroll	4	1	10	15	5	1	1	3	3	1	1
	"P" Triangle	12	1	3	16	6	0	2	2	6	0	0
	Triangular Scroll	8	1	0	9	6	0	0	0	3	0	0
	Composite Triangular Scroll	8	1	2	11	6	1	0	2	2	0	0
	Total Appearance of Motifs	92	33	45	170	73	8	18	17	41	8	5
	Average # of Motifs per Jar	3.8	2.2	2.4	2.9	2.5	2.7	3.0	2.8	4.6	2.7	2.5
	Simple	52	29	30	111	45	6	13	9	27	7	4
	Complex	40	4	15	59	28	2	5	8	14	1	1

Table 5.12 Comparative frequency of motifs in effigy jars for each polychrome type, museum sample, and effigy class

layout style (i.e., 4-Line with Stepped Triangle, Barbed, no Complex motifs; Semi-Panelled with "P" Triangle, Circles, Triangle, Hooked Triangle). Since the decoration on these effigies conforms to the patterns of the layout style, further discussion will emphasize broader patterns within the museum sample.

In general, effigies with Continuous layouts are dominated by Simple motifs (77%), regularly incorporate the Rectangular Scroll, and use fewer motifs per jar. Individual motif frequencies correspond to the basic parameters of the Continuous style with a reliance on the triangle-shaped motifs and a general lack of Triangles, Circles, Triangular Scrolls, and CTS that are common on Segmented vessels. If Zig-Zag effigies are excluded from

the Continuous style, these vessels become clearly associated with Simple motifs and few motifs per vessel. A further distortion of the results for the Continuous data is a sole Ramos effigy that has eight motifs, including several Complex designs.

Effigies decorated with Segmented layouts similarly conform to the basic patterns produced for the museum sample: a greater proportion of Complex motifs, increased number of motifs per jar, and a reliance on "P" Triangles, Triangular Scrolls, CTS, Triangles, and Hooked Triangles. A further point that distinguishes the Segmented effigies is that several motifs commonly found in Continuous layouts (i.e., Stepped Triangles,

Style	Motif	Effigy Sample		Continuous				Segmented	
		Continuous	Segmented	2-Line	3-Line	4-Line	Zig-Zag	Semi-Panelled	Panelled
		N=26	N=28	N=12	N=5	N=6	N=3	N=3	N=24
Simple	Triangle	1	11	0	1	0	0	1	10
	Hooked Triangle	5	11	3	0	2	0	1	10
	Hooked/Stepped Triangle	8	11	0	4	3	1	1	10
	Stepped Triangle	6	1	3	0	3	0	0	1
	Scrolled Triangle	8	2	6	0	1	1	0	2
	Barbed	6	1	4	0	2	0	0	1
	Ladder	1	4	0	0	0	1	0	4
	Checker	3	2	2	0	0	1	1	1
	Circles	0	7	0	0	0	0	1	6
	Diamond	2	0	1	0	0	1	0	0
	Spiral	0	2	0	0	0	0	0	2
	Miscellaneous	3	3	1	0	0	2	0	3
Complex	Macaw	1	1	0	0	0	1	0	1
	Feather	1	2	0	0	0	1	1	1
	Zoomorph	1	2	0	1	0	0	0	2
	Rectangular Scroll	6	7	5	1	0	0	1	6
	"P" Triangle	2	14	0	0	0	2	2	12
	Triangular Scroll	1	8	0	0	0	1	0	8
	Composite Triangular Scroll	1	9	0	0	0	1	1	8
	Total Appearances of Motifs	56	98	25	7	11	13	10	88
	Average # of Motifs per Jar	2.2	3.5	2.1	1.4	1.8	4.3	3.3	3.7
	Simple	43	55	20	5	11	7	5	50
	Complex	13	43	5	2	0	6	5	38

Table 5.13 Comparative frequency of motifs among effigies by layout style and class

Barbed figures, and Scrolled Triangles) are extremely rare in this style.

Design Styles and Type by Effigy Classes

Only Hooded and Bird effigies are compared according to design styles and type since the remaining classes are not found in sufficient quantities in each layout style or polychrome type. While the number of Bird effigies is also quite limited, the unique character of this class requires further investigation.

Hooded effigies are the best class for the comparison of design styles since they are equally distributed within both Layout styles and each of the polychrome types (Table 5.14a). The Hooded jars in Babícora and Villa Ahumada are predominantly decorated using the Continuous format (67% and 75%) and rely heavily on Simple motifs (76% and 75%). Rectangular Scrolls again play a fairly prominent role in the Villa Ahumada jars. By contrast, the Ramos examples are almost exclusively decorated with Segmented layouts (75%) and are filled with a greater proportion of Complex motifs (48%). Based on this information, no distinct patterning is detected between the Hooded effigies and the rest of the museum sample. This suggests that Hooded effigies were not decorated with a different strategy than ordinary polychrome jars in the Chihuahuan tradition.

Bird effigies, while not nearly as numerous as Hooded jars, also occur within each polychrome type (Table 15.4b). At a broad level, these pots are primarily distinguished from other effigy classes through the inordinate number of different motifs that are used to decorate each vessel. This trait generally transcends type distinctions, however it is most notable for Ramos polychrome. A further point that distinguishes the sample of Bird effigies is the juxtaposition presented by the use of Segmented layouts coupled with a significantly greater reliance on Simple motifs (66%). While it is not uncommon for Segmented jars to contain more Simple motifs, the ratio is normally much closer. Further comparison of individual types is complicated by considerations of sample size, however, one point worth noting is that the Miscellaneous motif is the only design shared by all three types. It is also interesting to note that each of the Ramos pots contained the Hooked Triangle and "P" Triangle and three incorporated Ladder, Circles, and Triangular Scrolls. This motif pattern is almost exactly repeated on the Bird effigy from the Naylor collection used to demonstrate the decoding process for this study (see Figure 4.4). Based on this information, the decoration of Bird effigies is unique among the effigy classes and appears to have been quite standardized, especially within Ramos polychrome.

Black-bordered Red

A detailed examination of individual motif and layout frequencies in relation to the use of BoR is complicated by the small sample of effigy vessels. Instead of examining each design level individually, the data presented for the effigy jars is summarized according to basic patterns of motif and layout style within each type and effigy class. These patterns are derived from the information presented in Tables 5.15 and 5.16 based on equal ratios of vessels with and without the BoR trait.

5.14a Hooded Effigy

Style	Motif	Ramos N=12	Babicora N=9	Villa Ah N=8	Museum N=29	Continuous N=15	Segmented N=13
Simple	Triangle	5	2	2	4	1	7
	Hooked Triangle	5	3	0	3	1	6
	Hooked/Stepped Triangle	8	2	2	4	6	6
	Stepped Triangle	0	3	0	3	3	0
	Scrolled Triangle	1	2	4	6	5	1
	Barbed	0	1	0	1	1	0
	Ladder	1	0	0	0	1	0
	Checker	1	0	0	0	1	0
	Circles	1	0	0	0	0	1
	Diamond	0	0	0	0	0	0
	Spiral	0	0	0	0	0	0
	Miscellaneous	1	0	1	1	1	1
Complex	Macaw	2	0	0	0	1	1
	Feather	2	0	0	0	1	1
	Zoomorph	1	0	0	0	0	1
	Rectangular Scroll	1	1	3	4	3	2
	"P" Triangle	5	1	0	1	1	5
	Triangular Scroll	5	1	0	1	1	5
	Composite Triangular Scroll	5	1	0	1	1	5
	Total Appearance of Motifs	44	17	12	29	28	42
	Average # of Motifs per Jar	3.7	1.9	1.5	2.5	1.9	3.2
Motif Style	Simple	23	13	9	45	20	22
	Complex	21	4	3	28	8	20
Layout Style	Continuous	3	6	6			
	Segmented	9	2	2			

5.14b Bird

Style	Motif	Ramos N=4	Babicora N=2	Villa Ah N=3	Museum N=9	Continuous N=1	Segmented N=6
Simple	Triangle	2	1	0	3	0	2
	Hooked Triangle	4	0	0	4	0	4
	Hooked/Stepped Triangle	2	1	0	3	0	3
	Stepped Triangle	0	0	1	1	0	0
	Scrolled Triangle	1	0	0	1	0	1
	Barbed	0	1	1	2	0	1
	Ladder	3	0	0	3	3	3
	Checker	0	1	0	1	0	1
	Circles	3	0	1	4	0	4
	Diamond	0	1	1	2	1	0
	Spiral	0	0	0	0	0	0
	Miscellaneous	1	1	1	3	1	1
Complex	Macaw	0	0	0	0	0	0
	Feather	0	0	0	0	0	0
	Zoomorph	0	0	0	0	0	0
	Rectangular Scroll	1	0	2	3	0	2
	"P" Triangle	4	0	2	6	1	5
	Triangular Scroll	3	0	0	3	0	3
	Composite Triangular Scroll	2	0	0	2	0	2
	Total Appearance of Motifs	26	6	9	41	6	32
	Average # of Motifs per Jar	6.5	3	3	4.6	6	5
Motif Style	Simple	16	6	5	27	5	20
	Complex	10	0	4	14	1	12
Layout Style	Continuous	0	0	1			
	Segmented	4	1	1			

Table 5.14a-b Comparative frequency of motifs in Hooded and Bird effigies by polychrome type and layout style

NoBoR

The majority of NoBoR vessels are decorated by Continuous layouts (79%) and populated with a specific range of Simple motifs (81%), which includes Triangles, Scrolled Triangles, Stepped Triangles, and Barbed figures. Typically, the Rectangular Scroll is the only Complex motif repeatedly found in association with this layout/motif combination.

By type, Babícora and Villa Ahumada account for all but one of the NoBoR effigies. All of the Babícora effigies are decorated almost exclusively with the same Continuous layout/Simple motif style, while one Villa

Style	Layout	Type Ramos		Babicora		Villa Ah		Museum		Effigy Class Hooded		H. Face		Animal		Bird	
		NoBoR	BoR	NoBoR	BoR	NoBoR	BoR	NoBoR	BoR	NoBoR	BoR	NoBoR	BoR	NoBoR	BoR	NoBoR	BoR
		N=2	N=22	N=11	N=4	N=16	N=3	N=29	N=29	N=14	N=15	N=4	N=2	N=2	N=4	N=2	N=7
Continuous	Basic	0	0	1	0	0	0	1	0	1	0	0	0	0	0	0	0
	2-Line	0	0	6	0	6	0	12	0	5	0	1	0	1	0	0	0
	3-Line	1	2	1	0	1	0	3	2	2	2	1	0	0	0	0	0
	4-Line	0	0	3	0	3	0	6	0	4	0	1	0	1	0	0	0
	Zig-Zag	0	1	0	0	2	0	2	1	1	1	0	1	0	0	1	0
Segmented	Semi-Panelled	1	2	0	0	0	0	1	2	0	1	1	1	0	0	0	0
	Panelled	0	16	0	3	1	3	1	22	1	11	0	0	0	4	0	6
	Rep. Figures	0	0	0	1	2	0	2	1	0	0	0	0	0	0	1	1
	Miscellaneous	0	1	0	0	1	0	1	1	0	0	0	0	0	0	0	0
	Continuous Style	1	3	10	0	12	0	23	3	12	3	3	1	2	0	1	0
	Segmented Style	1	18	0	3	1	3	2	24	1	12	1	1	0	4	0	6

Table 5.15 Distribution of layout class and style by BoR in effigy jars for each polychrome type, museum sample, and effigy classes

Ahumada displays a Segmented layout with multiple Complex motifs (Rectangular Scrolls, Macaws, CTS). Other than this singular anomaly, all of the Villa Ahumada effigies are decorated with the same decorative style. The two NoBoR effigies attributed to Ramos polychrome contain typical features of the type such as the greater reliance on Complex motifs and Segmented layouts.

Each of the effigy classes with NoBoR is dominated by Continuous style layouts. This is particularly evident for Hooded vessels, however, no individual layout appears more dominant from the sample. In terms of motif frequency, these effigies rely heavily on a wide range of Simple motifs; the only motifs shared across the four effigy classes are the Stepped Triangle and Rectangular Scroll. When compared according to the number of different motifs per vessel, the Hooded jars are considerably less elaborately decorated than any other class. Similarly, the average for Bird effigies is also very low. In general, the NoBoR effigies show no internal difference and present comparable patterns of layout and motif.

BoR

The effigy vessels with BoR present a very different decorative strategy. Firstly, the overwhelming majority of these effigies are decorated using the Segmented style and specifically with Panelled layouts. Motif frequency for this trait emphasizes the Complex style, yet Simple motifs still represent the larger proportion of the total recorded in the sample. The most common motifs include "P" Triangles, Hooked Stepped Triangles, Triangles, Hooked Triangles, CTS and Circles, each of which are found in association with Segmented layouts from the initial design analysis.

Ramos polychrome effigies account for 76% of all jars that contain BoR. With a few minor exceptions, this type is dominated by Segmented (i.e., Panelled) style layouts and is decorated most often with the same combinations

of motifs (i.e., "P" Triangle, Hooked/Stepped Triangle, Triangle etc.). The patterns produced by Ramos are basically mirrored in the much less frequent examples of Babícora and Villa Ahumada. These types are completely reliant on Panelled layouts and there is a definite consistency in the use of individual motifs (i.e., "P" Triangles, Triangular Scrolls, Triangles). The only notable difference is that Villa Ahumada has a higher ratio of Complex motifs, but this is likely a factor of sample size.

Decoration of the four most abundant effigy classes with the BoR trait is fairly homogeneous. The only variation in layout style, which is predominated by Segmented (i.e., Panelled) vessels, is the presence of three Continuous style jars in the Hooded class. Motif frequency varies due to the number of jars in each class, however the same basic suite of motifs is shared throughout. As discussed earlier, the Bird effigies are distinguished from other classes by the greater range and number of individual motifs depicted on their surfaces. Human Face and Animal effigies are less common than Hooded or Bird classes, but the motifs that are depicted conform to the general parameters of vessels decorated with the BoR trait.

Summary of Designs in Effigy Vessels

Comparison of the isolated study of effigy vessel decoration with the entire museum sample produces no obvious difference in painting strategies. This similarity is readily apparent in Figure 5.18, which summarizes the dominant patterns of motif frequencies for each of the polychrome types, layout styles and the presence or absence of the BoR trait for the effigy jars. Two distinct clusters appear within these comparative categories: firstly, Babícora, Villa Ahumada, Continuous style layout, and NoBoR, while the second group includes Ramos, Segmented style, and BoR.

The addition of effigy class into this discussion produces a similar degree of decorative diversity. Hooded jars,

| | | Type | | | | | | | Museum Sample | | Effigy Class | | | | | | | | |
| | | Ramos | | Babicora | | Villa Ahumada | | | | | Hooded | | Human Face | | Animal | | Bird | | |
Style	Motif	NoBoR N=2	BoR N=22	NoBoR N=11	BoR N=4	NoBoR N=16	BoR N=3	NoBoR N=29	BoR N=29	NoBoR N=14	BoR N=15	NoBoR N=4	BoR N=2	NoBoR N=2	BoR N=4	NoBoR N=2	BoR N=7
Simple	Triangle	1	9	1	2	2	1	4	12	2	7	1	1	0	0	0	3
	Hooked Triangle	1	9	3	1	5	0	9	10	2	6	2	0	0	0	0	4
	Hooked/Stepped Triangle	1	11	2	1	3	0	6	12	4	8	1	0	1	1	0	3
	Stepped Triangle	0	1	5	0	2	0	7	1	3	0	1	1	1	0	1	0
	Scrolled Triangle	0	2	4	0	6	0	10	2	6	1	2	0	0	0	0	1
	Barbed	0	0	3	1	4	0	7	1	1	0	2	0	1	0	1	1
	Ladder	0	5	0	0	1	0	1	5	0	1	0	1	0	0	0	3
	Checker	0	2	2	1	0	0	2	3	0	1	0	1	0	0	0	1
	Circles	0	6	0	0	0	1	0	7	0	1	0	0	0	2	0	4
	Diamond	0	0	0	1	2	0	2	1	0	0	0	0	1	0	1	1
	Spiral	0	1	0	0	0	0	0	1	0	0	0	0	0	1	0	0
	Miscellaneous	0	3	1	1	2	1	3	5	1	1	0	0	0	1	1	2
Complex	Macaw	0	2	0	0	0	0	0	2	0	2	0	0	0	0	0	0
	Feather	0	3	0	0	0	0	0	3	0	2	0	1	0	0	0	0
	Zoomorph	1	2	0	0	0	0	1	2	0	1	1	0	0	1	0	0
	Rectangular Scroll	1	3	1	0	7	1	9	4	3	2	1	0	1	2	1	2
	"P" Triangle	0	12	0	1	1	2	1	15	0	6	0	2	0	2	1	5
	Triangular Scroll	0	8	0	1	0	3	0	12	0	6	0	0	0	0	0	3
	CTS	0	8	0	1	2	0	1	9	1	6	0	0	0	2	0	2
	Total Appearance of Motifs	5	87	22	11	36	9	61	107	22	51	11	7	5	12	6	35
	Average # of Motifs per Jar	2.5	4	2	2.8	2.3	3	2.1	3.7	1.6	3.4	2.8	3.5	2.5	3	3	5
	Simple	3	49	21	8	27	3	51	60	19	26	9	4	4	5	4	23
	Complex	2	38	1	3	9	6	12	47	3	25	2	3	1	7	2	12

Table 5.16 Comparative frequency of motifs and motif styles by BoR in effigy jars for each polychrome type, the museum sample, and effigy classes

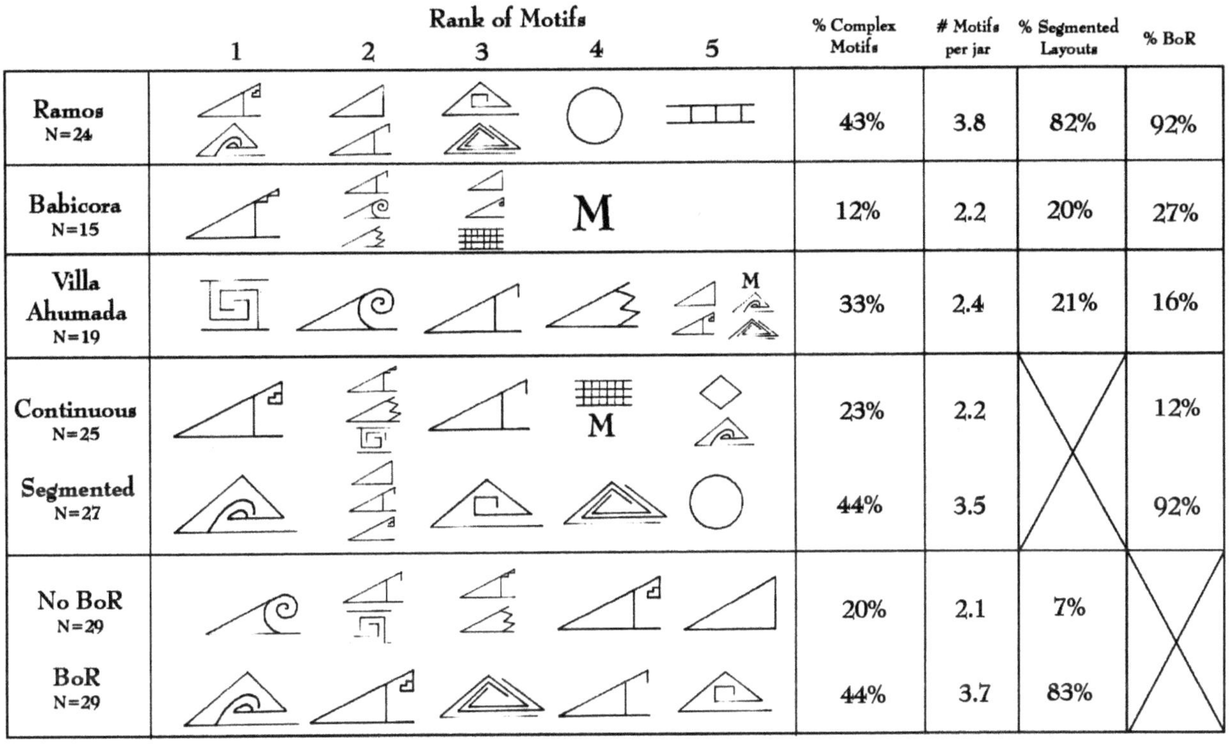

	Rank of Motifs					% Complex Motifs	# Motifs per jar	% Segmented Layouts	% BoR
	1	2	3	4	5				
Ramos N=24	*(motif)*	*(motif)*	*(motif)*	*(motif)*	*(motif)*	43%	3.8	82%	92%
Babicora N=15	*(motif)*	*(motif)*	*(motif)*	M		12%	2.2	20%	27%
Villa Ahumada N=19	*(motif)*	*(motif)*	*(motif)*	*(motif)*	*(motif)* M	33%	2.4	21%	16%
Continuous N=25	*(motif)*	*(motif)* M	*(motif)*	*(motif)* M	*(motif)*	23%	2.2		12%
Segmented N=27	*(motif)*	*(motif)*	*(motif)*	*(motif)*	*(motif)*	44%	3.5		92%
No BoR N=29	*(motif)*	*(motif)*	*(motif)*	*(motif)*	*(motif)*	20%	2.1	7%	
BoR N=29	*(motif)*	*(motif)*	*(motif)*	*(motif)*	*(motif)*	44%	3.7	83%	

Figure 5.18 Summary of motif frequencies in effigy jars for polychrome types, layout styles, and presence of BoR

		Type			Layout Style		Motif Style		BoR		Effigies
	Total	Babicora	Ramos	Villa Ah	Continuous	Segmented	Simple	Complex	No BoR	BoR	Effigies
ROM	161	54	58	49	76	72	256	189	80	81	34
WPM	200	54	102	44	94	95	318	225	83	117	24

Table 5.17 Relative frequency of polychrome type, layout and motif styles, BoR and effigies between the ROM and WPM

which represent the most abundant effigy class, are equally represented in both of the decorative 'styles' discussed above. The design differences within this effigy class suggest that the application of hoods to the basic jar form had considerable time depth or spatial breadth in the Chihuahuan tradition. The same can be said for each of the effigy classes, though with less certainty due to their significantly smaller sample size. One important exception to this general rule are the macaw effigies within the Bird class, which are predominantly associated with Ramos polychrome, decorated with Segmented layouts, Complex motifs, and all utilized the BoR trait. This standardization is a characteristic that has been identified numerous times in relation to the Ramos type but is particularly evident in this effigy sub-class. For example, comparable patterning of the macaw effigies is identified outside the ROM and WPM collections on the vessel owned by Harold Naylor in Figure 4.4 and also in the jars recovered from Paquimé.

While this study uncovered little variation in decoration between effigies and jars based on the frequency of layouts and motifs, the facial decoration and subjects depicted in hooded or appended form vary considerably. Further examination of the construction or content depicted on the appendages (i.e., facial decoration, type of animal) is merited, but is beyond the scope of this thesis.

Design Differences between the Museum Samples
As discussed in Chapter IV, the museum sample comprises only the jars attributed to Ramos, Babícora, and Villa Ahumada from the ROM and WPM museums. These vessels represent only a portion of the total number of Chihuahuan pieces, which include numerous other forms and types (including plain and textured wares), housed in these collections.

	Jars				Effigies*				Effigy Classes						
	Ramos	Babicora	Villa Ah	Total	Ramos	Babicora	Villa Ah	Total	Hooded	Reclining	H. Face	Animal	Bird	Snake	Fish
Layout	N=109	N=23	N=14	N=140	N=16	N=3	N=6	N=25	N=5	N=2	N=3	N=4	N=2	N=7	N=1
Basic	3	0	1	1	0	0	0	0	0	0	0	0	0	0	0
2-Line	1	6	1	7	0	0	1	1	1	0	0	0	0	0	0
3-Line	0	7	2	9	0	0	1	1	1	0	0	0	0	0	0
4-Line	1	0	0	0	0	0	0	0	0	0	0	0	0	0	0
Zig-Zag	6	1	1	2	0	0	0	0	0	0	0	0	0	0	0
Semi-Panelled	24	1	2	3	1	0	1	2	0	0	1	1	0	0	0
Panelled	58	2	4	6	6	1	1	8	3	0	1	2	2	0	0
Repeated Figure	3	3	1	4	0	0	0	0	0	0	0	0	0	0	0
Miscellaneous	13	3	2	5	8	2	2	12	0	2	1	1	0	7	1
Continuous	8	14	4	26	0	0	2	2	2	0	0	0	0	0	0
Segmented	82	3	6	91	7	1	2	10	3	0	2	2	2	0	0

	Jars				Effigies				Style	
	Ramos	Babicora	Villa Ah	Total	Ramos	Babicora	Villa Ah	Total	Continuous	Segmented
No BoR**	0	2	2	4	0	0	2	2	4	0
BoR	51	4	3	61	10	0	2	12	9	42

Table 5.18 Distribution of layouts in the Paquime Collection by polychrome type, effigy class and presence of BoR trait

*Horned Lizard effigy not included

**Sample reflects only those vessels with photographs in Di Peso et al. 1974a

Paquime Class	Total N=25	Babicora N=3	Ramos N=16	Villa Ahumada N=6
Hooded	5	0	3	2
Reclining Figure	2	0	2	0
Human Face	3	1	1	1
Animal	4	0	1	3
Bird	2	0	2	0
Snake	7	1	6	0
Horned Lizard	1	0	1	0
Fish	1	1	0	0

Table 5.19 Distribution of effigy classes by polychrome type from Paquimé

With the analysis of design levels, styles and secondary comparative tests now complete it is useful to examine whether there are any notable decorative differences between the ROM and WPM whole vessels. An extensive study could be undertaken by comparing this data, however, the aim of this summary is to identify broad trends rather than examine specific details. The basic categories used in this discussion are presented in relation to the ROM and WPM ceramics in Table 5.17. The most apparent difference is that the WPM has a substantially larger sample. If we disregard sample size and consider relative proportions between each collection, several important characteristics can be identified. In relation to type, the WPM contains a much greater quantity of Ramos than the ROM but has identical or very comparable numbers of Babícora and Villa Ahumada. Given the data collected for Ramos, it is therefore not surprising that the WPM sample should also display a greater ratio of BoR vessels. Effigy vessels, by contrast, are more abundant within the ROM collection. Each of these differences, however, appear less significant when compared with the near equal ratios of layout (51% to 50% Continuous) and motif styles (58% to 59%). While these styles represent arbitrary divisions of these design levels, these relationships suggest that neither sample is biased towards one particular decorative style and would produce a similar result if examined on an individual basis.

Paquimé Collection

Di Peso's data presented in the Ceramic volume (Di Peso et al. 1974) on whole vessels excavated from the site of Paquimé can be used to test the decorative patterns uncovered from the ROM and WPM sample. Due to restricted access to the actual pots or images of the vessels the only information available for each of the 140 vessels is type, layout, and effigy class (see Table 5.18). Partial information was recovered for the presence of BoR based on the examination of index cards held by INAH Chihuahua, however, numerous cards were missing from the inventory and are not included. As a result, only 65 pots are examined in relation to this decorative trait.

Jars

The number of Ramos polychrome whole vessels (78%) far surpasses any other type in the collection studied by Di Peso and colleagues. This imbalance in the Paquimé assemblage is directly reflected in the equally high ratio of Segmented style pots, of which 82 of the 91 examples are attributed to Ramos. Interestingly, the Continuous style is actually less frequent than Basic, Repeated Figure, and Miscellaneous layouts combined. The few examples of Babícora polychrome are predominantly Continuous in style and Villa Ahumada contains slightly more vessels decorated with Segmented layouts. These types produce a fairly wide range of different layouts, however, Babícora appears to be strongly associated with 2-Line or 3-Line structures. In terms of the frequency of BoR, all of the Segmented and a large proportion of the Continuous vessels include this trait while the results for each polychrome type suggest regular use of BoR designs. Unfortunately, this association is based on less than half of the sample published by Di Peso as access to clear photographs of the vessels was not available. This information was taken from a sample of the original index cards produced by the Amerind Foundation, courtesy of INAH Chihuahua.

Effigies

A total of twenty-five effigy jars are included in the vessels recovered from the excavations at Paquimé and contrasted at the level of layout according to type, class, and the presence of BoR (Table 5.18). Given the abundance of Ramos jars it is not unexpected that this type contains the greatest number of effigy vessels. What is surprising is that the ratio of effigy vessels to total jars is fairly comparable for both Bab8cora (13% of total) and Ramos (15%) and is actually much greater for Villa Ahumada (43%). The distribution of layouts in this small sample is also striking in that Miscellaneous layouts outnumber Segmented and Continuous styles combined. If we exclude the Miscellaneous jars, Ramos and Babícora are restricted to Segmented layouts while Villa Ahumada is evenly split between Continuous and Segmented styles.

Each of the effigy classes is represented by at least one vessel. Snake effigies, almost all of which are ascribed to Ramos polychrome, are more common than any other class and are individually responsible for the high number of Miscellaneous layouts in the Paquimé collection (see Table 5.19). Hooded jars display the dichotomy of layout style found within the museum sample but only occur the within Ramos and Villa Ahumada type categories. The remaining classes are all restricted to Segmented or other layouts and the Reclining Figure, Horned Lizard and Bird are only found within Ramos polychrome. While there is no motif information, the fact that the Ramos Bird effigies are decorated with a Panelled layout again suggests some degree of standardization within the class. The little information available to examine BoR for the Paquimé assemblage indicates that this trait, while obviously important among Ramos effigies, is not so clearly defined for Villa Ahumada. Access to the original data set would no doubt lead to firmer conclusions, however, based on the trends for all the excavated vessels, it appears that Ramos is very much linked to the use of BoR designs.

Overall, this data corroborates the basic premise that, at the level of layout, the decorative strategies of each type and effigy class are not distinguished from polychrome jars that lack clay appendages attached to the side or rim.

CHAPTER VI

ANALYSIS OF DESIGN AND PRESENTATION OF EXPLANATORY MODELS

Following the goals outlined in Chapter III, the data derived from the design analysis of the ROM and WPM samples is used to address two separate lines of archaeological investigation. First, this information will contribute to the Chihuahuan typology by providing a list of specific layouts and motifs depicted within each polychrome type. The second part will examine any significant decorative overlap using the design horizon concept. By testing the typological information against models of temporal or spatial variation, we can investigate the cultural implications of specific design trends.

TYPE DESCRIPTIONS

Ramos

Ramos polychrome is perhaps the most famous of the Chihuahuan ceramic types. Its white paste and fine decoration represent the pinnacle of artistic development that few styles of prehistoric types achieved. From the design analysis (see Figure 6.1), we learn that this type is distinguished by the reliance on Panelled layouts (Segmented style) that are filled with a regular suite of seven different motifs and a wholesale use of black borders around red motifs (Figures 6.2a and 6.2b). Composite Triangular Scroll (CTS) and "P" Triangle motifs, as well as frequent depictions of life-based designs (i.e., plumed serpent in Figure 6.2a #105, double macaw head in Figure 6.2b #167), represent the core motifs that separate Ramos from the majority of Babícora and Villa Ahuamada jars. Overall, the "P"-triangle is a fairly good indicator of this type since its appearance transcends the layout classes. Another factor that contributes to the unique character of this type is the near absence of multiple layouts (Table 6.1).

The appearance of several Continuous layouts (see Table 5.6) is somewhat misleading as the vast majority of non-Segmented vessels actually fit within the Zig-Zag class. As explained in Chapter V, the motifs used in Zig-Zag layouts do not comply with the other Continuous layout classes, sharing more in common with Segmented style jars. If these vessels are included as part of the Segmented style, the remaining Continuous layouts are extremely infrequent. It should be noted that even though the layout may differ on these vessels they share the white paste, black bordered red motifs, and (sometimes) Complex motifs associated with the Segmented style.

Effigies

Ramos effigies are decorated with the same basic motif and layout combinations found on regular jars (Figures 6.3a and 6.3b). The most noticeable stylistic variation occurs in the decoration and depiction of the appendages attached to the side and /or rim of the vessel. Hooded effigies, which represent the most common class, are decorated with a fairly consistent motif/layout combination on the body of the vessel but show significantly different patterns of facial decoration (i.e., Figure 6.3a #37, #36, #38, Figure 6.3b #170, #175). Research being undertaken by Maria Sprehn (personal communication, March 2000) on a large sample of effigy vessels will shed further light on the actual range of variation present on the faces of Hooded jars. The range of animal species represented in the museum sample, which includes the owl (Figure 6.3a #58, #57), badger (Figure 6.3b #165), and possibly deer, (Figure 6.3b #168) similarly provide an interesting point for future study into the importance of animals to prehistoric inhabitants of the region. The only non-local animal represented in the lexicon of Ramos effigies is the macaw. The macaw, but more specifically, the scarlet macaw, is a Mesoamerican import that was brought into Chihuahua and bred for the use of its feathers during the Medio period (Di Peso 1974:599-600). As discussed in Chapter V, the macaw jars are distinguished from other Ramos jars through the large number of different motifs used to fill the Segmented layout, and the head-tail (Figure 6.3a #54), head-head (Figure 6.3a #53) appended combination is consistent throughout the museum sample. These effigies represent the most elaborate form of Ramos polychrome.

The classification of Ramos polychrome decoration is the easiest of the three polychrome types: a Segmented layout, several different Simple and Complex motifs (specifically CTS and "P" Triangle), red motifs outlined by black, painted on vessels made with a light or white paste. On the whole, Ramos polychrome is a polythetic type, whereby any one of the tell-tale characteristics of this type can be absent from a pot (i.e. use of Complex motifs, Segmented layout). In this situation the jar normally contains at least two other traits that bind it within the parameters of the type, such as the ROM Hooded effigy (Figure 6.3a #30) with Simple motifs but Semi-Panelled layout, BoR, and white paste.

Babícora

Historically, Babícora has been viewed as a 'junk' category used to classify any sherd or vessel that does not quite fit the description of another type. A direct result of this practice is that the classification of Babícora has often been defined by traits that it does not display rather than those that it does. The root of the problem with this 'dark paste' type lies in the variety of ways that it is decorated. Indeed, the results of the design analysis presented in Figure 6.4 reflect the diversity indicated by previous type descriptions. From the examination of layout and motif frequencies in Chapter V, we can explain the divergent frequency of Panelled layouts, CTS and "P" Triangle motifs, and BoR by recognizing two distinct styles of decoration.

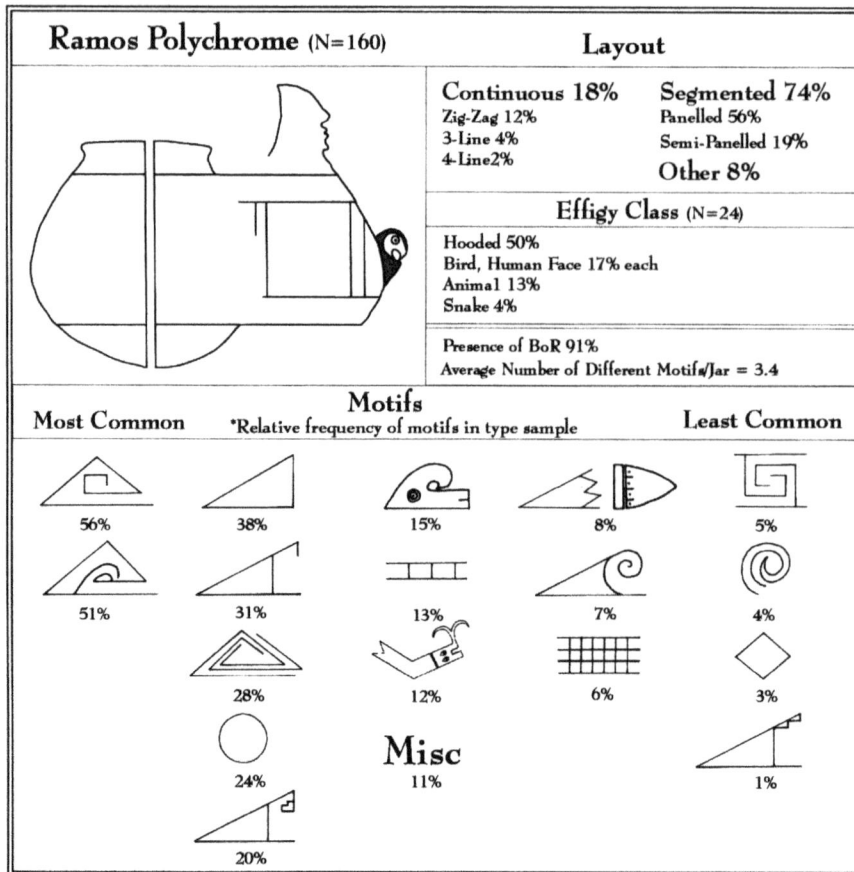

Figure 6.1 Decorative characteristics of Ramos Polychrome

Number of Band Layouts	Ramos N=160	Babicora N=108	Villa Ahumada N=93
One Band	98	73	68
Two Bands	2	25(3)*	23
Three Bands	0	2	9

Table 6.1 Relative frequency of multiple bands for each polychrome type (note - * indicates number of DH II jars)

Vertical Section	Ramos N=160	Babicora N=108	Villa Ahumada N=93
Ellipsoid	52	75	76
Ovoid	26	13	13
Spheroid	13	4	5
Corner Point	9	8	5
Rounded Base	87	93	82
Sub-conoidal Base	13	6	12
Flat Base	1	1	6

Table 6.2 Frequency of vertical sections for each polychrome type

74

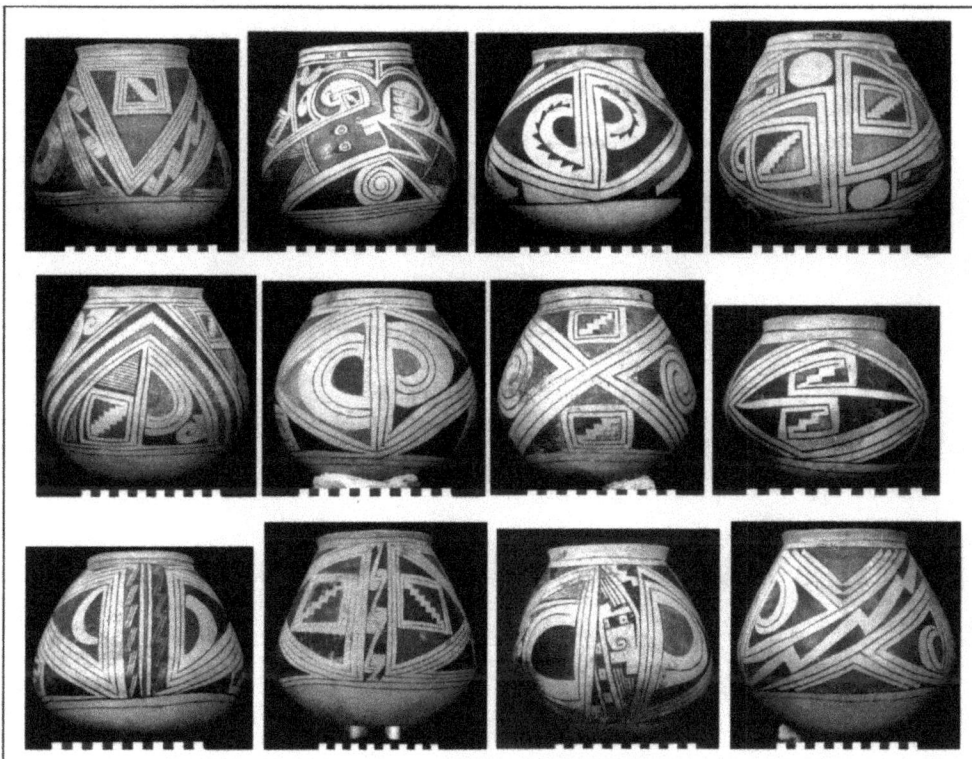

Figure 6.2a Ramos polychrome jars from the ROM decorated with Segmented layout/Complex motifs (top row - l to r - #122, #105, #123, #137, middle row - #145, #149, #151, #89, bottom row - #155, #47, #79, #77)

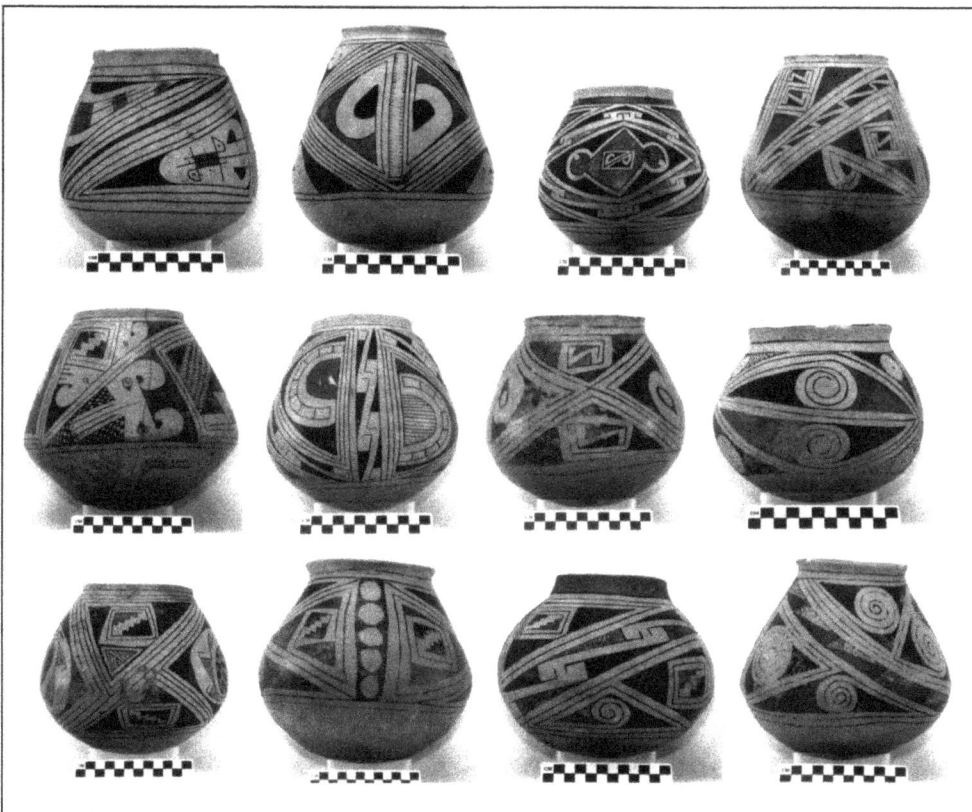

Figure 6.2b Ramos polychrome jars from the WPM decorated with Segmented layout/Complex motifs (top row - l to r #159, #200, #167, #187, middle row - #174, #30, #31, #35, bottom row - #48, #51, #72, #80)

Figure 6.3a Ramos polychrome Effigy jars from the ROM decorated with Segmented layout/Complex motifs (top row - l to r - #37, #36, #38, middle row - #35, #30, #58, #57, bottom row - #43, #42, #54, #53)

Figure 6.3b Ramos Effigy jars from the WPM decorated with Segmented layout/Complex motifs (top row - l to r - #206, #170, #175, middle row - #165, #208, #176, bottom row - #166, #168, #198 [hood broken off])

76

Babícora A

A typical (or at least more common) Babícora jar (Figures 6.5a and 6.5b) contains a layout constructed of a series of lines running continuously around the vessel that are appended with or terminate in one or two different triangle-based motifs, such as Hooked/Stepped Triangles, Hooked Triangles, or Scrolled Triangles. This Continuous layout/Simple motif combination (or Babícora A) is also normally associated with red motifs that are very rarely found outlined with black borders. Another general characteristic that typifies Babícora polychrome (but was not directly examined in the previous design analysis) is the presence of multiple bands on a single vessel. The actual count and relative percentage of vessels decorated with one to three band layouts (Table 6.1) shows that Babícora A has the largest proportion of two band layouts within the museum sample.

Returning to the problem of identifying different types, the decorative characteristics of these Babícora jars share much in common with the trends outlined for the Dublan

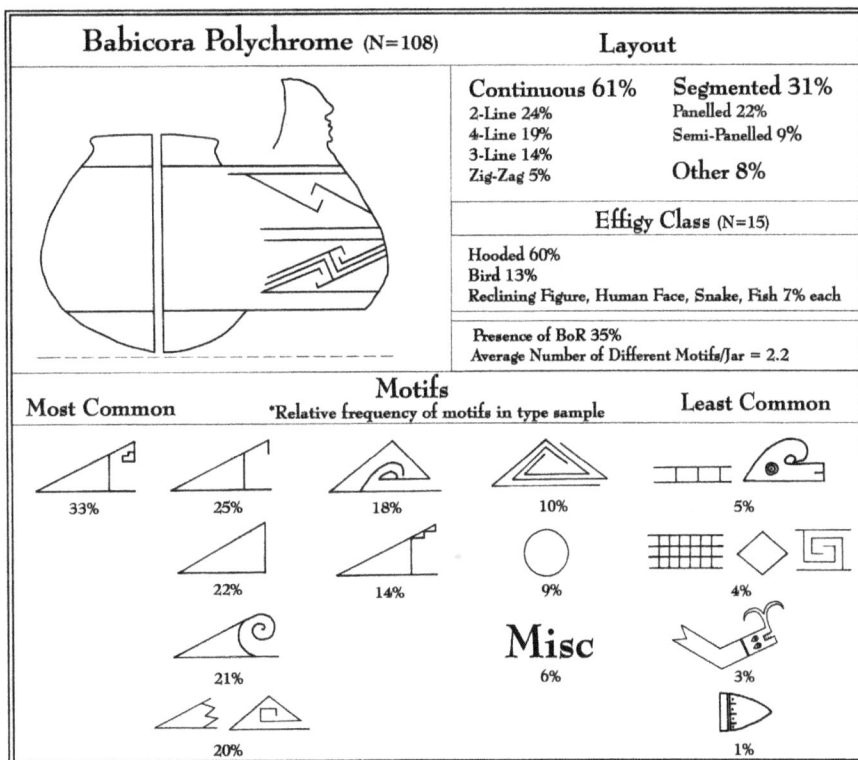

Figure 6.4 Decorative characteristics of Babícora Polychrome

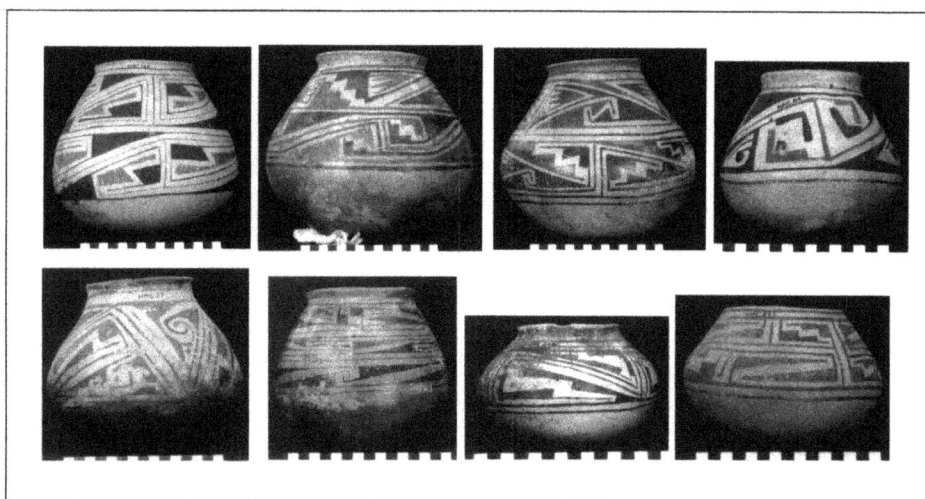

Figure 6.5a Babícora polychrome jars from the ROM decorated with Continuous layout/Simple motifs (top row - l to r - #152, #160, #162, #172, bottom row - #182, #195, #93, #97)

Figure 6.5b Babícora polychrome jars from the WPM decorated with Continuous layout/Simple motifs (top row - l to r #100, #103, #105, #111 middle row - #113, #117, #118, #122 bottom row - #163, #193, #52, #54)

Figure 6.6a Babícora polychrome jars from the ROM decorated with Segmented layout/Complex motifs (top row - l to r - #130, #154, #134, #140, middle row - #76, #136, #110, #129, bottom row - #41, #51, #56, #131)

78

Figure 6.6b Babícora polychrome jars from the WPM decorated with Segmented layout/Complex motifs (top row - l to r #162, #63, #73 bottom row - #77, #83, #97)

Figure 6.7   Babícora Effigy jars from the ROM decorated with Continuous layout/Simple motifs (top row - l to r - #28, #26, #33, #66, bottom row - #44, #63, #62)

and Carretas types by Di Peso (Di Peso et al. 1974:98; 194). The difference between these is not found in the depiction of painted elements but in the presence of textured decoration (Dublan) and the use of orange paste and black sub-glaze paint (Carretas). As a result, vessels that lack these 'defining' features are often attributed to Babícora polychrome.

Babicora B

The type description of Babícora polychrome is complicated by the presence of a second decorative style that relies on Panelled layouts filled with a significantly different range of motifs, including the CTS, "P" Triangle, and Triangular Scroll. The proliferation of these

Complex motifs (Figures 6.6a and 6.6b) coincides with the adoption of black borderlines around red designs and is very similar to the decoration used on Ramos polychrome. Twenty-six (24%) jars in the Babícora sample jars conform directly to this style, while up to thirty-four vessels incorporate just one of the defining traits (i.e., BoR).

Unlike the frequent use of multiple bands in Continuous layout/Simple motif jars, only three Babícora jars decorated with Segmented layouts contain more than one band on their surface (see Table 6.1). In combination, the Segmented layout/Complex motif/BoR style incorporated in this small sample of Babícora B jars mirrors the

79

patterns that are backbone of the Ramos decorative strategy. As with the typological overlap that occurs with Dublan and Carretas, the only noticeable difference between the Babícora and Ramos jars is the paste/surface colour (dark brown versus white).

The chameleon-like character that has been attributed to Babícora polychrome has aided the identification process of other types while simultaneously hindering the development of a more concise type definition. A comparable situation is evident from the design analysis of the museum collections, where two distinct styles are identifiable. While the majority of jars fit within a decorative style that consists of Continuous layouts, Simple motifs, and lack of black borders around red motifs, Babícora may also be typified by its stylistic opposite. This raises the question of whether the type description developed by Di Peso accurately reflects a Babícora variant of Ramos, rather than the reverse. Further discussion of the direction of development between these polychrome types will be presented within the context of outlining possible temporal and spatial models.

Effigies

The design and class patterning for Babícora effigy vessels would be better tested by a much larger sample, however, some basic trends do appear from the ROM and WPM data. Hooded effigies are the most common effigy class painted within the Continuous layout/Simple motif

style or Babícora A (Figures 6.5b [bottom row] and 6.7). The most significant variability in these jars is found in the representation of the hood rather than the painted decoration, which is similar to jars without appendages. Interestingly, the Hooded class contains one vessel shaped like an owl, suggesting that it is not restricted to human representation. A wide range of effigy classes, such as Human Face, Animal, and Snake, are also individually represented in this style of Babícora polychrome.

Hooded and Bird effigy jars are commonly found decorated with Panelled layouts and use BoR (Figures 6.6a bottom row, 6.6b #162), but show minor variations in specific motifs (i.e., Figure 6.6a #41, #51). In contrast to the limited range of birds represented in the Babícora A style, an owl, macaw, and duck (?) (Figure 6.6a #56 [beak has been broken off], #51, #41) are each found in the small sample of Babícora B. The representation of owls in both decorative styles (Figure 6.5b, #163 and Figure 6.6a #56) suggests some ideological continuity within this category.

Villa Ahumada

In the classification system developed for Chihuahua, any white-slipped jar is attributed to Villa Ahumada polychrome. The only other type with a white slip, Huerigos polychrome, is restricted to bowls and often displays a black sub-glaze paint (Di Peso et al. 1974:244-245). For this study, the results (see Figure 6.8) for the

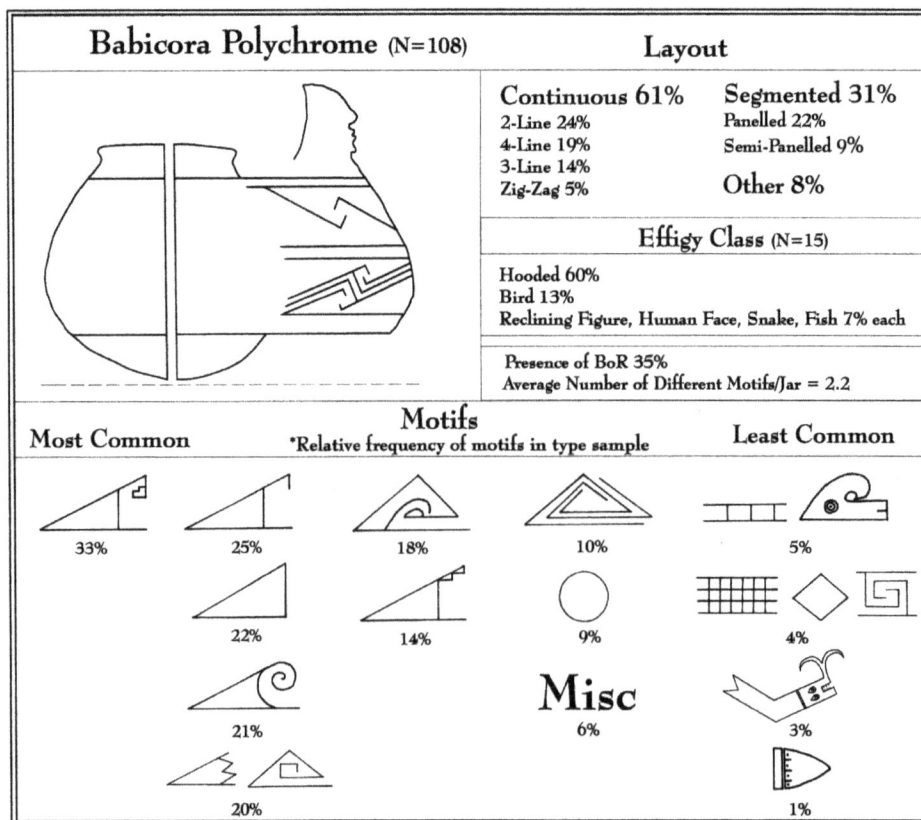

Figure 6.8 Decorative characteristics of Villa Ahumada Polychrome

white-slipped jars housed at the ROM and WPM are in direct opposition to those that define Ramos polychrome.

Villa Ahumada A

Continuous layouts, specifically focussed on 2-Line and 4-Line, are filled with triangular designs and almost never incorporate black borders around red motifs. Rectangular Scrolls represent the only motif that has a definite association with this type. These patterns are quite clear within the jars in Figures 6.9a and 6.9b. Secondary characteristics of design or form that typically recur in Villa Ahumada A are the presence of multiple band layouts on a single vessel (Table 6.1) and the addition of pairs of handles to the rim of the jar (i.e., Figure 6.9b. #129, #154, #134).

Villa Ahumada B(?)

A second style that appears infrequently within the museum sample conforms to the design parameters established for Ramos and the less common style in Babícora polychrome (Figure 6.10). The Villa Ahumada jars rely on Panelled layouts (and employ the same suite of "P" Triangles, CTS, Circles, and Macaws. With the exception of one vessel (e.g., Figure 6.10 #34) the execution on these jars is quite good (e.g., Figure 6.10 #185, #103) and show a consistent degree of decorative elaboration. One motif that appears more regularly than in the Ramos or Babícora sample is the macaw (e.g., Figure 6.10 #135, #108, #109). Whether this is attributed to sample size or is an actual characteristic of this style is uncertain.

Like Babícora polychrome, the classification of Villa Ahumada generally conforms to one decorative style. The problem is the small, but definite, cluster of vessels that share the same patterns as Ramos polychrome. One aspect of the type definition for Villa Ahumada that should be considered in conjunction with the decorative differences is the white paste. While this trait has proven to be the benchmark for classification of this type, there appears to be considerable variation (at least macroscopically) in the thickness and treatment of the slip itself. For instance, the slip on the Segmented layout/Complex motif jars (e.g., Figure 6.10 #185, #194) was much brighter and thicker than the majority of those vessels decorated in the Continuous/Simple style (e.g., Figure 6.9b #154, #191) which tend to be more of a wash than a solid background.

Effigies

The decoration on the Hooded and Animal effigies reflects the same patterns of the two styles identified for Villa Ahumada jars (see Figures 6.9b bottom row, 6.10 WPM #185, ROM #103, #34, 6.11). One important source of variation in the effigies is that there is no apparent standard form for the human heads placed on the Hooded effigies, nor for the decoration of the jars beneath them (i.e., Figure 6.9b #130, #160, #191; Figure 6.10 #32, #29). In addition to the only representation of fish

(Figure 6.11 #60), the Villa Ahumada sample also contains a turtle (#61), dog (#101), and frog? (#104) effigy. The macaw effigy (Figure 6.11 #52) represents the only non-Ramos, non-Segmented layout/Complex motif jar in the entire study. The use of multiple bands is also present in the effigy jars (Figures 6.9b #191 and 6.11 #29).

The few effigies decorated with the Villa Ahumada B style display a similar range of effigy classes to Villa Ahumada A (see Tables 5.10 and 5.11). Single examples of Hooded (Figure 6.10 #34), Animal (#103 - bear), and Bird (WPM #185 - double-headed quail) effigies suggest a fairly broad use of subject matter for this type. A nearly identical double-headed quail vessel was examined in the collection of Mr. Ken Burlingham of El Paso during the summer of 1999. Given the sample size, the only other differences between the effigies are attributed to the design execution (i.e., Figure 6.10 #34, poor execution) and basic vessel form.

Formal Patterning in the Polychrome Types

In addition to the presence of multiple bands, several general trends can be identified that appear to vary in accordance with type or Design Horizon categories. Based on the data in Appendix A, the average jar height for Babícora (16.1cm) and Villa Ahumada Jar (15.8cm) is very comparable, while that of Ramos polychrome jars is greater (18.5cm). In comparing the vertical section (Table 6.2), Ramos differs from the other types in the high frequency of ovoid jars. As discussed in Chapter II, this ovoid shape is often referred to as the 'classic' form in the Chihuahuan tradition (see Figure 2.14). Interestingly, the use of sub-conoidal bases is very comparable between Ramos and Villa Ahumada, the two most divergently decorated types in the design analysis. This brief discussion of formal characteristics suggests that the comparison of decoration and shape characteristics is a viable avenue for future research.

Comparison with Paquimé Collection

Discussion of the whole vessel data from Paquimé is included for two reasons. First, these jars were the source data from which Di Peso developed the type descriptions used throughout Chihuahuan archaeology. Since this classification system was used for the ROM and WPM collections, the jars from the museum and Paquimé contexts are defined according to the same descriptive assumptions. The second, and perhaps more important reason for incorporating this data set, is that it is from a well-described archaeological context. By contrasting with an excavated sample, we can begin to examine the cultural implications of decorative patterning found in the museum jars.

The rank order of polychrome types between the museum and Paquimé samples are the same, however, the proportion of each type is markedly different: Ramos

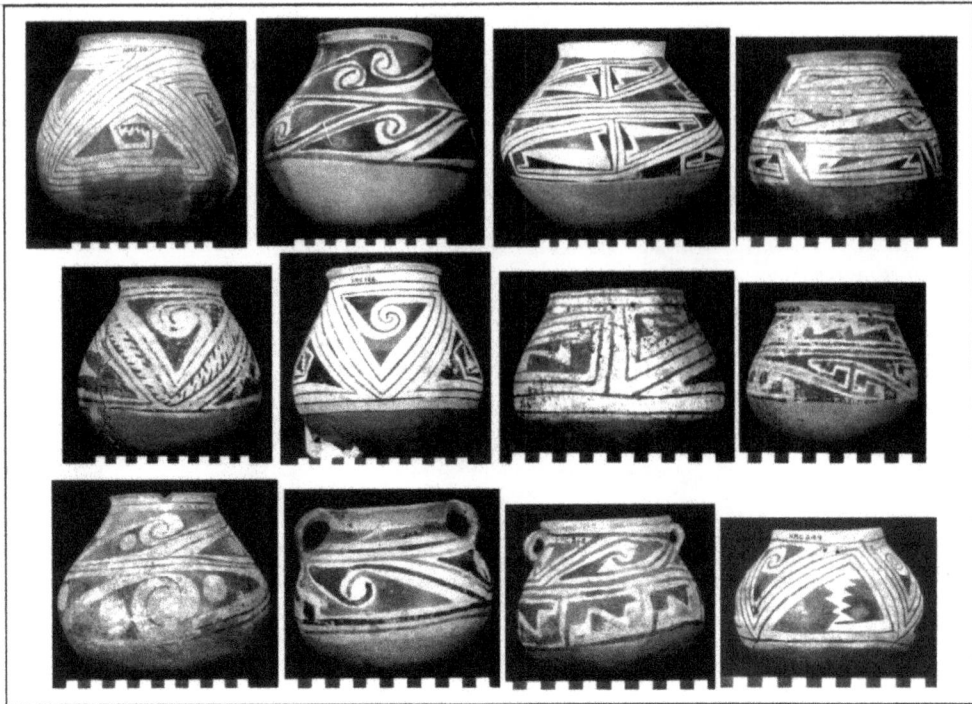

Figure 6.9a Villa Ahumada jars from the ROM decorated with Continuous layout/Simple motifs (top row - l to r - #144, #161, #185, #170, middle row - #178, #186, #175, #169, bottom row - #181, #194, #190, #171)

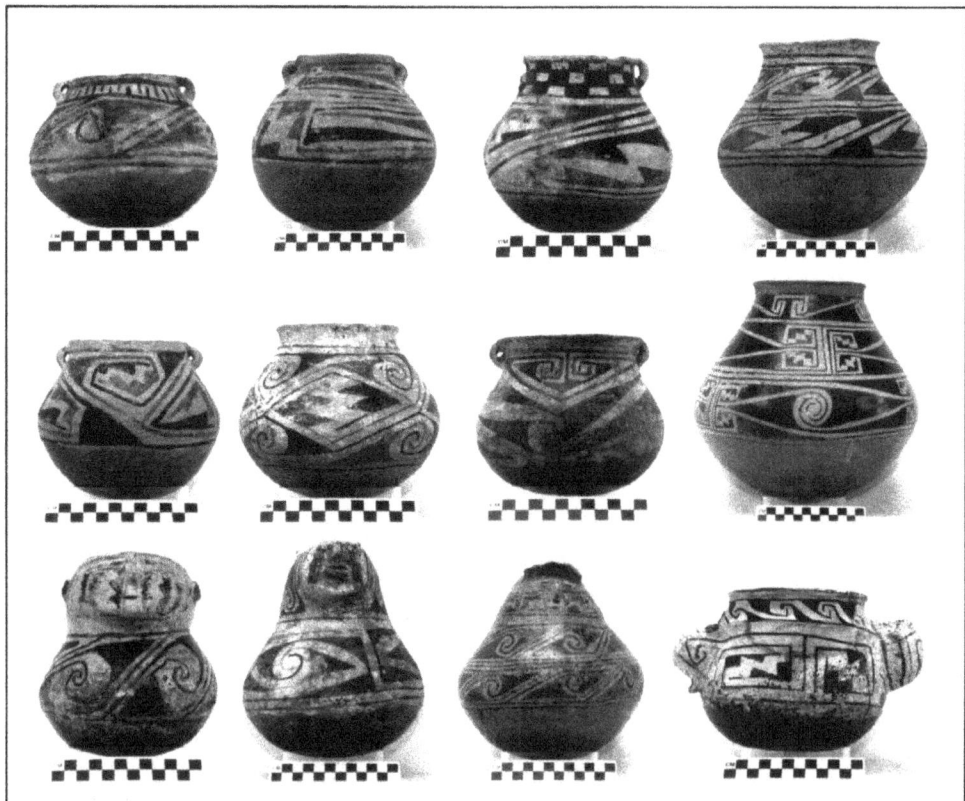

Figure 6.9b Villa Ahumada jars and effigies from the WPM decorated with Continuous layout/Simple motifs (top row - l to r #128, #154, #134, #139, middle row - #140, #143, #144, #189, bottom row - #130, #160, #191, #157

Figure 6.10 Villa Ahumada jars from the WPM and ROM decorated with Segmented layout/Complex motifs (top row - l to r - WPM #13, #135, #204, #194, #185, bottom row - ROM #108, #109, #103, #34)

Figure 6.11 Villa Ahumada Effigy jars from the ROM decorated with Continuous layout/Simple motifs (top row - l to r - #60, #61, #101, bottom row - #32, #29, #104, #52)

(ROM/WPM - 44% to Paquimé - 75%), Babícora (30% to 15%), and Villa Ahumada (26% to 10%) (see Tables 5.1 and 5.18). A cursory evaluation of the sherd count from Paquimé reveals a similar pattern with Ramos at 11.6%, Babícora at 1.5%, and Villa Ahumada constituting 1.3% of the total number of sherds recovered (Di Peso et al. 1974a). This evidence clearly emphasizes the importance of Ramos polychrome over any other painted ware found at Paquimé.

Layouts on Ramos and Babícora from Paquimé display comparable patterns to the same types at the ROM and WPM. Ramos jars decorated in the Segmented style (75%, most being Panelled [53%]), and Babícora jars associated with Continuous layouts (61%) illustrate this point. The Babícora from both Paqimé and the museum sample are also infrequently decorated with Segmented style designs. This similarity is contrasted with the results

for Villa Ahumada which show a greater association with Segmented style layouts (43%). Excluding the large number of Snake effigies, the distribution, type and layout association of the remaining effigy classes corresponds to the jars from the museum sample.

The ceramic remains from Paquimé are weighted towards Ramos polychrome and, often regardless of type, the use of Panelled or Semi-Panelled layouts. However, the overlapping styles present in the museum sample seem to correspond to the general descriptions of type variants. Further discussion of the variant concept and its utility for archaeological research is required before we attempt to explain the reason for this overlap.

Di Peso's Variants and the Museum Sample
Trait overlap has been a significant issue throughout the study of Chihuahuan polychrome ceramics. Simple

descriptions provided by Carey, Brand, Sayles, and Gladwin narrowed the immense variation in the Chihuahuan tradition into identifiable and 'useable' types. Problems began with the publication of Di Peso's analysis of the sherd and whole vessel remains recovered from Paquimé. The once 'clear' type descriptions devised through the research in the 1930s became clouded by a remarkable degree of decorative overlap. To compensate for this problem, Di Peso proposed to further divide the assemblage into smaller, inter-related categories such as the Paquimé and Ramos variants of Babícora and Villa Ahumada polychromes. Essentially, both of these variants are decorated in the same manner as Ramos but with a darker paste colour or white slip. Since the ceramic definitions established by Di Peso were used to classify the ROM and WPM pots, it is not surprising that comparable 'variants' are present. Babícora and Villa Ahumada share two distinct styles A and B, with the less common style (B) conforming to the basic characteristics of Ramos. This mirrors the patterns produced in the Paquimé and Ramos variants of Babícora and Villa Ahumada identified by Di Peso. That such a pattern should repeat in two unrelated whole vessel analyses requires us to consider two important questions. First, if not for the differences in paste colour, would the Babícora jars have been classified as Ramos? And, more importantly, do Di Peso's original variant categories contribute to our knowledge of the development and processes that occurred within the Chihuahuan culture? Instead of simply recognizing the existence of such overlap, we need to account for the considerable decorative similarity between these types.

The Problem of Paste

One of the key traits traditionally employed to separate pottery types is the paste used to construct the pot. Paste has often provided a key marker in identifying points of cultural change or variation in an assemblage. Braun's (1985) research on grit and shell temper in Eastern Woodlands pottery is perhaps one of the most successful examples whereby differences in ceramic materials are shown to reflect diachronic change across a long time span and a broad geographical area. The situation in Chihuahua, however, has yet to show any significant patterning in material other than the association of Ramos with white clay, Babícora with brown clay, Villa Ahumada with a brown clay (and white slip), and other types such as Carretas with orange clay. Obviously, differences in clay source, firing, and use will effect the final hue of each vessel body; however, should comparably decorated vessels be slotted into different types based on differences in paste or surface colour? Graves' ethnographic work with the Kalinga (1991:114-116) questioned whether paste colour should influence classification at all, and that design was a much better aspect of variation to understand differences in an assemblage. Based on this perspective we can put considerations of paste colour aside and focus solely on the overlap found in the design analysis. It is argued that the shared decorative traits present on white or brown jars will more likely yield a better understanding of commonly-held cultural structures than is obtained through divisions based on paste/surface colour.

DESIGN HORIZONS IN THE CHIHUAHUAN TRADITION

The solution proposed here is to temporarily disregard differences of paste colour and consider the implications of using the design horizon concept. As defined previously, a design horizon is identified through the co-occurrence of two or more decorative characteristics across multiple types in a ceramic assemblage. Using the data from the museum samples, Design Horizon A is comprised of the Continuous layouts, Simple motifs, NoBoR, and few motifs per vessel (Figures 6.12 top row). Jars that are decorated with Segmented layouts, show an increased reliance on Complex motifs, an affinity for BoR, and three to four different motifs per vessel, are therefore classified as Design Horizon B (Figure 6.12 bottom row). For the individual polychrome types, Babícora and Villa Ahumada are therefore represented in Design Horizon A and B (WPM #124, ROM #131), while Ramos is restricted to Design Horizon B (WPM #167, #73, ROM #122, #123, #37). Returning briefly to the issue of diagnostic traits, we can clarify the role of black borderlines around red motifs (BoR) in making type associations. David Phillips's suggestion (1999, personal communication) that this trait is directly related to Ramos polychrome is, for the most part, correct. The problem is that black borderlines are also typical of Design Horizon B examples of Babícora and Villa Ahumada polychrome. For this reason, the presence of BoR is better seen as a Design Horizon marker, rather than an indicator of type.

Shifting the focus to the level of Design Horizon allows more freedom to explore new reasons for the variation evident in the Chihuahuan tradition. As discussed in Chapter III, explanations for these trends are considered here within models of temporal and spatial variation, as well as the implications of decorative standardization and complexity to cultural development.

Is There Temporal Variation?

The test of temporal change devised for this study is based on the identification of decorative structures that correspond with the archaeological evidence known prior to and near the end of the Medio period. Pottery design in the Viejo period, which is dominated by lines and chevron motifs, represents the marker of an early 'style' in the Chihuahuan tradition. The whole vessels recovered from Paquimé are used as the 'later' boundary within the tradition. Close parallels are readily identifiable from the museum sample. Design Horizon A is similar to Viejo period decorative structure in the use of line-based designs and the small range of basic motifs. By

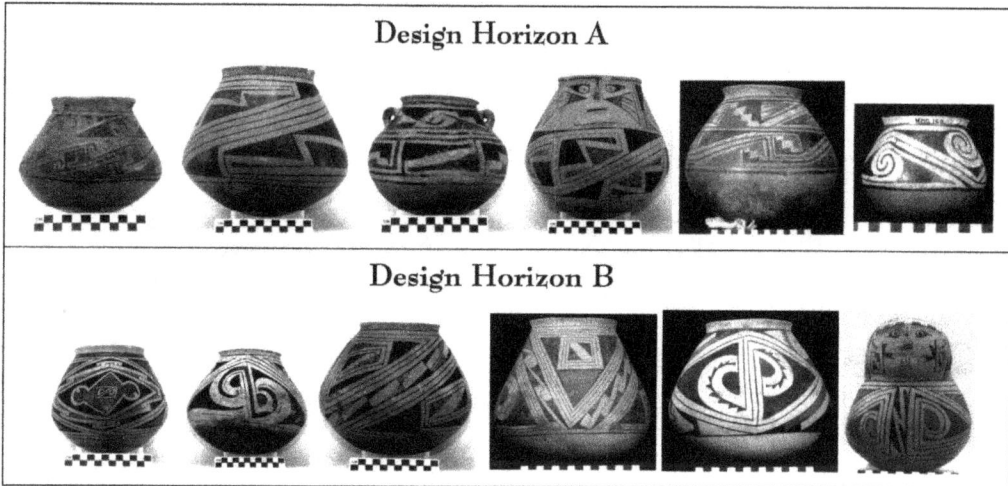

Figure 6.12 Polychrome jars decorated representing Design Horizons A and B from the WPM and ROM (top row - l to r WPM #110 [Babicora], #116[Babicora], #146 [Villa Ahumada], #177[Ramos], ROM#160[Babicora], #167[Villa Ahumada], bottom row - WPM #167[Ramos], #124[Villa Ahumada], #73[Babicora], #122[Ramos], #123[Ramos], #37[Ramos])

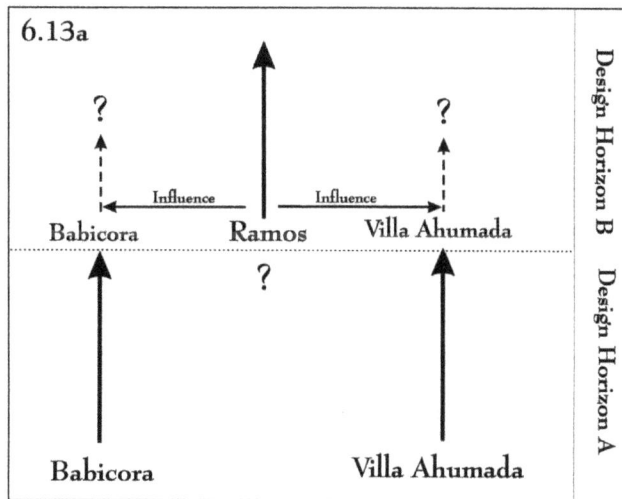

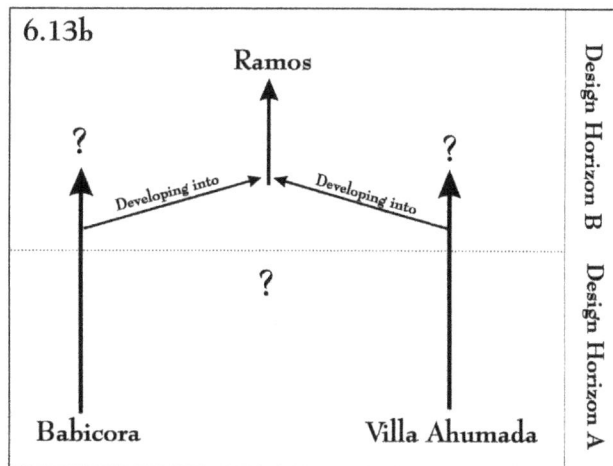

Figure 6.13a-b Models of temporal development and direction of influence of the Chihuahuan polychrome types using the design horizon concept

comparison, Design Horizon B shares a nearly identical pattern in the range and frequency of layouts (Panelled), type association (mostly Ramos), and also the use of black-outlined red motifs found at Paquimé. By combining the museum and the archaeological information, we are presented with the initial basis for identifying decorative markers of temporal variation: the earliest pottery in the Medio period proper is associated with continuous line-based layouts and triangle-based motifs appended to the design structure; this eventually gives way or evolves into a greatly elaborated style composed of a diverse range of motifs employed within vertically-divided design fields. These differences offer the basis for establishing temporal signifiers within this 250-year span of cultural development and can be examined for their impact on understanding the diachronic ordering of each polychrome type, effigy class, and decorative evolution.

Temporal Change: Polychrome Types

A potential order of type development can be examined from the temporal association of each Design Horizon. Contrary to Di Peso's view of unilateral type development, the decoration on Babícora, Ramos, and Villa Ahumada suggests that each type is associated with a particular era in the Medio period sequence. The high frequency of Design Horizon A decoration in both Babícora and Villa Ahumada indicates that these types are earlier in the Medio period. By contrast, few Babícora and Villa Ahumada jars are decorated with Design Horizon B, while nearly all Ramos jars exhibit this style. Since this pattern mirrors the type frequencies and design characteristics from Paquimé, Ramos likely represents a later type within the ceramic sequence.

The horizon dichotomy presented for these types is complicated by the fact that Babícora and Villa Ahumada both display a small percentage of Design Horizon B jars in the museum sample. If we use the argument that the Design Horizons are separated in time, Babícora and Villa Ahumada must be viewed as having considerable time depth. The number of Design Horizon A vessels in these types suggests that this style was replaced in favour of the decorative structures employed by the artisans making Ramos polychrome (see Figure 6.13a). Borrowing from Lyman, O'Brien, and Dunnell's (1997:113) suggestion that varieties or variants of pottery types may represent transitional forms in a sequence, we must consider the possibility that Ramos is actually a variant of Babícora polychrome, instead of the other way around. Regardless of the actual relationships between these types, Ramos still represents the pinnacle of decorative complexity. Figure 6.13b illustrates this developmental trajectory, where changes in Babícora and Villa Ahumada evolve into Ramos polychrome. Since there is no evidence of a Ramos A (other than the odd example using a Continuous layout) its origin in the sequence is uncertain.

Returning to the original sequence suggested by Sayles (see Figure 2.9), the results from the museum sample indicate some strong parallels of temporal development within the Chihuahuan ceramic tradition. Using the painted wares as our guide, we now have the basic grounds for identifying an Early and Late phase for the Medio occupation, with Babícora and Villa Ahumada made at an earlier date than Ramos polychrome. It is impossible to determine from the data whether the smaller proportion of Design Horizon B in Villa Ahumada reflects the actual amount of this type produced during the later part of the Medio sequence. However, if these patterns are discovered from archaeologically-derived materials, this new information will counter Di Peso's conclusion that the polychrome types are contemporary from the beginning of the Medio period to its collapse two-hundred and fifty years later.

Temporal Change among Effigy Classes

Effigy vessels show little decorative differentiation as a sub-set of the jar shape and, therefore, fit nicely within the Design Horizons identified for the entire museum sample. Examination of the range, frequency, and depiction of each effigy class between these Design Horizons (Figure 6.14) provides little concrete evidence of temporal change. Only two classes, Reclining Figure and Fish, are not represented in Design Horizon B, while the rest are found at least once in both Horizons. Due to the small sample size it is difficult to say if these pots are truly representative, but we can state with some confidence that the Hooded effigy was commonly used throughout the Medio period. The frequency of Bird effigies within the Late phase suggests greater use, however the remaining classes are equally represented. In comparison with the effigies from Paquimé, which also have at least one example of each effigy class, all of the Hooded, Bird, Animal, and Human Face jars are affiliated with Design Horizon B (i.e., Ramos, BoR, Panelled). Interestingly, these classes are outnumbered by Snake vessels decorated with Miscellaneous layouts, yet these are rarely encountered in the museum sample.

The most significant evidence for temporal variation from the individual effigy classes are the Ramos polychrome macaw effigies (Figure 6.15). These effigies are distinguished not only by the Design Horizon B painted characteristics, which include an increased number and standardized combination of motifs per vessel, but also by the manner in which the macaws are depicted. Either single head/tail, double head/tail, or entire bird appendage combinations are used, but the actual macaw is usually painted with the same style: red head, round eyes with a central dot, tongue extended from beak that is (usually) painted black. Evidence of painted macaws from the ROM and WPM, may also represent non-appended forms of this effigy class (Figure 6.15, bottom row). The reason for singling out these vessels is that macaws played an important role at Paquimé and throughout Medio period sites, as evidenced by the presence of burials, breeding

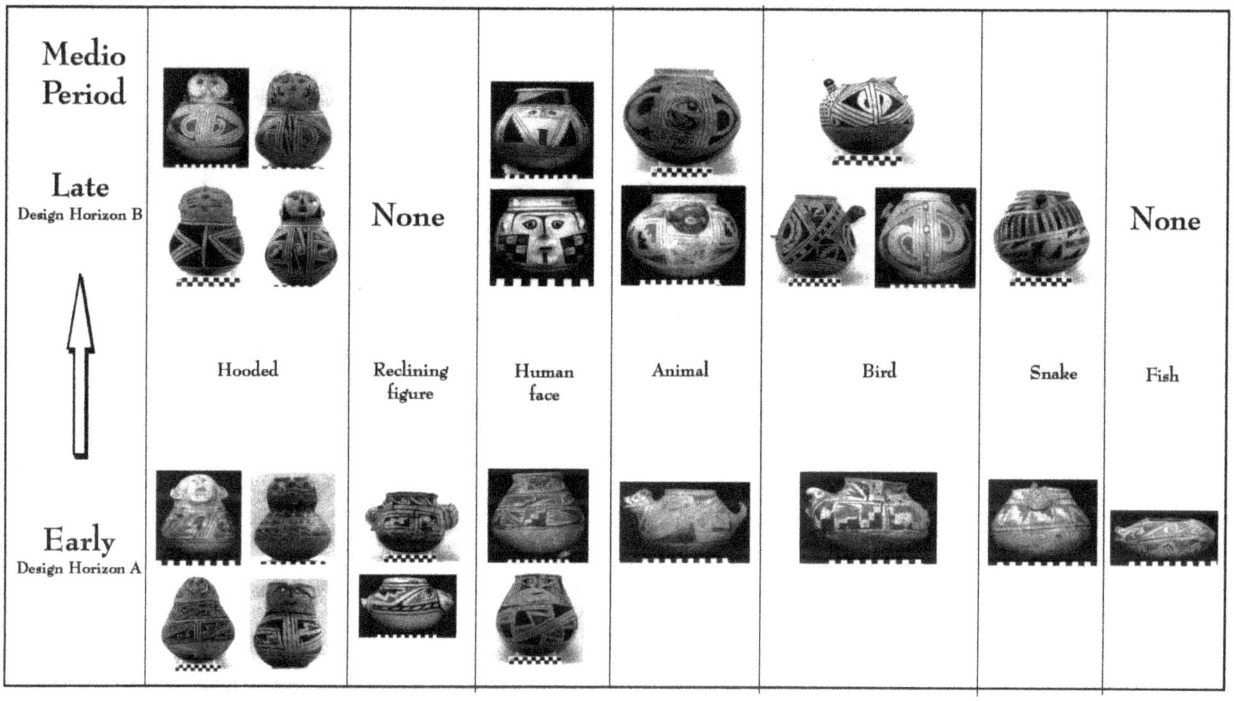

Figure 6.14 Comparison of effigy classes between Design Horizons A and B from the museum sample

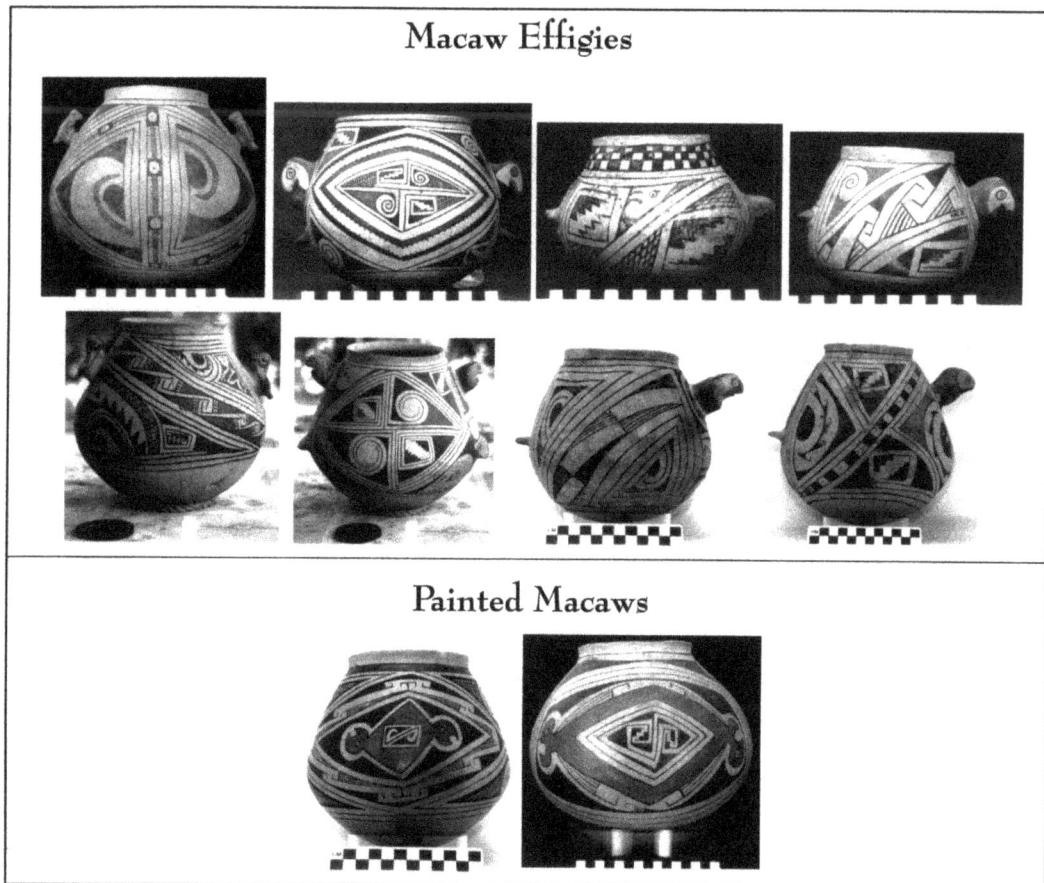

Figure 6.15 Macaw effigies and painted macaw designs (top row - l to r - ROM #102, #54, #51, #53, middle row - Naylor collection, Naylor collection, WPM #168, #166,bottom row - WPM #167, ROM #50)

pens, and the circular entrance stones (Minnis et al. 1993). Combined with the design analysis presented here, the sudden proliferation and standardization of this effigy class within Design Horizon B is perhaps indicative of an increased socio-economic importance of this animal to local inhabitants, or even as a marker of when the bird was first brought into the area. Using the temporal model presented in this discussion, any direct correlation between decorative patterning and time for the macaw effigies is complicated by the single Villa Ahumada macaw jar decorated with Design Horizon A (see Figure 6.14, bottom row, third from right). More data is required to test the validity of this association; however, for the time being, there is enough evidence to support the idea that these effigies represent a later phenomenon in the Chihuahuan sequence.

Evolution of the Chihuahuan Decorative Tradition

The association of museum jars with an Early or Late phase is the first step towards understanding the variation in the ceramic assemblage. Taking this information one step further, it is unlikely that the Design Horizons are isolated in time, and we can begin to examine a developmental sequence or flow from one style into the other. The Design Horizons identified in this study are not differentiated by single characteristics, but by the combination of different decorative features on more than one design level. Following this logic, the decorative overlap that has plagued our comprehension of the Chihuahuan tradition can now be used positively to look for incremental changes between the Design Horizons (i.e., for Design Horizon A jars with BoR, and Design Horizon B jars with Simple motifs, lacking BoR).

At a broad level, it is feasible to posit a simple evolutionary trajectory of structural layouts as moving from 2-Line through to Panelled (Figure 6.16). While there are multiple variations within each layout class the basic progression between these extremes is not that difficult to grasp. The first alteration is the movement towards a vertical division of the design field, ultimately resulting in the formation of Panelled structures (Figure 6.17a). Precursors of this vertical division are found in 4-Line layouts, however, these divisions do not touch the upper and lower borderlines, and the design is repeated upwards of five times around the vessel surface. The trademark of the Segmented style is a vertical partition of the design field into two sides and further division of the area into four parts. The second change is the appearance and elaboration of a secondary band that runs through the middle of the layout (Figure 6.17b). Creation of this open space within the Line-based layouts is isolated and eventually filled with motifs in Zig-Zag, Semi-Panelled, and Panelled layouts. It should be pointed out that the decoration of this band is not always presented in Design Horizon B, however, it is a feature that does not occur within Design Horizon A jars.

The frequency of motifs within this projected evolution of design layout also produces some fairly conclusive patterning of a temporal sequence (Figure 6.16). Earlier motifs are those that interact well with, or are easily appended to, the structural lines of a Continuous layout, such as Scrolled Triangles, Barbed figures, and Stepped Triangles. Rectangular Scrolls are similarly incorporated into this Design Horizon representing the only Complex motif used with any regularity at this stage of stylistic development. By contrast, jars corresponding to the latter part of the Medio period are dominated by motifs constructed of multiple lines (i.e., "P" Triangle, Triangular Scrolls, and CTS), showing a much greater affinity for life designs (Macaw, Zoomorph, Feather), and other basic motifs (Circles). From the perspective of design construction, these motifs are well-adapted to fill the design field constructed in Segmented layouts. Other motifs, such as Triangles, Circles, and Macaws, are employed to fill secondary bands or vertical panels (see Figure 6.17a-b).

Not all motifs can be associated with a single era in Chihuahuan prehistory. Several motifs are universally common (Triangles, Hooked Triangles, and Hooked Stepped Triangles) or rare (Diamonds, Spirals, Checkers) in the museum sample. Another feature that bridges the formal boundaries between Design Horizon A and Design Horizon B, is the application of black borders around red motifs. This trait appears in association with some Design Horizon A vessels and is suddenly adopted *en masse* by Chihuahuan potters in the later style. More detailed investigation of the use of black outlines is required to determine if this trait is found associated with a suite of motifs or is simply a new technique that was popularly employed in Design Horizon B.

Spatial Variation in the Chihuahuan Tradition

It was suggested by Di Peso that the decorative variation in the Chihuhauan tradition is not the result of temporal differences. If we are to follow this line of reasoning, then we must consider the existence of regional styles. Following the survey and archaeological data compiled for the polychrome types, which suggests that each is associated with a specific region in Chihuahua (i.e., Babicora-south, Ramos-north/central, Villa Ahumada-east), we can apply the design horizon information to the issue of space. Two distinct 'regions' can be identified from the design analysis. The first 'style zone' is associated with the southern and eastern reaches of the Chihuahuan culture and is characterized by Design Horizon A. A second style zone, identified through the repeated production of vessels painted in Design Horizon B, is centered along the Río Casas Grandes and the site of Paquimé to the north and west of the other groups (Figure 6.18).

The most significant problem with the regional association of decorative styles is the overlap of Design

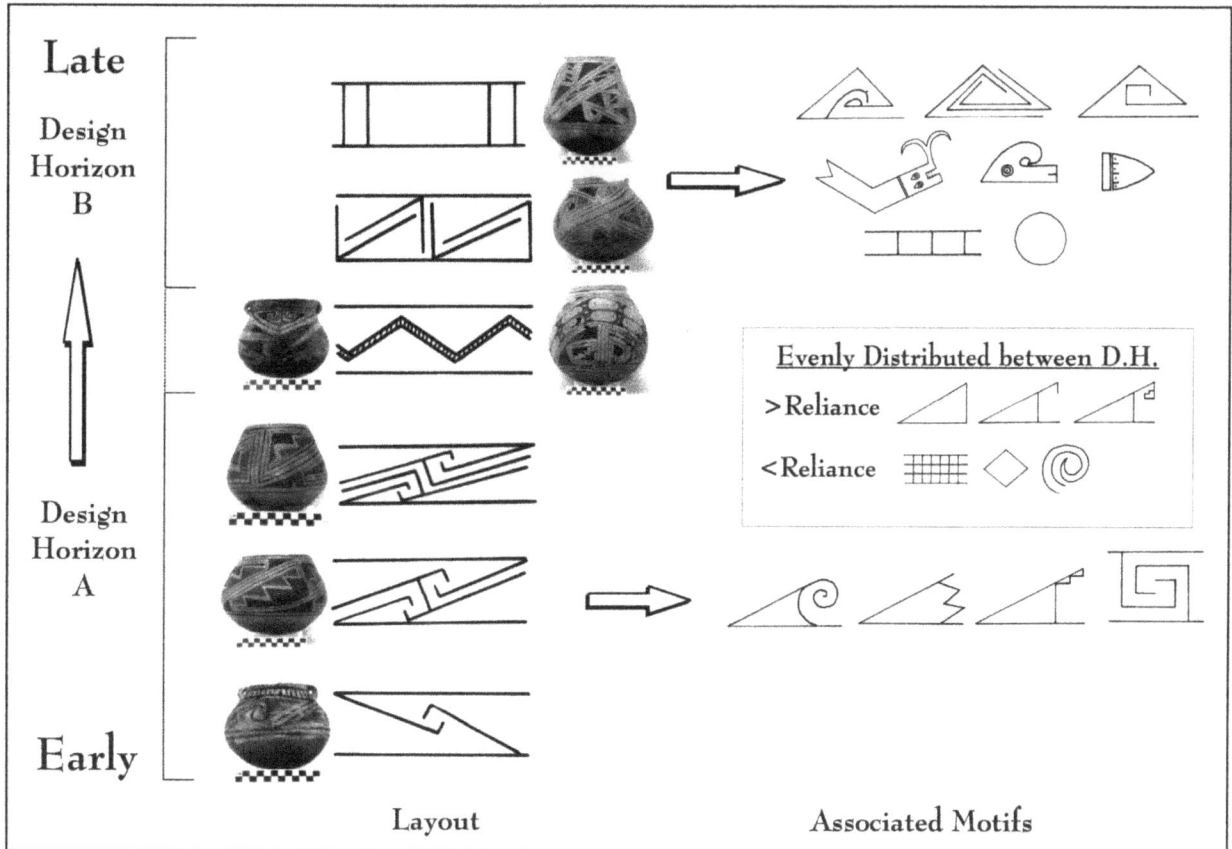

Figure 6.16 Proposed development of layout through Design Horizon A and B with associated motifs (top to bottom WPM #187, #63, #188, #52, #117, #144)

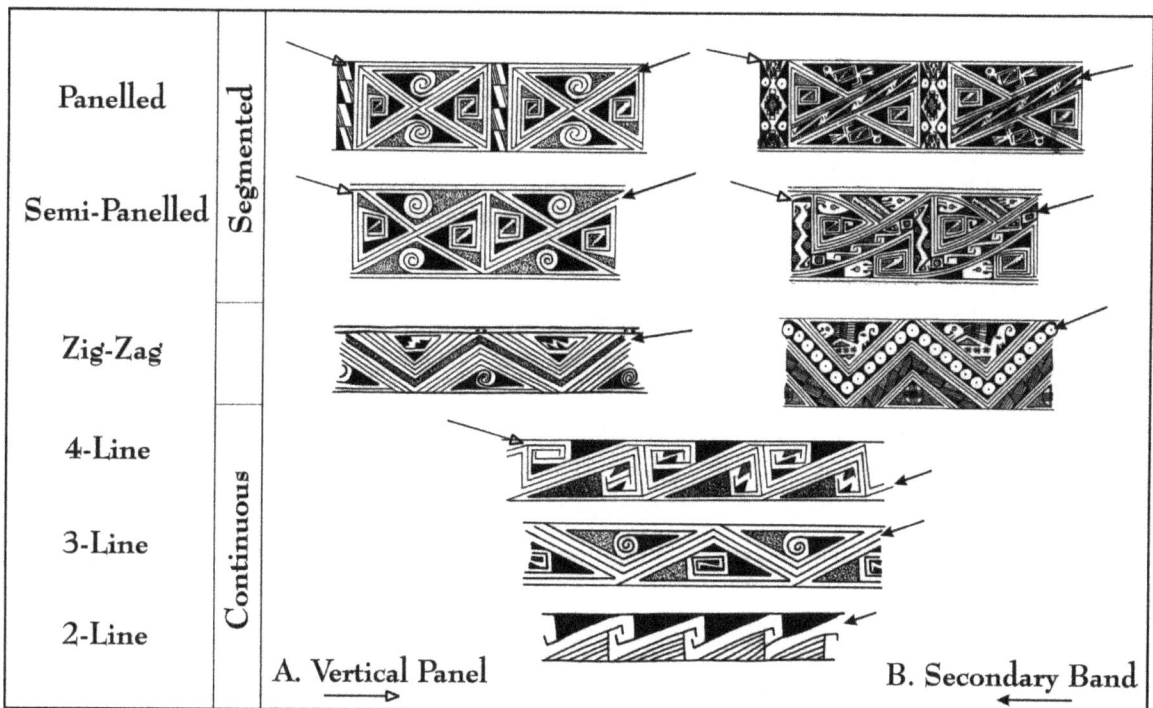

Figure 6.17a-b Evolution of the vertical division (Panelled layout) and secondary bands in the Chihuahuan polychrome tradition (bands adapted from Di Peso et al. 1974a:262, 267, 272, 273, 308)

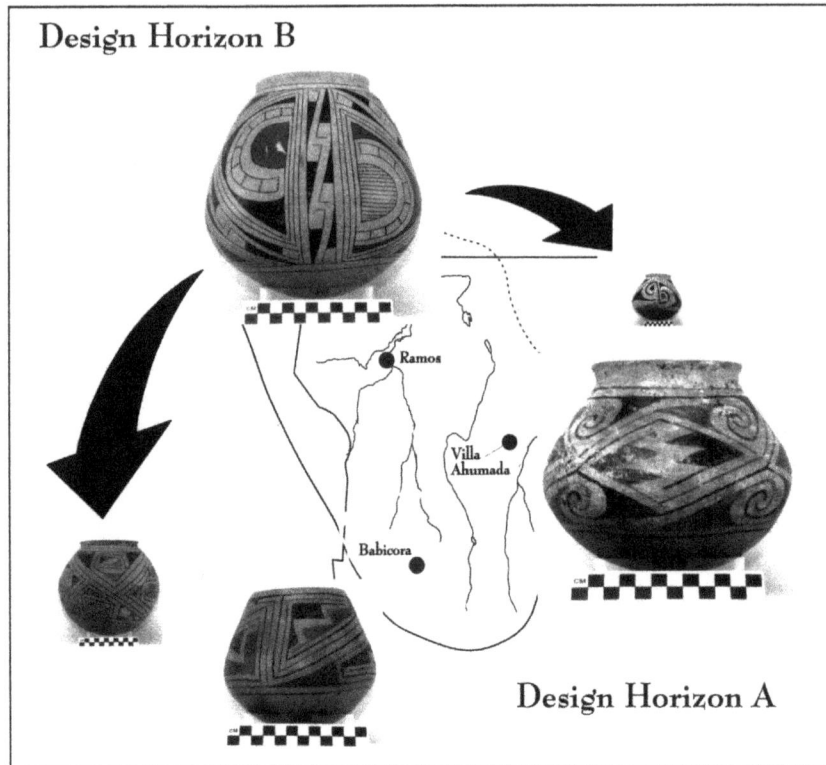

Figure 6.18 Regional distribution of polychrome types and Design Horizons in each area. Arrows demarcate relative proportion of Design Horizon B moving from Ramos into Babicora and Villa Ahumada

Horizons between the types. One potential solution is perceived through the adoption of interaction theory, where the less common variations within each type represent the borrowing or exchange of decorative ideas from another. Due to the infrequent occurrence of Design Horizon A in Ramos polychrome, the direction of influence appears to be predominantly one-way: Panelled layouts, CTS, "P" Triangle, and life figure motifs moving from the central region into the south and east. In this model, these decorative ideas spread out from the 'core' area and represent imitations or adaptations of the style used on Ramos polychrome. In the unlikely event that the museum sample reflects a true proportion of Design Horizons in each type, the higher ratio of Design Horizon B for Babícora in this study suggests that the people to the south had more contact with the producers of Ramos polychrome. The implication of this result is important since one of the proposed sources of Villa Ahumada polychrome, the Galeana site, is considerably closer to Paquimé than any site that is dominated by Babícora.

Obviously, these spatial interpretations are limited by the lack of provenience information for the museum sample and by whether the sample is a true representation of the relative frequency of each type. However, given the very large distribution of Chihuahuan culture, the likelihood that some form of regional patterning is buried within the ceramic assemblage must be considered.

Regional Distribution of Effigy Vessels

There is little evidence to suggest that the individual effigy classes are differentially distributed through space according to the comparison of Design Horizon and type. On a general level, the greatest variation between the effigies lies in the actual shape or subject matter of the appendages or hoods and the designs used to paint these additions (see Figure 6.14). Because of the sample size from both the museum (see Table 5.10) and Paquimé (see Table 5.19) contexts, it is impossible to tell if the frequency of effigies is typical of each type; however, the comparison of Design Horizon and effigy class produces minor variations that may reflect regional choices. Combining both the museum and excavated samples, the Fish jar is the only class restricted to Babícora polychrome and Design Horizon A, and may be associated with a southern distribution. A more likely geographical distinction is the association of the macaw Bird effigies with the style used in the area around Paquimé. The association of macaw jars with the sites around Paquimé is important because of the evidence of macaw breeding pens, burials, and the numerous painted renditions included by Di Peso in the ceramic volume (see Di Peso et al. 1974a:263-274). If this painted sample reflects a 'true' representation of the frequency of macaw depictions on Paquimé jars, then we have evidence of physical and decorative 'control' over this bird at the site.

Cultural Impulses in Decorative Variation

The final aspect of this design analysis is to consider the implications of two decorative trends, standardization and complexity, within the context of cultural development and individual agency or choice in Chihuahua.

Standardization

From the perspective of the ceramic tradition, the Design Horizons broadly reflect specific choices made by a group or groups of potters using the same style unit pool or symbolic reservoir. As Di Peso argued in the report from Paquimé, the Chihuahuan tradition represents a 'school' of production that was maintained throughout the Medio period. While this thesis might dispute the existence of a school and aspects of temporal development presented by Di Peso, there is a definite standardization that links the Design Horizons. Such standardization becomes more apparent at the level of type, as each polychrome type shows a marked degree of decorative homogeneity, at least within the Design Horizon. The most obvious case of standardized representation from the design analysis is found on the Ramos polychrome jars. Both the museum and Paquimé examples of Ramos utilize the Panelled layout and one of every two jars incorporates the CTS or "P" Triangle motifs. Based on the assumption that Design Horizon B is associated with the apex of cultural development in Chihuahua, it is likely that these jars were being produced for a specific purpose and by a specific group of individuals. The use of this style on Babícora and Villa Ahumada jars indicates that the standardization of Design Horizon B is more widespread than Paquimé. If this style is being produced at distant locations it suggests that some form of craft specialization took place. A useful test of the regional implications of this process would be to incorporate vessel shape and size into the analysis of design. This form of study would enable us to determine whether vessel size or shape predetermines the kind of decoration applied to the exterior (i.e., larger motifs, such as CTS, are more difficult to incorporate onto smaller design fields). As mentioned in the discussion of type definitions, the regularity of vessel form in Ramos offers an excellent means to evaluate the standardization that occurs in the decoration of this type.

Complexity

A second trend within the polychrome tradition is the increased decorative complexity defined in the progression from Design Horizon A to B. Following the temporal sequence, the Continuous layout/Simple motif style found in Babícora and Villa Ahumada develops into, or is eventually eclipsed by, vessels decorated with the Segmented layout /Complex motifs/ BoR associated with Ramos polychrome. If we look at the presence of large sites (i.e., Paquimé) in the area associated with Ramos polychrome, we may see this change as the result of an increase in economic activity or social complexity in the central part of the Chihuahuan culture area. A second possible explanation related to this increased complexity is that the new style represents group affiliation. Hardin (1991:46-49) noted this process in her ethnohistoric research on Zuni pottery, which experienced a major florescence of artistry during the 1880s. The complexity of design and number of different motifs during this period represented an apex for the tradition and was associated with a period of strong tribal identity. Zuni people were distinguishing themselves from other Puebloan groups through their decorative style. The disintegration of this painted tradition was brought about by the abandonment of traditional pottery in favour of metal pots (Ibid.:51-54). Design Horizon B within the Chihuahuan tradition may represent a similar era focussing on group identity or status. In contrast with slow deterioration of the Zuni tradition, the prehistoric sequence from Chihuahua gives us no indication of a similar decrease in decorative elaboration. This may be attributed to the sacking and abandonment of the site of Paquimé and the subsequent collapse of the entire socio-economic web based on this cultural hub.

A second aspect of complexity that can be discussed within the museum data actually appears within the guise of standardization. While Design Horizon B jars illustrate a significant degree of standardization of motifs and layouts, the variety of different Panelled layouts and "P" Triangle motifs provide intriguing possibilities for the study of regional styles or individual agency.

Complexity in Layouts: Panelled

Design Horizon B is dominated by the Panelled layout; however, on closer inspection it is apparent that the number of ways that the design is executed is remarkably varied. Based on the classification devised by Di Peso, which identified forty-seven variations of the Panelled layout, this study recorded twenty-three variations within this single layout class (see Appendix A). What links these jars together is the presence of a common layout incorporating two distinct panels. The primary difference between these jars is found in the further division of the field into smaller zones and the motifs used to fill them. Such variation may be indicative of shorter temporal phases or represents groups of potters or individuals in different parts of the Chihuahuan culture area. A study focussed on this variety would no doubt produce useful insights that may reveal further patterning of motif association.

Complexity in Motifs: "P" Triangle

Of all the motifs recorded for the museum sample, the only design that demonstrates any significant variety in depiction is the "P" Triangle. Normally found in conjunction with Panelled layouts, this motif varies in colour balance, use of hatching, and the addition of secondary elements such as ticks, triangles, and eyes. The end result is that at least twenty-seven and forty-seven different incarnations of the "P" Triangle are found in the ROM and WPM samples respectively, and comparable variations were also noted in Di Peso's study of the Paquimé assemblage (Figure 6.19). The complexity in motif construction and elaboration offers an excellent opportunity to establish important geographical trends or identify patterns that could be attributed to production locales or individual potters (where the provenience of the vessel is known). The complex nature of this design is made more apparent through its formal similarities to the Macaw and Zoomorph (specifically Plumed Serpent) motifs. Discussion of the relationship, origin and direction of evolution between these motifs is beyond the scope of this thesis but has been investigated by the author (Hendrickson 2000). Further examination of the diversity found in both the Panelled layouts and "P" Triangles needs to be undertaken if we are to eventually perceive variation at a level nearing a production center or individual painter.

Broader Implications: Variation through Time and Space

A more realistic perspective for the overlap and variation within the Chihuahuan tradition is that it reflects decorative evolution (i.e., simple to complex) and geographical location (i.e., type association with place). By combining both models together we are presented with a more dynamic and realistic picture of regional development. The temporal model indicates that Babícora and Villa Ahumada are stylistically earlier within the Medio period sequence. However, a concurrent analysis using the geographical model reveals decorative overlaps with Ramos polychrome that cannot be explained through temporal development alone.

In order to understand the broader implications of decorative change, we must expand our scope beyond the ceramic medium and consider the social, economic and ideological implications of the entire archaeological assemblage.

The Archaeological Evidence

The most important development in the history of Chihuahuan archaeology is, without a doubt, the excavation of the site of Paquimé. This site represents the pinnacle of Medio period, and many of its diagnostic architectural features, including multi-story, rectangular roomblocks, ballcourts, ceremonial mounds, and avian breeding pens, are shared throughout the Chihuahuan culture area. Imported materials were also stock-piled at the site, suggesting the importance of Paquimé as a regional trade center. This differs dramatically from the picture for the Viejo period whose settlements consisted of small clusters of circular, semi-subterranean houses and a more even distribution of trade goods, such as shell (Ronna Jane Bradley, personal communication 2000, see also Kelley et al. 2000a). The archaeological data presents a distinct and possibly sudden change in architectural and economic practice.

Returning to the ceramic data, however, we are presented with a situation that suggests a more continuous development between these periods. For example, the proposed temporal evolution of design within the museum sample indicates a steady progression from simple to complex design structures. New evidence from the Viejo period Calderon site on the southern edge of the Chihuahuan culture area (Kelley et al. 2000a; Kelley et al. 2000b) suggests that the recently discovered Santa Ana polychrome may be an early form of the Medio period Babícora type. Unfortunately, Viejo sites in the area around Paquimé are rare, which has led to the speculation that the numerous Medio period sites are built on top of the older habitations (Art MacWilliams, 2000 personal communication). We can conclude that the dramatic change seen in the adoption of a new architecture is not matched in the pottery. Graves' examination of decorative changes within the Kalinga

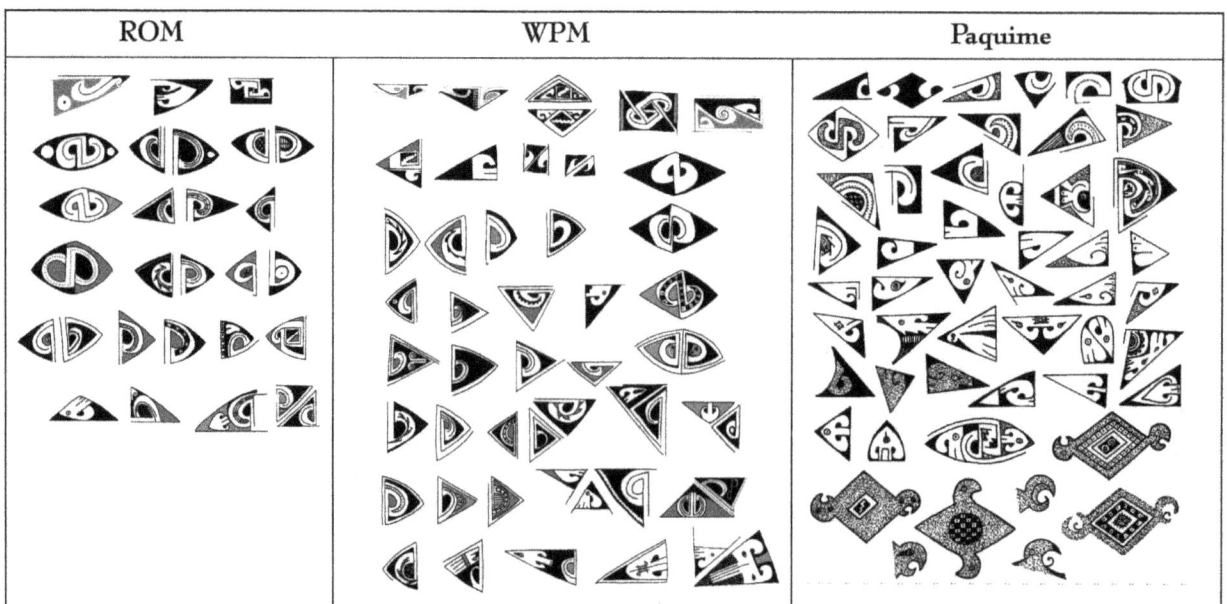

Figure 6.19 Variation in "P" Triangle and macaw motifs from the ROM, WPM, and Paquime vessels (Paquime motifs taken from Di Peso et al. 1974a:282)

92

ceramics presents a potential reason for the transition into Design Horizon B,

> rapid design changes... [or] the complete replacement of one design system by another within 25 to 50 years, are probably owing to factors other than inter-cohort differences expressed over time through cohort succession. More likely these kinds of changes reflect rapid sociocultural developments that lead to large-scale population alterations (1985:33).

Taking this position, it is possible that the change in pottery is related to the increase in socio-economic practice and the influx of new ideas (i.e., macaws, ballcourts, etc.) into a ceramic tradition already well-established in Chihuahua. In relation to the individual polychrome types, Ramos is the culmination of this new development and represents the hybridization of local and external influences. Helms' idea (1988, 1991) that an object obtained from afar is often ascribed more socio-religious importance is perhaps one of the most salient concepts for understanding this new style. Painted and modelled renditions of 'foreign' imagery, such as macaws and plumed serpents, are combined with the locally-produced design structures found predominantly in Ramos polychrome, and more specifically, in the vessels produced at Paquimé. In turn, since this site displays numerous other 'Mesoamerican' architectural and trade goods, the depiction of this imagery on ceramics may have been used to spread an ideology to other regions.

If Babícora and Villa Ahumada are produced in specific areas of the Chihuahuan culture, then the appearance of Design Horizon B in these types suggests that they were borrowing or buying into the symbols and power associated with Paquimé. In this scenario the use of the white slip on Villa Ahumada could be attributed to the lack of white clay that is characteristic of Ramos polychrome. A second, but less likely possibility, is that Ramos is the culmination of a style initiated by Babícora polychrome. The question of whether people were reproducing or copying this style in different areas needs to be addressed with clay sourcing studies currently being undertaken by Daniela Triadan (Jane Kelley, personal communication, September 2000).

The Origin of Effigy Jars
The archaeological evidence of effigies, whether produced from clay, stone, or shell, in Chihuahua dates back to the Viejo period. Examples of stone and ceramic effigies from the Calderon site (800-900 A.D.) indicate that the representation of the human form has considerable time depth in this region (Jane Kelley, personal communication 2000). The polychrome ceramic effigies (in a wide range of classes) are also distributed throughout both the Medio sequence and Chihuahuan culture area. The quantity and standardized character of

Ramos and Design Horizon B effigies is therefore interpreted as the florescence of this ceramic form, rather than the beginning. The only class that likely developed out of Paquimé's sudden florescence is the macaw effigy. The archaeological data for breeding and burial, as well as the elaborate painting and regular placement of head and tail appendages on these jars suggests that these birds played a significant role in the socio-religious complex that developed with the site's increased economic status.

Summary of the Design Analysis
Incorporation of the design horizon as a unit of analysis has enabled the formulation of patterns that expand our conception of type. It also provides models of decorative variation according to time, space, and broad cultural factors. On the whole, the most convincing argument from this analysis is the issue of temporal variation. At present, there is sufficient evidence to suggest that variation in motif and layout frequency in the museum collections is at least partly the result of temporal changes. Using the proposed Design Horizon divisions, both Villa Ahumada and Babícora polychrome would pre-date Ramos polychrome in the Medio period sequence. Ramos appears or evolves out of these older ceramic types and eventually comes to dominate the assemblage until the collapse of the Chihuahuan culture in the 15th century.

While prohibited from making any direct claims for the origin or spread of decorative characteristics across the Chihuahuan culture area, my analysis clearly illustrates the potential for uncovering regional styles. The most obvious candidate from the museum sample are Ramos polychrome and Design Horizon B which are likely products of an increase in socio-economic power at the site of Paquimé. Increased survey and focus on regionalized assemblages that emphasize the role of design horizon and type will no doubt clarify the presence of synchronic variation in the Chihuahuan tradition.

At present, the number of questions that can be asked of the data far outweighs the number of answers. However, this study has demonstrated the value of considering the dynamic structural characteristics of decorative variation while we search for vertically- and/or horizontally-stratified sites.

THE QUESTION OF FORGERIES

As mentioned briefly within Chapter IV, a serious caveat with using museum collections as the primary database is the question of vessel authenticity. During the analysis of both the ROM and WPM, notes were made of those vessels that displayed exceptional traits that 'felt wrong', such as cracked or flaking paint, errant shapes, very poorly or oddly articulated designs, or, on the opposite

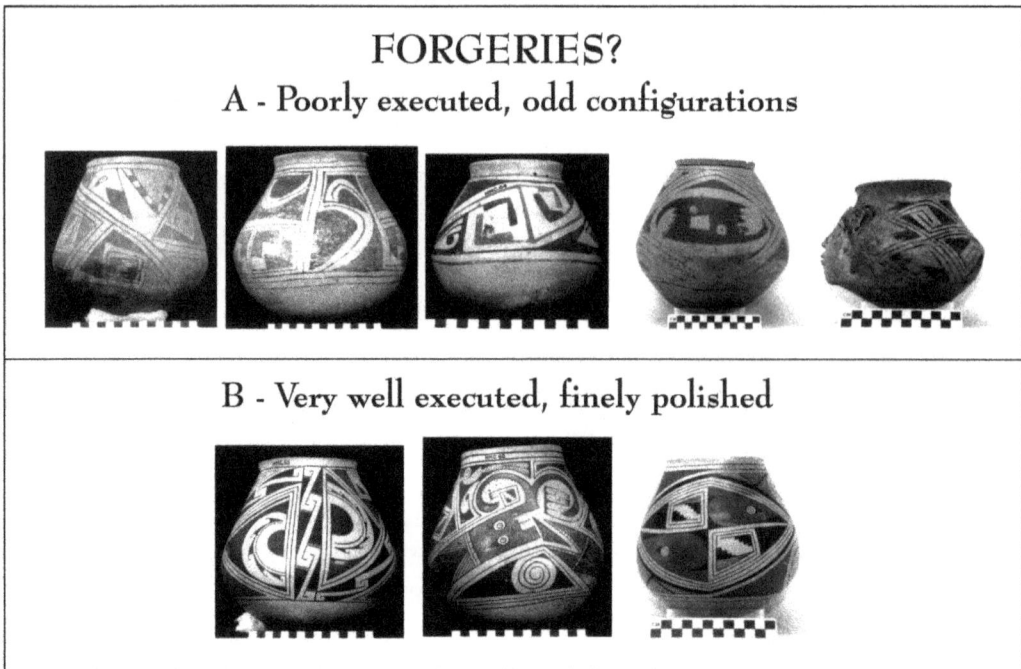

Figure 6.20 Anomalous examples of Chihuahuan polychrome jars from the ROM and WPM (upper row - l to r - #119, #143, #172, WPM #148, #190, bottom row ROM #105, #147, WPM #180)

Figure 6.21 Chihuahuan polychrome vessels from the collection of Mr. Harold Naylor (top row - l to r - Ramos polychrome, Ramos polychrome, Ramos polychrome, bottom row Ramos polychrome, Ramos polychrome, Babicora polychrome, Ramos polychrome)

end of the spectrum, very well articulated designs (Figure 6.20). An example of a vessel that appears 'too good' is seen in the finely polished surface, exceptional line construction, and overall decorative elaboration on a large jar from the ROM (Figure 6.20, #147). This combination of techniques shares more in common with modern vessels being produced at the small town of Mata Ortiz, located one hour to the west of the site of Paquimé, than with the majority of vessels recovered from prehistoric contexts. The economy of Mata Ortiz has been revitalized over the past two decades by the trade of its distinct ceramic wares across the globe, however, the root of this economic change began through mimicking prehistoric jars (Estes, in press). Similarly, there are rumours that families have been forging and selling pots to tourists for more than four generations (Kirk Gittings, personal communication, June 1999). While this is hearsay, it emphasizes the potential problem in blindly using museum collections. In combination with this historical evidence is the more tangible fact that Chihuahuan vessels are found in extremely large quantities, relative to other culture areas, in museums and private collections throughout the US Southwest and across North America. David Phillips (personal communication, November, 2000) suggests that there may be as many as 20,000 whole Chihuahuan pots housed in these collections. In the case of private collections, Mr. Harold Naylor (see Figure 6.21) and Mr. Ken Burlingham of El Paso each own over a dozen polychrome jars and effigy vessels. According to Marc Thompson (personal communication, July 1999) there are several other collectors in the immediate area with similar numbers of Chihuahuan jars. For the purpose of this study, however, the database was restricted to vessels located in museum contexts.

The solution to the question of whether forgeries exist can be approached by two ways. The first involves the incorporation of technical analyses, such as Thermoluminescence, Neutron Activation Analysis, and X-radiography, to assess date of manufacture, firing conditions, chemical composition of raw materials, and construction (Rice 1987:443-444; 374-5). The second approach is to compile a detailed history of pot production in Chihuahua during the late 19th to mid 20th, prior to the development of the modern ceramic trade in Mata Ortiz. This will not tell us exactly which pots were made as prehistoric copies but may provide a means of identifying characteristics of individual potters.

Unfortunately, such tests were not available for this study and as a result only those pieces that could not be classified, or lacked a recognizable design structure, were excluded from consideration. Of the vessels recorded in the museum setting, five jars were not included from the ROM, and eight jars were not used from the WPM. Detailing the inherent danger of forgeries is not meant to belittle the use of museum collections, but rather to raise awareness of the possibility that some jars may be modern copies of Medio period ceramics. Until the problem of forgeries is solved, the stigma of incorporating this data into archaeological research should be recognized in the production of prehistoric interpretations.

CHAPTER VII

CONCLUSION

The primary motivation for using the whole vessels housed in museum collections is to demonstrate the potential of this little-used medium for archaeological research. To illustrate the utility of this oft-scorned data set, a design analysis was undertaken to address a critical problem in the Chihuahua tradition: type descriptions, or more succinctly, the problem of decorative overlap. The first contribution of this design analysis is the establishment of a more explicit list of motif and layout frequencies for each of the polychrome types. While these descriptions proved to be somewhat fluid, it is possible to interpret the overlap between polychrome types using the Design Horizon concept.

The two Design Horizons identified in the Chihuahuan tradition offer a more useful perspective for understanding the overlap than the adoption of Di Peso's variant categories created at Paquimé. Using a combination of the museum and archaeological information, it is possible to formulate models of temporal and spatial development to explain the existence of separate Design Horizons. For temporal variation, this study has provided the methodological and empirical evidence lacking from Sayles' decorative assumption that there is an evolution of polychrome types in the Medio Period: Babícora and Villa Ahumada are both earlier in the sequence than Ramos polychrome. The overlap of Design Horizons between these types can also be explained according to regional distributions, with the production of each type corresponding to particular regions in Chihuahua. Overall, the decorative variation is reflecting factors of both time and space. By comparing the motif patterns from the museum sample to assemblages of provenienced sherds, we will greatly increase our understanding of regional developments and, in the case where an undisturbed site is discovered, assist in establishing finer-grained temporal divisions within the Medio period.

Based on the definitions and models presented in the previous chapters, it has been argued that the museum collection can be usefully employed outside the realm of art historical description and contribute to our knowledge of cultural variation. The key to this thesis is the adoption of a rigorous contrastive approach aimed at uncovering patterns or structures from multiple levels of decorative characteristics. Design analysis is seen as an appropriate means for initiating the study of stylistic comparison among whole vessels whether they come from excavated or museum contexts. Given the variety of traits found within the whole vessel, the opportunity exists to expand the use of museum collections to eventually include a comparison of manufacturing and finishing properties as well as design.

PERSPECTIVES AND QUESTIONS

Looking In and Looking Back

This report represents an archaeological step backwards in many ways. The general bias of this thesis is aimed at recognizing internal distinctions within the Chihuahuan culture. As discussed in the history of ceramic analysis in Chihuahua, the research focus has emphasized external relations, rather than introspective concerns. First, this thesis suggests a return to the insights of the original work undertaken in Chihuahua (i.e., Kidder 1916; Carey 1931; Sayles 1936) to clarify the more recent data from Paquim0, which has dominated intellectual thought about regional prehistory since the publication of Di Peso's eight-volume treatise. Second, it attempts to map the patterning from a single artifact class to inform on broader cultural changes. Recent publications have, and for good reason, moved away from such monolithic (ceramic) explanatory mechanisms in favour of a holistic material evaluation. Ironically, the re-contextualized museum pieces can become instrumental in identifying phases that have yet eluded context-based archaeological endeavours.

Looking Out

Not surprisingly, the search for internal variation and potential for a developmental sequence in the ceramic tradition is a reaction to the frequent attempts to cut and paste foreign origins overtop of indigenous development. Now that the descriptions and analysis of the Chihuahuan types have been examined in detail, it is possible to expand our conceptions to external implications. The question of Mesoamerican influence outlined in Chapter II cannot be denied and the presence of these motifs suggests some form of interaction. Based on the ceramics alone, Kidder's summary of the analysis of the ceramic decoration in Chihuahuan polychromes provides a useful perspective on the importance of incorporating this data into future research, "we conclude…that Casas Grandes pottery is a highly specialized and somewhat abherrant sub-group of the great Southwestern family" (1916:267). Having answered, or at least addressed, the basic questions outlined for this thesis, it is necessary to expand consideration to new avenues of investigation both internally and externally.

BIBLIOGRAPHY

Adams, W. Y. and E.W. Adams
1991. *Archaeological Typology and Practical Reality*. Cambridge University Press, Cambridge.

Amsden, Monroe
1928. *Archaeological Reconnaisance in Sonora*. Southwest Museum Papers 1, Los Angeles.

Ayeleyra, Arroyo de Anda, Luis
1961. El Primer Hallazgo Folsom en Territorio Mexicano y su Relacion con el Complejo de Puntas Acanaladas en Norte Americana. In Homenaje a Pablo Martinez del Rio, en el *Vigesimoquinto Aniversario de la Primera Edicion de Los Origenes Americanos*, Mexico D.F., 31-48.

Bandelier, Adolph F.
1890. The Ruins of Casas Grandes – Part I. *Nation* 1313, 166-168.

Beckett, Patrick H. and Richard S. MacNeish
1994. The Archaic Chihuahua Tradition of South-Central New Mexico and Chihuahua, Mexico. In *Contributions in Anthropology, Archaic Hunter-Gatherer Archaeology in the American Southwest*, 13(1). Eastern New Mexico University Press: Las Cruces.

Bradley, Ronna J. and Jerry M. Hoffer
1985. Playas red: a preliminary study of origins and variability in the Jornada Mogollon. In *Proceedings of the Third Jornada-Mogollon Conference*, edited by M. S. Foster and T. C. O'Laughlin. The Artifact 23(1-2):161-177.

Brand, Donald D.
1935 The Distribution of Pottery Types in Northwest Mexico. *American Anthropologist* 37:287-305.
1933. *The Historical Geography of Northwest Chihuahua*. Unpublished doctoral dissertation. Department of Geography, University of California: Berkeley.

Braniff, Beatriz C.
1986. Ojo de Agua, Sonora and Casas Grandes Chihuahua: A Suggested Chronology. In *Ripples in the Chichimec Sea: New Considerations of Southwestern-Mesoamerican Interactions*, edited by Frances J. Mathien and Randall H. McGuire, pp. 70-80. Southern Illinois University Press: Carbondale.

Braun, David P.
1985. Ceramic Decorative Diversity and Illinois Woodland Regional Integration. In *Decoding Prehistoric Ceramics*, edited by Ben A. Nelson, pp. 128-153. Southern Illinois University Press: Carbondale.

Brew, Otis John
1946. Archaeology of Alkali Ridge, Southeastern Utah. *Papers of the Peabody Museum of American Archaeology and Ethnology*, Volume XXI. Harvard University: Harvard.

Brooks, Prudence
1973. An analysis of painted pottery designs of the Casas Grandes culture. *Awanyu* 1(2):11-33.

Bourdieu, Pierre
1973. The Berber House. In *Rules and Meanings*, edited by Mary Douglas, pp.98-110. Penguin: Harmondsworth.

Broekman, Jan M.
1974. *Structuralism.* D. Reidel Publishing Company: Boston.

Callaghan, Richard T. and Claire P. Allum
1992. Technological Development and Shared Chemical Process: An Andean Example. *Archaeomaterials* 6:123-129.

Cantwell, Anne-Marie, James B. Griffin and Nan A. Rothschild, eds.
1981. *The Research Potential of Anthropological Museum Collections.* New York Academy of Sciences: New York.

Carey, Henry A.
1931. An Analysis of the Northwestern Chihuahua Culture. *American Anthropologist* 33:325-374.

Carlson, Roy L.
1982. The polychrome complexes. In *Southwestern Ceramics: A Comparative Review*, edited by Albert H. Schroeder, pp. 201-235. The Arizona Archaeologist No. 15: Phoenix.

Carpenter, John P. nd.
The Animas Phase and Paquimè, (Casas Grandes): A Perspective on Regional Differentiation and Integration from the Joyce Well site, New Mexico. Unpublished paper submitted for MA, University of New Mexico: Las Cruces.

Chapman, Kenneth M.
1923. Casas Grandes Pottery. *Art and Archaeology* 16(1-2):25-34.
1922. Life Forms in Pueblo Pottery Decoration. *Art and Archaeology* XIII(3):120-122.

Chilton, Elizabeth
1998. The Cultural Origins of Technical Choice: Unravelling Algonquian and Iroquoian Ceramic Traditions in the Northeast. In *The Archaeology of Social Boundaries*, edited by Miriam T. Stark, pp. 132-160. Smithsonian Institution Press: Washington, D.C.

Clarke, David L.
1968. *Analytical Archaeology.* Methuen and Co.: London

Colton, Harold S. and Lyndon L. Hargrave
1937. *Handbook of Northern Arizona Pottery Wares.* Museum of Northern Arizona, Bulletin 11.

Cordell, Linda S.
1993. Charles Di Peso's Gran Chichimeca: Comments in Retrospect and Prospect. In *Culture and Contact: Charles C. Di Peso's Gran Chichimeca*, edited by Anne I. Woosley and John C. Ravesloot, pp. 219-226. Amerind Foundation New World Stuides Series Number 2: Dragoon.

Crown, Patricia L.
1994. *Ceramics and Ideology: Salado Polychrome Pottery*. University of New Mexico Press: Albuquerque.
1991. The Hohokam: Current Views of Prehistory and the Regional System. In *Chaco and Hohokam: Prehistoric Regional Systems in the American Southwest*, edited by Patricia L. Crown and W. James Judge, pp. 135-158. School of American Research Press: Santa Fe.

Cruz, Rafael Antillon and Timothy D. Maxwell
1999. The Villa Ahumada Site: Archaeological Investigations East of Paquimé. In *The Casas Grandes World*, edited by Curtis F. Schaafsma and Carroll L. Riley, pp. 43-53. University of Utah Press: Salt Lake City.

Dean, Jeffrey S. and John C. Ravesloot
1993. The Chronology of Cultural Interaction in the Gran Chichimeca. In *Culture and Contanct: Charles C. Di Peso's Gran Chichimeca*, edited by Anne I. Woosley and John C. Ravesloot, pp. 83-104. Amerind Foundation Publication: Dragoon.

DeBoer, Warren R.
1991. The Decorative Burden: Design, Medium, and Change. In *Ceramic Ethnoarchaeology*, edited by William A. Longacre, pp. 144-161. University of Arizona Press: Tucson.
1990. Interaction, Imitation, and Communication as Express in Style: The Ucayali Experience. In *The Uses of Style in Archaeology*, edited by Margaret Conkey and Christine Hastorff, pp. 82-104. Cambridge University Press: Cambridge.

Dietler, Michael and Ingrid Herbich
1998. Habitus, Technology, Style: An Integrated Approach to the Social Understanding of Material Culture and Boundaries. In *The Archaeology of Social Boundaries*, edited by Miriam T. Stark, pp.232-263. Smithsonian Institution Press: Washington, D.C.

Di Peso, Charles J.
1974. *Casas Grandes: A Fallen Trading Center of the Gran Chichimeca*. Northland Press: Flagstaff.
1969. *Casas Grandes Pottery Types*. 11th Ceramic Conference, Amerind Foundation: Dragoon.

Di Peso, Charles C., J. Rinaldo, and G. Fenner
1974a. *Casas Grandes: A Fallen Trading Center of the Gran Chichimeca: Ceramics and Shell (6)*. Northland Press: Flagstaff.
1974b. *Casas Grandes: A Fallen Trading Center of the Gran Chichimeca: Burials and Economy (8)*. Northland Press: Flagstaff.

Douglas, John E.
1996. Distinguishing Change During the Animas Phase (A.D. 1150-1450) at the Boss Ranch Site, Southeastern Arizona. *North American Archaeologist* 17(3):183-202.
1992. Distant Sources, Local Contexts: Intepreting Nonlocal Ceramics at Paquime (Casas Grandes), Chihuahua. *Journal of Anthropological Research* 48(1):1-25.

Ford, James A.
1954. On the Concept of Types: The Type Concept Revisited. *American Anthropologist* 56:42-53.

Glassie, H.
1975. *Folk Housing in Middle Virginia*. University of Tennessee Press: Knoxville.

Goodby, Robert G.
1998. Technological Patterning and Social Boundaries: Ceramic Variability in Southern New England, A.D. 1000-1675. In *The Archaeology of Social Boundaries*, edited by Miriam T. Stark, pp.. Smithsonian Institution Press: Washington, D.C.

Graves, Michael W.
1998. The History of Method and Theory in the Study of Prehistoric Puebloan Pottery Style in the American Southwest. *Journal of Method and Theory* 5(4):309-343.
1991. Pottery Production and Distribution Among the Kalinga: A Study of Household and Regional Organization and Differentiation. In *Ceramic Ethnoarchaeology*, edited by William A. Longacre, pp. 112-143. University of Arizona Press: Tucson.
1985. Ceramic Design Variation within a Kalinga Village: Temporal and Spatial Process. In *Decoding Ceramics*, edited by Ben A. Nelson. Southern Illinois University Press: Carbondale.

Harcum, C. G.
1923. Indian pottery of the Casas Grandes region, Chihuahua, Mexico. *Bulletin of the Royal Ontario Museum of Archaeology* 2:4-11.

Hard, Robert J. and John R. Roney
1998. A Massive Terraced Village Complex in Chihuahua, Mexico, 3000 Years Before Present. *Science* 279:1661-1664.

Hardin, Margaret Ann
1991. Sources of Ceramic Variability at Zuni Pueblo. In *Ceramic Ethnoarchaeology*, edited by William A. Longacre, pp. 40-70. University of Arizona Press: Tucson.
1984. Models of Decoration. In *The Many Dimensions of Pottery: Ceramics in Archaeology and Anthropology*, edited by S.E. van der Leeuw and A.C. Pritchard, pp. 573-608. Amsterdam: Universiteit van Amsterdam.

Hedrick, Basil C., J.C. Kelley, and C.R. Riley, eds.
1974. *The Mesoamerican Southwest*. Southern Illinois Press: Carbondale.

Helms, Mary
1991. Esoteric knowledge, geographical distance and the elaboration of leadership status: dynamics of resource control. In *Profiles in Cultural Evolution: Papers in Honour of Elman R. Service*, edited by Terry Rambo and Kathleen Gillogly, pp. 333-348. Anthropological Papers of the Museum of Anthropology No. 85, University of Michigan.
1988. *Ulysses Sail: An ethnographic odyssey of power, knowledge, and geographical distance*. Princeton University Press: Princeton.

Hendrickson, Mitch J.
2001. Are You My Type? Styles in Classification for Medio Period Polychrome Jars, Casas Grandes Culture, Chihuahua, Mexico. In *Jornada Mogollon Archaeology: Collected Papers from the 11th Jornada Mogollon Conference*, edited by Patrick H. Beckett, pp. 119-131. Coas Publishing and Research: Las Cruces.
2000. *The Macaw and the "P": Evolution and Origins of Two Motifs in the Chihuahuan Decorative Tradition*. Paper presented at Art and Archaeology 33rd Chacmool Conference of the University of Calgary Department of Archaeology.

Hegmon, Michelle
1998. Technology, Style and Social Practices: Archaeological Perspectives. In *The Archaeology of Social Boundaries*, edited by Miriam T. Stark, pp. 132-160. Smithsonian Institution Press: Washington, D.C.
1995. *The Social Dynamics of Pottery Style in the Early Puebloan Southwest*. Occasional Paper No. 5. Crow Canyon Archaeological Center: Cortez.

Hill, James N.
1985. Style: A Conceptual Evolutionary Framework. In *Decoding Prehistoric Ceramics*, edited by Ben A. Nelson, pp. 362-388. Southern Illinois University Press: Carbondale.

Hill, Warren D.
1992. *Chronology of the El Zurdo site, Chihuahua (Mexico)*. Unpublished MA thesis, Department of Archaeology, University of Calgary: Calgary.

Hodder, Ian
1982a. Sequences of structural change in the Dutch Neolithic. In *Symbolic and Structural Archaeology*, ed. by Ian Hodder, pp. 162-177. Cambridge University Press: Cambridge.
1982b. *Symbols in Action*. Cambridge: Cambridge University Press.

Hole, Frank
1984. Analysis of Structure and Design in Prehistoric Ceramics. *World Archaeology* 15(3):326-347.

Hough, Walter
1923. Casas Grandes Pottery in the National Museum. *Art and Archaeology* 16:34.

Jernigan, E. W.
1986. A Non-Hierarchical Approach to Ceramic Decoration Analysis: A Southwestern Perspective. *American Antiquity* 51(1):3-20.

Kelley, J. Charles
1986. The Mobile Merchants of Molino. In *Ripples in the Chichimec Sea: New Considerations of Southwestern-Mesoamerican Interactions*, edited by Frances J. Mathien and Randall H. McGuire, pp. 81-104. Southern Illinois University Press: Carbondale.
1971. Archaeology of the Northern Frontier: Zacatecas and Durango. In *Archaeology of Northern Mesoamerica: Part Two*, edited by G.F. Ekholm and I. Bernal, pp.768-801. Handbook of Middle American Indians, volume 11, R. Wauchope, general editor, University of Texas Press: Austin.
1966. Mesoamerica and the Southwestern United States. In *Archaeological Frontiers and External Connections*, edited by G.F. Ekholm and Gordon R. Willey, pp. 95-110. Handbook of Middle American Indians, volume 4, R. Wauchope, general editor, University of Texas Press: Austin.
1956. Settlement Patterns in North-Central Mexico. In *Prehistoric Settlement Patterns in the New World*, edited by Gordon R. Willey, pp.128-139. Viking Fund Publications in Anthropology 23. Wenner Gren Fund for Anthropological Research: New York.

Kelley, Jane H. and Joe D. Stewart.
1991. El Proyecto Arqueologico de Chihuahua: Informe de la Temporada de 1990. In *Tercer Congres Internacional de Historia Regional Comparada*, edited by R. L. García, pp. 47-50. Universidad Autónoma de Ciudad Juarez: Juarez.
1991b. Proyecto Arqueologico de Chihuahua Trabajos de Campo 1991. In *Boletin del Consejo de Arqueología*, pp. 157-161. Instituto Nacional de Antropología e Historia: Mexico, D.F.

Kelley, Jane H., Joe D. Stewart, A.C. MacWilliams, and Loy C. Neff
1999a. A West Central Chihuahuan Perspective on Chihuahuan Culture. In *The Casas Grandes World*, edited by Curtis F. Scaafsma and Carroll L. Riley, pp. 63-77. University of Utah Press: Salt Lake City.

Kelley, Jane H., Arthur C. MacWilliams, and Joe D. Stewart
1999b. *Proyecto Arqueologico Chihuahua Informe del Temporada 1998.* Informe al Consejo de Arqueologia Instituto Nacional de Antropologia e Historia.

Kelley, Jane H., Karen Adams, Karin Burd, Richard A. Garvin, Mitch Hendrickson, Joe D. Stewart, and Monica Webster
2000a. *Proyecto Arqueologico Chihuahua Informe del Temporada 1999.* Informe al Consejo de Arqueologia Instituto Nacional de Antropologia e Historia.

Kelley, Jane H., Karin T. Burd, and Mitch J. Hendrickson
2000b. *Ceramics As Temporal and Spatial Indicators inChihuahuan Cultures.* Paper presented at the Meetings for the Society of American Archaeology, Philadelphia, April 2000.

Kidder, Alfred V.
1924. *An Introduction to the Study of Southwestern Archaeology.* Yale University Press for Phillips Academy: Andover.
1916. The Pottery of the Casas Grandes District, Chihuahua. In *Anthropological Essays Presented to William Henry Holmes in Honor of his 70th Birthday*, pp. 253-268. AMS Press Inc.: New York.

Kintigh, Keith W.
1985. Social structure, the structure of style, and stylistic patterns in Cibola pottery. In *Decoding Prehistoric Ceramics*, ed. by Ben A. Nelson, pp. 35-74. Southern Illinois University Press: Carbondale.

Leach, Edmund
1954. *Political Systems of Highland Burma.* Beacon Press: Boston.

Lechtman, Heather
1977. Style in Technology: Some Early Thoughts. In *Material Culture: Style, Organization, and Dynamics of Technology*, edited by Heather Lechtman and Robert Merrill, pp. 3-20. West Publishing: St. Paul.

Lekson, Stephen H.
2000. *Chaco, Aztec and Paquimé: Centers of Political Power in the Ancient Southwest.* Paper presented at Ancient Casas Grandes: Spheres of Influence at the Museum of Man, San Diego, March 25, 2000.
1999. Was Casas A Pueblo? In *The Casas Grandes World*, edited by Curtis F. Schaafsma and Carroll L. Riley, pp. 84-92. University of Utah Press: Salt Lake City.

Levi-Strauss, Claude
1963. *Structural Anthropology.* Basic Books: New York.

Lister, Robert H.
1946. Survey of Archaeological Remains in Northwestern Chihuahua. *Southwestern Journal of Anthropology* 2(4):433-453.
1938. *Some Aspects of Chihuahua Archaeology.* Unpublished MA Thesis, Department of New Mexico, Albuquerque.

Longacre, William A. ed.
1991. *Ceramic Ethnoarchaeology.* University of Arizona Press: Tucson.

Lumholtz, C.
1902. *Unknown Mexico: Explorations in the Sierra Madre and Other Regions, 1890-1898* (2 Volumes). New York: Charles Schribner & Sons.

Lyman, R. Lee, Michael J. O'Brien and Robert C. Dunnell
1997. *The Rise and Fall of Culture History*. Plenum Press: New York.

MacEachern, A. Scott
1998. Scale, Style, and Cultural Variation: Technological Traditions in the Northern Mandara Mountains. In *The Archaeology of Social Boundaries*, edited by Miriam T. Stark, pp. 107-131. Smithsonian Institution Press: Washington, D.C.

MacIntosh, Roderick J.
1992. From Traditional African Art Into the Archaeology of Form in the Middle Niger. In *Dall'Archeologia all'Arte Tradizionale Africana*, edited by G. Pezzoli, pp. 145-151. Centro Studi Archeologia Africana: Milan.

MacNeish, Richard S. ed.
1993. *Preliminary Investigations of the Archaic in the Region of Las Cruces, New Mexico*. Historic and Natural Resources Report No. 9. Cultural Resources Management Program Directorate of Environment, United States Army Air Defense Artillery Center: Fort Bliss.

MacNeish, Richard S. and Patrick H. Beckett
1987. *The Archaic Chihuahua Tradition*. COAS Monograph Series, No. 7. COAS Publishing and Research: Las Cruces.

Malagón, Maria Sprehn
2001. Tattoos, Women, and Rites of Passage: Body Art in the Casas Grandes World. In *From Paquimé to Mata Ortiz: The Legacy of Ancient Casas Grandes*, edited by Grace Johnson, pp. 65-72. San Diego Museum of Man: San Diego.

Mann, June R.
1980. Symbolism in Casas Grandes Effigies. *The Artifact* 28(2):63-68.

McGuire, Randall H.
1993. Charles Di Peso and the Mesoamerican connection. In *Culture and Contact: Charles C. Di Peso's Gran Chichimeca*, edited by A. I. Woosely and J. C. Ravesloot, pp. 23-38. Amerind Foundation New World Studies Series No. 2: Dragoon.
1992. *A Marxist Archaeology*. Academic Press: Toronto.

McGuire, Randall H. and Maria E. Villalpando
1993. *An Archaeological Survey of the Altar Valley, Sonora, Mexico*. Arizona State Museum Archaeological Series 184. Arizona State Museum, University of Arizona: Tucson.

Mills, Barbara J.
1999. Ceramics and social contexts of food consumption in the Northern Southwest. In *Pottery and People: A Dynamic Interaction*, edited by James M. Skibo and Gary M. Feinman, pp. 99-114. Foundations of Archaeological Inquiry, University of Utah Press: Salt Lake City.

Minnis, Paul E.
1989. The Casas Grandes Polity in the International Four Corners. In *The Sociopolitical Structure of Prehistoric Southwestern Societies*, edited by Steadman Upham, Kent G. Lightfoot, and Roberta A. Jewett, pp. 269-305. Westview Press: Boulder.
1984. Peeking under the tortilla curtain: regional interaction and integration on the northeastern periphery of Casas Grandes. *American Archaeology* 4(3):181-193.

Minnis, Paul E., M. E. Whalen, J. H. Kelley, and J. D. Stewart
1993. Prehistoric macaw breeding in the North American Southwest. *American Antiquity* 58(2):270-276.

Minnis, Paul E. and Michael E. Whalen
1995. *El sistema regional de Casas Grandes, Chihuahua: Informe Presentado al Instituto Nacional de Antropogía e Historia*. Manuscript on File. University of Oklahoma: Norman.
1990. El Sistema Regional de Casas Grandes, Chihuahua. *Actas del Segundo Congreso de Historia Regional Comparada* 1990, pp. 45-55. Universidad Autonoma de Ciudad Juárez: Juárez.

Nelson, Ben A.
1992. *Constructions of the Past in the Northern Mesoamerican Periphery*. Paper Presented at the Roundtable of the Center for Indigenous Studies in the Americas entitled "Cultural Dynamics of the Precolumbian West and Northwest Mesoamerica, Phoenix.

Nelson, Ben A. and Steven A. LeBlanc
1986. Short-Term Sedentism in the American Southwest: The Mimbres Valley Salado. *Maxwell Museum of Anthropology Publication Series*, Maxwell Museum of Anthropology and the University of New Mexico Press: Albuquerque.

Pailes, R. A.
1980. The Upper Rio Sonora Valley in Prehistoric Trade. *Transactions of the Illinois Academy of Science* 72(4):20-39.
1978. The Rio Sonora Culture in Prehistoric Trade Systems. In *Across the Chichimec Sea*, edited by Carroll L. Riley and B.C. Hedrick, pp. 134-143. Southern Illinois University Press: Carbondale.

Phillips, David. A. jr.
1991. *Mesoamerican-Northern Mexican Relationships: An Intellectual History*. Paper presented at the Symposium Navigating the Chichimec Sea: Internal Developments and External Involvements in the Prehistory of Northern Mexico of the 47th International Congress of Americanists: New Orleans.
1989. Prehistory of Chihuahua and Sonora, Mexico. *Journal of World Prehistory* 3(4):373-401.

Plog, Stephen
1980. *Stylistic Variation in Prehistoric Ceramics*. Cambridge University Press: Cambridge.

Rakita, Gordon F. M.
2001. *Social Complexity, Religioius Organization and Mortuary Ritual in the Casas Grandes Region of Chihuahua, Mexico*. Unpublished Ph.D Dissertation, University of New Mexico: Albuquerque.

Ravesloot, John C.
1988. *Mortuary Practices and Social Differentiation at Casas Grandes, Chihuahua, Mexico*. Anthropological Papers of the University of Arizona No. 49. University of Arizona Press: Tucson.

Raymond, J. Scott, Warren R. DeBoer and Peter G. Roe
1975. *Cumancaya: A Peruvian Ceramic Tradition*. Occasional Papers No. 2. University of Calgary, Department of Archaeology Press: Calgary.

Rice, Prudence M.
1987. *Pottery Analysis*. University of Chicago Press: Chicago.

Sayles, E.B.
1936a. *Some Southwestern Pottery Types*. Medallion Papers No. 21.
1936b. *An Archaeological Survey of Chihuahua, Mexico*. Medallion Papers No. XXII: Globe.

Schaafsma, Curtis F.
1979. The "El Paso Phase" and its Relationship to the "Casas Grandes Phenomenon". In *Jornada Mogollon Archaeology*, edited by Patrick H. Beckett and Regge D. Wiseman, pp. 383-388. New Mexico State University Press: Las Cruces.

Schaafsma, Curtis F. and Carroll L. Riley, eds.
1999. *The Casas Grandes World*. University of Utah Press: Salt Lake City.

Schaafsma, Polly
1999. Tlalocs, Kachinas, Sacred Bundles, and Related Symbolism in the Southwest and Mesoamerica. In *The Casas Grandes World*, edited by Curtis F. Schaafsma and Carroll L. Riley, pp. 164-192. University of Utah Press: Salt Lake City.

Schmidt, Robert H.
1973. *A Geographical Survey of Chihuahua. Texas Western Press*, Monograph No. 37. University of Texas at El Paso: El Paso.

Scott, Stuart D.
1966. *Dendrochronology in Mexico. Papers of the Laboratory of Tree-Ring Research* No. 2., The University of Arizona Press: Tucson.

Shafer, Harry J. and Robbie L. Brewington
1995. Microstylistic Changes in Mimbres Black-on-White Pottery: Examples from the NAN ruin, Grant County, New Mexico. *Kiva* 61(1):5-30.

Shepard, Anna O.
1956. *Ceramics for the Archaeologist*. Publication 609, Carnegie Institute of Washington: Washington, D.C.

Sillitoe, Paul
1980. The art of war: Wola shield designs. *Man* 15:483-501.

Stark, Miriam T., ed.
1998. *The Archaeology of Social Boundaries*. Smithsonian Institution Press: Washington, D.C.

Steponaitis, Vincas P.
1983. *Ceramics, Chronology, and Community Patterns: An Archaeological Study at Moundville.* Academic Press: New York.

Stewart, Joe D.
1984. Jornada Ceramics at Casas Grandes: Chronology and Interaction. *Pottery Southwest* 11(2):1-3.

Stoppard, Tom
1991. *Rosencrantz and Guildenstern Are Dead: the Film.* Faber and Faber: Boston.

Thompson, Marc
1999. *Mimbres Iconology: Analysis and Interpretation of Figurative Motifs.* Unpublished Ph.D. Dissertation, University of Calgary: Calgary.

Van der Leeuw, S. E.
1991. Variation, Variability, and Exploration in Pottery Studies. In *Ceramic Ethnoarchaeology*, edited by William A. Longacre, pp.11-39. University of Arizona Press: Tucson.

Van Keuren, Scott
1999. *Ceramic Design Structure and the Organization of Cibola White Ware Production in the Grasshopper Region, Arizona.* Arizona State Museum Archaeological Series 191. Arizona State Museum, University of Arizona: Tucson.

Van Pool, Christine S.
2001. Birds, Burials, and Beliefs at Paquimé, Chihuahua, Mexico. In *From Paquimé to Mata Ortiz: The Legacy of Ancient Casas Grandes*, edited by Grace Johnson, pp. 73-88. San Diego Museum of Man: San Diego.

Vansina, Jan
1984. *Art History in Africa.* Longman Group: London.

Washburn, Dorothy
1983. Symmetry analysis of ceramic design: two tests of the method on Neolithic material from Greece and the Aegean. In *Structure and Cognition in Art*, edited by Dorothy Washburn, pp. 138-164. Cambridge University Press: Cambridge.

Whalen , Michael E. and Paul E. Minnis
1999. Investigating the Paquimé Regional System. In *The Casas Grandes World*, edited by Curtis F. Scaafsma and Carroll L. Riley, pp. 54-62. University of Utah Press: Salt Lake City.
1996. Studying Complexity in Northern Mexico: The Paquimé, Regional System. In *Debating Complexity, Proceedings of the 26th Annual Chacmool Conference*, edited by Daniel T. Meyer, Peter C. Dawson, and Donald T. Hanna, pp. 282-289. The Archaeological Association of the University of Calgary: Calgary.

Wheat, Joe-Ben
1948-1949. A Double-Walled Jar from Chihuahua. *The Kiva* 14(1-4):8-10.

Willey, Gordon R.
1948. A Functional Analysis of Horizon Styles in Peruvian Archaeology. In *A Reappraisal of Peruvian Archaeology*, edited by Wendell C. Bennett, pp.8-15. Society for American Archaeology Memoirs No. 4.

Winters, Howard D.
1981. Excavating in Museums: Notes on Mississippian Hoes and Middle Woodland Copper Gouges and Celts. In *The Research Potential of Anthropological Museum Collections*, edited by Anne-Marie E. Cantwell, James B. Griffin, and Nan A. Rothschild, pp. 17-33. New York Academy of Sciences: New York.

Woosley, Anne I. and Bart Olinger
1993. The Casas Grandes Ceramic Tradition: Production and Interregional Exchange of Ramos Polychrome. In *Culture and Contact: Charles C. Di Peso's Gran Chichimeca*, edited by Anne I. Woosley and John C. Ravesloot, pp. 105-132. Amerind Foundation Publication: Dragoon.

www.ingramcontent.com/pod-product-compliance
Lightning Source LLC
Chambersburg PA
CBHW061006030426
42334CB00033B/3388